The Naked Lady
Who Stood on
Her Head

The Naked Lady Who Stood on Her Head

A Psychiatrist's Stories of His Most Bizarre Cases

GARY SMALL, M.D.,
AND GIGI VORGAN

wm

WILLIAM MORROW

An Imprint of HarperCollins*Publishers*

Designed by Richard Óriolo

ISBN 978-1-61129-800-0

This book is dedicated to all the people who have suffered from mental illness and found the strength to get help

Those modern analysts! They charge so much! In my day, for five marks Freud himself would treat you. For ten marks, he would treat you and press your pants. For fifteen marks, Freud would let you treat him—that included a choice of any two vegetables.

WOODY ALLEN

CONTENTS

PREFACE

HOW COULD SOMEONE GET SO ANGRY that he suddenly becomes mute? Yank at his hair nervously until he goes bald? Or pass out just because he sees someone else pass out? Questions like these have always fascinated me. So when I was in medical school, it came as no surprise to anyone that I picked psychiatry as my specialty, and I've never regretted that choice. Now, after three decades of practicing psychiatry, I have seen patients whose bizarre behavior was too intriguing to forget. The mind sometimes pushes people to the extreme, and I was taught that a good psychiatrist can help bring them back.

In this book, I will tell all about my most unusual patients and how I was able to help many of them return from the brink of insanity. I will share my feelings, thoughts, and reactions to these bizarre cases, because it should be understood that being a psychiatrist and neuroscientist is not only a professional journey but a personal one as well. As I illustrate the challenges I faced with each case, I want you to join me in unraveling the puzzles underlying my patients' mental issues and to observe how solving these cases and gaining experience made me a better doctor.

I relate these cases in chronological order—from my early training throughout the next thirty years—as they shaped the way I have matured as a psychiatrist. Throughout these accounts, I explore several dynamics, particularly how the mind can make the body sick, as well as how the body can imbalance the mind. In working with my patients, I used a variety of approaches—what has been described as an *eclectic* psychiatric style—drawing upon both physical and mental explanations for psychological problems and treating problems with talk therapy, medication, or both.

In more recent years, I have also focused my career on understanding and preventing memory loss and Alzheimer's disease. While I helped my patients preserve their memories, it struck me that many of them had memories they wished to forget, driven by unresolved psychological issues, conflicted relationships, and insurmountable challenges that sometimes made them flee reality. Helping memory-challenged individuals overcome their mental struggles can be as essential to their well-being as preserving their memories.

It surprises me that many people, even those with crippling mental disorders, still fear psychiatry and never get treatment. Often what seems to keep people away is the lingering stigma of "seeing a shrink" and admitting one has a problem. Thanks in part to the media, there exists an unwarranted pessimism about psychiatry that dissuades many from getting the help they need. Psychiatrists are sometimes viewed as probing mental detectives who take control of their patients' minds rather than heal them. With this book, I hope to debunk such misconceptions and demystify the treatment of mental illness.

In any given year, an estimated one in four adults—nearly sixty million people—in the United States suffer from a mental disorder. Despite the public's misconceptions, psychiatric interventions have been shown to diminish and often eradicate the symptoms of psychosis, depression, and anxiety; yet many people do not have access to care, and often those who could improve with treatment never seek out a specialist.

I have described the events in this book as I experienced them, in the first person. My co-author and wife, Gigi Vorgan, has been essential to the writing of this book, helping me shape the narrative so that readers can better grasp the events and the science behind them.

The people and situations portrayed in this book are based on real patients and their emotional struggles. The details are derived from my case histories and vivid memories; however, many of the particulars have been altered to protect the confidentiality of my colleagues, patients, and their families The cases have been re-created as accurately as possible to give readers a true sense of my experiences as they occurred. Some dialogue, locations, and situations have been altered or fictionalized, as well as traits of some patients embedded onto others, to further protect the privacy of those involved. Any similarities to real people are unintended.

It is my hope that this book will both entertain and help those who fear psychiatry to overcome their fears and get help if they need it.

GARY SMALL, M.D.
LOS ANGELES, CALIFORNIA

ACKNOWLEDGMENTS

WE WISH TO THANK THE PATIENTS and mentors who inspired us to write this book, as well as our friends and colleagues who contributed their energy and insights, including Rachel Champeau, Michela Gunn, M.D., Jeff Gandin, M.D., Melinda Gandin, Robert Gandin, D.D.S., Jonathan Hiatt, M.D., Shirley Impellizeri, Ph.D., Don Seigel, and Lawrence Warick, M.D., Ph.D.

This book would not have been possible without the support and input from our longtime editor and friend, Mary Ellen O'Neill, as well as our dear friend and literary agent, Sandra Dijkstra. We also want to thank our children, Rachel and Harry, as well as our parents, Dr. Max and Gertrude Small, and Rose Vorgan and Fred Weiss, for their love and encouragement.

GARY SMALL, M.D.
GIGI VORGAN

The Naked Lady
Who Stood on
Her Head

CHAPTER ONE

Sexy Stare

Winter 1979

I BOBBED AND WEAVED MY WAY through the crowded waiting area of what we called "the APES," short for the Acute Psychiatric Service, Boston's busiest walk-in psychiatric clinic. It was just down the hallway from the emergency room of Massachusetts General, the major teaching hospital at Harvard Medical School. Our group of young psychiatric trainees nicknamed it the APES because of its jungle-like ambience—a perpetual array of troubled souls found their way here, either by their own free will or thanks to the assistance of the local police or emergency technicians.

I was twenty-seven and had finished medical school and a year of internal-medicine internship before leaving my hometown of Los Angeles for Boston. Only six months earlier, I had sold my car and everything else I owned and shown up at my empty one-bedroom Cambridge apartment with three boxes and a duffel bag. I had been anxious about moving and starting a new training program but excited to begin my career in psychiatry. Even though I was Phi Beta Kappa and summa cum laude, I still couldn't believe I was going to Harvard—although part of me thought, if they were letting *me* in, how good a school could it really be?

As I inched through the cramped waiting room, I almost bumped into a woman with bloodstained white gauze wrapped around her wrists, being escorted by two emergency technicians. I finally made it to the coffee room, where some of the other psych residents were taking a break between patients. There was something about being thrown into this intense environment that created an immediate bond between us. Humor was our favorite coping mechanism, and we constantly tried to one-up one another with jokes and patient horror stories to both shock and impress.

The first year of psychiatry residency combined rotations in emergency settings and inpatient units. In addition to these medically oriented training experiences, we were expected to begin taking on at least three long-term outpatient psychotherapy cases. I felt like I was finally jumping out of the textbook into a whirlwind of clinical experience. At the same time, I was dealing with a plethora of real people and their very real suffering. I found it overwhelming, frightening, and often exhilarating. Although I was energized by the intensity of the work, I was usually exhausted and always relieved when my shift ended.

The next morning was Saturday and I could have slept in, but the sunlight on my face woke me up early. I hadn't gotten window shades for my apartment yet. My girlfriend, Susan, was still sleeping, so I cuddled up to her for warmth—the narrow beam of sun didn't do much to heat the room. January was not my favorite month in Boston. Had Susan not been there, I would have already been huddled by my space heater reading Jung and Freud, looking like the Michelin Man in my three-pound parka and wool cap. Instead I threw the blankets over my head and imagined myself back in Los Angeles, where everybody always pretends it's such a fluke that it's eighty-five degrees in January. I knew that calling the landlord to turn on the steam heat for more than five minutes twice a day was fruitless, so I stayed where I was until Susan, an ICU nurse at Cambridge Hospital, stirred and mumbled that she had a shift that morning and had to go.

Sometimes on the weekends I felt a little homesick. Rather than hunker down and start studying for the day, I decided to run out to get a cappuccino and a croissant at my local coffee joint, where I might bump into Mike Pierce.

After completing his residency the previous year, Mike had started a part-time private practice while remaining half-time at the hospital as an attending physician supervising the residents. He was only three years ahead of me, but seemed to have a decade more experience and knowledge. His edgy humor reminded me of George Carlin, and he used it to teach us and help us deal with the tension that was constantly palpable. Mike was already married and had two young kids. Although he was an attending, we got to be good friends. He usually had Saturday-morning patients at his practice in the Back Bay, so sometimes we met early to get coffee and have a few laughs.

I saw Mike in line reading the *Boston Globe* sports page, so I cut in. "Skipping out on the twins on Saturday morning? I bet Janey is delighted."

Mike laughed. "I'm just giving them some special mommy time to bond."

"How's the practice going?" I asked.

"Great. Ever since I hung out my shingle, it's been a magnet for every desperate psychopath on the East Coast. Another couple of months and *I'll* be an inpatient at Lindemann," referring to the nearby psychiatric hospital. We took our coffees and croissants over to a small table by the windows.

"So what's up for you today?" Mike asked.

"I've got tons to read. Lochton assigned me every psychotherapy manual ever written."

"Ouch, you got the Loch Ness Monster as a supervisor? Have you picked out your plot at Forest Hills?"

Dr. Herman Lochton was my first assigned psychotherapy supervisor. He was well known in Harvard psychiatry circles and had edited several popular textbooks. He was also the team psychiatrist for the Boston Celtics, and treated senators and other VIPs who flew their private planes in from the Bahamas for therapy sessions. He had created a reputation for himself as a skilled diagnostician and therapist. When he wasn't busy telling people about his great accomplishments, he saw patients in his private practice. He volunteered one morning a week to supervise psychiatry residents in order to keep his title as a Harvard clinical professor.

"Okay," I said. "He is a bit of a tyrant, and he does have a touch of narcissism."

Mike laughed. "A *touch* of narcissism? The man thinks that he's personally responsible for the Celtics beating the Suns for the championship in '76."

"Yeah, I know, the guy's a little nuts. But I am learning from him."

"Just be careful," Mike said. "He knows a lot, but I don't think he's necessarily the greatest psychotherapy supervisor in the world." He took a sip of coffee and asked, "So what else is happening? How are you doing?"

"You know, Mike, it's weird. I've had some interesting cases, and I'm getting better at listening and talking with patients, but I still haven't worked with a psychotherapy patient in long-term treatment yet, and I'm not sure I'll know what to do."

"What do you mean?" Mike asked.

"I keep flashing back to med school," I said. "Those first experiences as a *real* doctor—whether I was doing a physical or taking out a gallbladder—I felt like I was acting, you know, playing the *role* of what I imagined a doctor to be. And I'm worried that doing psychotherapy is going to feel the same way."

"Welcome to the club. I have my own practice, and I still feel like I'm faking it from time to time. But it does seem like the more experience I get, the less I feel that way." Mike finished his coffee and looked at his watch. "I gotta run. I've got my multiple personality at eight-thirty. I never know who's going to show up."

The following Tuesday, Lochton was scheduled to lecture at group supervision in the psychotherapy clinic. I was the first resident to arrive and caught him combing his hair while holding a small hand mirror. I didn't know why he bothered because his hair was so stiff with Brylcreem that it never moved.

I couldn't resist and said, "You're looking very sharp this morning, Dr. Lochton."

"Gary, you can never look too professional for your patients. It shows respect."

As I noticed his shiny black dress shoes, I pulled at my khakis in a feeble attempt to mask the scruffy hiking boots that I wore in the snow. I was thankful that I had at least remembered to wear a tie that day.

A few other residents filed in and took seats in the conference room. Lochton checked his watch and began.

"Today I want to talk about the perfect patient for psychotherapy; we call it the YAVIS. The term stands for *young, attractive, verbal, insightful,* and *wealthy*—the *s* standing for the dollar sign of course." He picked up a piece of chalk and drew a large *$* on the board. As he continued on about his ideal patient, I kept thinking he was living in a dream world, because we residents almost never saw a YAVIS. We were used to treating the sociopathic, drug-addicted dropouts who frequented our clinic. Rich, intelligent people solved their problems with experienced private practitioners, not first-year psychiatry residents at bargain-basement prices.

At the end of his lecture, Lochton instructed us to look through the file cabinets lining the walls of the clinic. They contained brief evaluations of patients seeking psychotherapy in the resident clinic. He told us to find a teaching case so we could get started doing real therapy. As soon as he finished, we all raced from the room, practically trampling over one another to get to the file cabinets, knowing how ridiculous it was because we had all been rummaging through those files for weeks looking for a decent case.

Searching the files was futile anyway because the typical folder contained only a patient's basics—age, marital status, and reason for referral. It seldom had enough information to tell us if we had stumbled upon a YAVIS or not. In fact, if it really was a YAVIS, the evaluating resident would have snagged the patient for himself. The real way to find good psychotherapy patients was through personal referrals or word of mouth, not unlike landing an awesome apartment or being set up on a great blind date.

Despite all that, I still routinely thumbed through those tired files, and after a few weeks, I thought I had found my first YAVIS. Sherry Williams was a housewife in her early thirties who lived in the suburbs. She was a college graduate and had never been arrested or hospitalized in a psych ward. She came to the clinic complaining of chronic anxiety. I knew Lochton would approve. I called her and arranged our first appointment.

The first-year psychiatry residents had to use whatever offices were available in the clinic for the day. I scored an office with a little window, although part of the view was obstructed by a file cabinet. There was a small desk that I kept bashing my knee on and a chair and sofa for patients. It had the bare necessities of a psychotherapy practice, including a telephone with intercom and a box of tissues.

At our first meeting, Sherry Williams entered my office dressed like a teenage girl, wearing tight jeans, sneakers, and braided hair. She sat on the sofa cross-legged, looked up at me, and waited. Clearly, it was my move.

I broke the ice by asking about her drive in from the suburbs. It seemed to relax her and start her talking. "You know those Boston drivers; they think traffic laws are optional."

Not sure what to say next, I ventured, "So tell me about yourself, Sherry."

"Well, I'm married to my college sweetheart"—she flashed her big diamond ring—"who's still gorgeous. We have a brand-new fabulous house with a step-down living room and an incredible deck." She went silent again, waiting for me to say something. Okay, I thought, now what would a *real* therapist ask?

"So what brings you to the clinic today?"

She stared at me for a moment and finally said, "I just can't stop feeling nervous, Doctor."

At the word *Doctor*, I almost giggled. I felt like such a phony.

Thankfully she went on. "The feeling gets worse when my husband travels, and he travels a *lot* for work since he got his promotion to regional manager. I feel lonely in that big house—it's boring. Sometimes I get so edgy that I can't even handle the housework. The laundry piles up, and nothing gets done."

It sounded like her anxiety was so overwhelming that it might be paralyzing her at home. My instincts told me not to discuss her mental paralysis at our first session. Instead, I tried to be supportive and get her to talk more about her feelings. "The anxiety must be very difficult for you," I said in my most empathic voice.

"It is, Dr. Small. It really is." She uncrossed her legs and sat in what seemed to be a slightly seductive pose on the sofa. "I just worry about everything . . . my husband's job, the mortgage payments—which is stupid, because I don't even know what our mortgage is. Eddie takes care of all the bills." She sighed and looked at the file cabinet in front of the little window.

"What are you thinking about?" I asked.

"I don't understand why I can't feel happy. All of my friends seem to be happy. I have the biggest house, and my girlfriends are all jealous that I got Eddie, but I can't seem to have any fun anymore. What's wrong with me? Do you think I'm depressed?"

I didn't know about that yet. I was just glad she didn't call me Doctor again.

"What do *you* think is wrong?" I asked, following Lochton's advice by avoiding yes/no questions and instead asking open-ended ones that would encourage her to talk.

"I feel empty . . . It's like I have a giant hole inside . . . here." She wrapped her arms around her chest and rubbed her shoulders in what I could have sworn was a seductive gesture.

As Sherry continued her story, I got the feeling she was holding something back. She told me that she couldn't have children and both she and Eddie were fine with that. Neither of them was really into kids. But the way she spoke seemed rehearsed, almost as if she *knew* the answers I wanted to hear. I started to wonder whether she was really just an anxious, bored, possibly depressed housewife who wanted to understand herself better or a sociopath who practiced her story after reading some psychotherapy text.

"Tell me about your marriage," I said.

"I think I fell in love with Eddie the first time I looked into his dreamy blue eyes. We were both juniors at Boston College, and he was the first-string quarterback. My mother loved him, his family had big money, and he was great in bed . . . at least for the first few years."

"So things have changed between you?" I asked.

"He works so hard now that he's too tired for sex. I really miss that, you know?" She grinned mischievously.

It seemed like she was flirting with me. I had read about seductive patients in textbooks, but to actually experience one was strange and uncomfortable. She was a confusing case, but I did have some ideas about what might be going on. Sherry seemed to focus on appearances and possessions—her dreamy-eyed husband with the family money, her big new house, and her jealous friends. Perhaps she had a narcissistic personality disorder—a condition wherein the individual pursues superficial pleasures in attempts to fill an underlying emotional emptiness and insecurity. But she could also be depressed because of her husband's frequent travel. Her flirtatious behavior could also reflect a histrionic personality, typical of people who seek attention through dramatic and emotional behavior.

I needed to know more about her before I could make a diagnosis and plan a therapeutic strategy. I continued to gently ask questions, but she was evasive about details and just kept returning to the angst she felt as a lonely housewife.

"You know, if you're going to be my psychiatrist, I need to know more about you," she said as if challenging me to go mano a mano.

"What would you like to know?" I asked.

"Where you're from, how old you are, and whether you have a girlfriend," she listed in quick succession.

Most patients are curious about their psychotherapist, but Sherry's series of questions felt intrusive. All patients are entitled to know their doctor's professional qualifications, fees, and treatment policies, but disclosure beyond that standard information can be a delicate matter and impede the therapeutic process.

Not all psychotherapists agree on how much self-disclosure is appropriate. Freud took the position that the therapist should be impenetrable to the patient. This Freudian approach encourages the patient to project his fantasies onto the therapist, who serves as a sort of mirror for the patient's inner life. The process of working through those projections, or transferences, helps patients understand themselves better and diminishes their mental symptoms.

Some clinicians endorse a more humanistic approach and don't mind revealing additional information about themselves—where they are vacationing, how many children they have, and so on. They view these disclosures as a way to enhance their therapeutic alliance with the patient, but it depends on the nature of the patient's problems. Therapist self-disclosure can be a burden for patients, who might feel a need to care for the therapist, or get angry or jealous, which can interfere with their own progress.

I could have told Sherry my age and where I was from, but I felt that the question about a girlfriend was over-the-top. My instincts told me that if I answered any of her questions, it would only encourage her to ask more, and where would it end? I decided to deflect. "You know, Sherry, it's natural to want to know about your therapist, but I can help you more if we focus on you."

She looked stung. "Fine, if that's how you want to play it." Her body language changed from the seductive teenager to a hurt little girl.

"What do you remember about your childhood, Sherry?"

"Look, I'm thirty-three, I graduated Boston College, I'm married, and I feel like crap. Okay? There's nothing else to tell," she replied, annoyed.

"Did you get along with your parents? Your mother?" I asked.

"Yes. Everything was fine."

"You mentioned that your parents really like your husband."

This made her smile. "Everybody loves Eddie. He's a real charmer. I just wish he was around more. I wouldn't be so nervous all the time."

As we continued, Sherry relaxed; it was as if she had forgiven me. We talked more about her marriage and her chronic anxiety. I ended the session by suggesting that we meet weekly. "This will give us an opportunity to understand your feelings and try to sort things out."

"Finally, someone wants to understand me. Thank you, Dr. Small," Sherry said, smiling, as she rose to leave. She grabbed my hand to shake it but held it so long that I eventually had to pull it away. It was an uncomfortable moment for me that she didn't seem to notice.

The next day was my supervision meeting with Lochton. His office was on the first floor of his Beacon Hill brownstone, a short, steep, uphill walk from the hospital. By the time I got there, lugging my backpack, I was panting. Those long shifts in the clinic didn't really motivate me to get out and jog very often, especially in the winter. I caught my breath before buzzing the intercom.

"Identify yourself," an officious voice blasted through the little box.

"It's Gary Small for supervision, Dr. Lochton." He buzzed me in and I opened the door to his waiting room, which was a converted entry hall. It was old Beacon Hill style—white walls with wainscoting, hardwood floors, Stickley furniture, and old *New Yorker* magazines. He made me wait for ten minutes, probably while he added globs of Brylcreem to his hair.

Finally a door opened. "Come in, Gary," Lochton said in his deep, radio-announcer voice. His wood-paneled office walls were covered with framed diplomas, awards, and journal covers. The bookshelves were jammed with medical and psychiatric texts. "Please sit down."

"Thank you, Dr. Lochton," I said as I took a seat. He was wearing a smoking jacket and holding an unlit pipe. He looked like an overweight, Freudian version of Hugh Hefner.

"Please, call me Herman," Lochton said.

The name Herman Hefner popped into my mind, and I almost laughed out loud. "Yes, sir," I managed to say with a straight face.

"So how is it going with your YAVIS, Gary?"

I pulled my copious notes out of my backpack and began. "She's a thirty-three-year-old college-educated housewife from Belmont whose main complaint is chronic anxiety. I tried, but she wouldn't give me much early history. She says she's in love with her husband but keeps talking about feeling empty inside, especially when he travels for work, which he does often."

When I said her husband traveled, Lochton lit up. "So he deserts her, over and over. Any kids?"

"She can't have them, and they don't seem to want to adopt."

"Interesting," he said as he lit his pipe, deep in thought.

As I continued to describe Sherry, I could see that Lochton was enthralled. His pipe smoke filled the room. I coughed and waved away some of the smoke. He was completely oblivious.

"So what we have here is an educated, verbal young woman with the capacity for a long-term relationship, but barren and probably so ashamed of her infertility that she's unwilling to adopt, even though her life is empty, boring, and unfulfilled." He leaned forward. "This will be an excellent case to help you learn about psychotherapy. I'm intrigued by the husband's frequent travel."

"Her symptoms do get worse when he's away—"

"Yes, but *why* does he travel so much, and what does *she* do in private to cope with her anxiety? She must be sensitized to separation and loss because of some early life trauma. Her evasiveness about her childhood proves my point."

I didn't see how he had proven his point at all, but I knew Lochton had a reputation for being obsessed with early separation and loss. His primary psychodynamic explanation for nearly every patient's problem was a psychological loss early in childhood—whether it was a death in the family, a traumatic divorce, or a beloved cat gone missing. He theorized that these types of childhood experiences made patients overly vulnerable to separations and losses later in life. Lochton believed that childhood losses explained most psychiatric symptoms, from anxiety and depression to obsessions and compulsions.

He encouraged me to get Sherry to talk about her childhood. He said

I should delve into her past and start seeing her twice a week. Increasing the frequency of her sessions would intensify our explorations and help her to open up more quickly.

"Find out about her relationship with her father," he said. "Did he also travel when she was a child? Or maybe he deserted the family and she felt abandoned just as she does now."

When I told Lochton about Sherry's seductiveness, his expression completely changed. "In what way was she flirting with you?" he asked.

"It wasn't so much overtly flirting, but more her body language, the way she moved around on the sofa and how she looked at me, the lingering handshake at the end of the session. It felt intrusive."

Lochton stared at me silently. Finally he said, "Go on . . ." His response was odd. He was talking to me as if I were a patient.

"She asked me personal questions like whether I had a girlfriend."

"How did that make you feel?" he asked.

"Strange. It was a therapy session, not a pickup bar."

"Did you answer the personal questions?"

"No. I told her we were there to talk about her feelings, not about my personal life," I said, trying not to sound defensive.

"That's good, Gary, but do you think you did anything that might have provoked her seductive behavior?"

"Absolutely not, Dr. Lochton. I was completely professional." I was starting to get annoyed. Lochton hadn't seen Sherry's behavior, and he was insinuating that I was the seducer.

He looked at his clock and said, "Our time is up here." Now he was really talking to me like I was a patient.

As I got up to leave, he added, "You know, Gary, a patient like this woman can stir up discomfort in her therapist. Be careful of that, and keep delving into her past. I'm sure you'll find the trauma that's driving her neurosis."

Although Lochton's theory seemed like a stretch, I followed his advice and started meeting with Sherry twice a week. I kept probing her past but didn't seem to get anywhere. At the same time, what I perceived as her seductive behavior escalated. She began wearing heavy makeup, short skirts, and plunging necklines to her sessions, and I noticed a pattern—when her husband was out of town, Sherry's outfits were more provocative than when he was home.

I discussed the possibility of confronting her about it, but Lochton told me to ignore it and press on about her early trauma. I was relieved because I sensed that if I pointed out the sexy-apparel pattern, she would take it as a rejection of her possible seductive overtures and perhaps stop therapy.

After about a month of my futile attempts to pry into her past, Sherry became exasperated with me and finally said, "Look, I had a normal childhood, okay? No abuse. My parents never went anywhere, and I did well in school. Your questions are making me uncomfortable."

It was clear that if she was going to talk about it, I needed to take a different approach. "That's fine, Sherry. I don't want to make you uncomfortable."

"Thank you, Dr. Small. Can I call you Gary?"

"I don't have a problem with that." After a long pause I asked, "Is there anything else making you uncomfortable?"

She stared at me. "Actually, yes. I need to confess something."

"Go ahead," I said.

"Ever since Eddie started traveling more, I've been going to this bar at night," she said. "At first I would just stop in for a quick drink with a friend, but eventually I started going there on my own." She stopped and looked away.

"Are you concerned that you might be drinking too much?" I asked.

"No, that's not it. I only have one or two glasses of wine to relax me." She paused and then continued, "One night I met this guy. We had a lot of laughs, and I took him home with me when the bar closed."

"How did you feel about that?" I asked.

"When I woke up the next day he was gone. I felt dirty, disgusted, and I threw the sheets in the trash," she said, looking down.

"Did you ever go back to that bar?"

"At first, no. I stayed away. But after a couple of weeks, I did go back. That's part of my confession. I've done it more than once."

"So you're going to a bar and having affairs when your husband is out of town?" I asked, trying to keep the surprise out of my voice and face.

"They're not really affairs; they're just one-night stands. And I always feel dirty and hate myself the next day. I mean, I still love Eddie."

"If it makes you hate yourself and you feel dirty afterward, why do you think you keep going back?" I asked.

She paused for a moment and then said, "I don't really think about the dirtiness at the beginning. I just feel bored and empty, and I want to be with someone. It's weird, when we're having sex, it feels like these guys really love me; but once I orgasm, everything changes. I want these strange men to disappear." She shuddered. "Eddie would die if he knew."

"How long has this been going on, Sherry?"

"I don't know, a year maybe, but it's all different now that I started seeing you, Gary. You're the first man who has shown that you really care about me. You always want to know how I feel, and I can see that look in your eyes. I know you mean it." She smiled at me again in her provocative way.

It was odd that she would say I was the first man who really cared about her. What about her husband and her father?

Although I thought it was progress that Sherry trusted me enough to reveal this secret side of her life, I was concerned. Her behavior was dangerous and could not only destroy her marriage but expose her to physical harm. I needed some supervision—fast.

"I think we both have to understand this better, Sherry. Do you think you can keep from going back to that bar until we've had a chance to talk again on Friday?"

Her smile was a caricature of sexiness. "For you, Gary, I'd do anything."

Later that afternoon I hiked up to Lochton's office. He had a field day over my session with Sherry. He paced and puffed his pipe as he expounded excitedly. "She's acting out sexually to compensate for her unmet emotional needs as a child. She must have been sexually abused as a girl. That's why she feels unloved and keeps searching for it with these strange men."

I tried to tell him that I wasn't convinced there had been abuse, but it was like talking to a tornado. He kept whirling about the room saying that Sherry was repeating these demeaning sexual acts as an adult repetition compulsion. And now her seductive behavior with me was perfect. She was developing a classic transference. At least he finally believed me about her seductiveness.

He stopped pacing and went into lecture mode. He said that transference was one of the most important aspects of insight-oriented psychotherapy. It meant that the patient was transferring feelings she had toward a parent or authority figure onto the therapist. Therapists who can remain neutral and nonjudgmental—suppressing their own issues and emotional reactions during the therapy—allow the patient to fill in what they imagine to be the therapist's reaction. When the time comes for the therapist to point out the reality of the relationship, the patient can gain insight into her distortions and realize how she transfers past distortions onto other relationships in her life. With the therapist's help, the patient can come to grips with this pattern, put her distortions into perspective, and move on.

I understood the lecture on transference, just as I had the first three times I'd heard it. And as for Lochton's explanations about Sherry's early-childhood losses, they were plausible—maybe she was still hiding something from me.

Before the next session on Friday, I had decided to focus on Sherry's self-destructive barhopping behavior and try to help her to stop. I was taken aback when Sherry showed up dressed like a prostitute.

She struggled to sit down in her tight miniskirt and started talking. "I want to thank you, Gary, for listening to me on Wednesday and helping me to stop doing what I was doing. It was crazy, and I know that you really do care about me."

"I'm relieved you've stopped. How are you feeling?" I asked.

"You know the answer to that. It's our little secret." She winked, as if there was some inside joke between us.

"What do you mean?"

She didn't say anything, just smiled.

"I thought we were beyond secrets, Sherry. For psychotherapy to work, you have to try to tell me what's on your mind."

She finally said, "But you know what's on my mind—every time you look into my eyes." She reached into her purse. "Here's a little thank-you for our last session. I hope you enjoyed it as much as I did." She handed me a gift and darted out of the office before I could say anything.

The gift was beautifully wrapped. I wasn't sure what to do, so I opened it. Inside was a Rolex watch—a real one. I ran into the hall and looked toward the elevator, but she was already gone.

A basic tenet of psychotherapy is to help people put feelings into words, not action. Sherry had crossed the line with the watch. There's a general rule in therapy that no gifts can be accepted. I called Lochton for advice, and he just told me to return the watch and explore the patient's motivation for the gift. He also said I shouldn't worry about her mini-skirts and plunging necklines. They were just expressions of her transference. It really had nothing to do with me. It was her father that she was pursuing.

At our next session, Sherry entered my office in a red cocktail dress and matching pumps. She seemed to bubble with joy—like a newlywed in love. As she sat down, she saw the Rolex on the coffee table and became serious.

I pushed the watch toward her and said, "Sherry, there are rules in therapy. No gifts, no—"

She interrupted angrily, "You're returning my watch? Fine." She threw the watch into her bag. "And how dare you? *You* seduced *me.*"

"What are you talking about?"

"Oh, please. You stared into my eyes and had sex with me. You and your sexy stare—as far as I know, I could be pregnant from your raping, peering eyes."

I had been taught to maintain eye contact as patients spoke, as a way to express interest and empathy and to try to listen and not interrupt. I was dumbfounded. Sherry had experienced my eye contact as a sexual assault. She was more than a neurotic housewife; she was talking crazy. Having sexual intercourse by looking into someone's eyes sounded more like a psychotic losing touch with reality than an angst-ridden woman expressing her neurotic woes.

"Let's slow down here, Sherry," I stammered.

She stood up and inched toward the coffee table. "You should have thought about that before you looked into my eyes."

Confused, I stood up too. My heart was pounding as she moved forward around the coffee table, and I backed away toward the door. Was she going to grab me? Embrace me? She was acting insane, and I had lost control of the session.

"Sherry, sit down. Let's talk about this." My attempt to bring order back to the session only worsened the situation.

Her face reddened with rage. "How dare you give me back my gift. That came from my heart."

"Sherry, I didn't mean to hurt you. It's just that there are rules for therapy—"

"Therapy?" she shouted. Suddenly, she lunged forward and slapped my face, hard. She was about to strike me again when I grabbed her wrist and said, "That's enough! This meeting is over." I quickly left the office and retreated down the hall.

Fortunately, the clinic secretary was at her desk. I asked her to check on Sherry and escort her from the clinic. After ducking into another office to hide, I heard Sherry stomp down the hallway in a huff.

I was shaken. Was this a rite of passage for a neophyte psychiatrist, or had I made some major tactical error? I had never been hit by a patient, despite numerous threats. I recalled a chronic schizophrenic that I sent to the state hospital the previous month calling out to me, "I'll get back at you for this, Small. I never forget!" But somehow he didn't feel as threatening. With Sherry, I never saw it coming. I let her chase me out of my own office. Could I continue treating her? Would she try to slap me again next time? I needed some supervision, but I no longer thought Lochton was the guy to help. In fact, I was angry at him. Following his advice had gotten me into this mess.

There were many skilled therapy supervisors at Mass General who knew about tough patients and tricky supervision situations. I was able to schedule some time the next day with Joe Sandler, a seasoned analyst and psychodynamic therapist who specialized in borderline and psychotic patients. I had attended a few of his seminars and liked his style. He was a cross between an opinionated Irish bartender and a caring Jewish mother.

Sandler agreed with what had become obvious to me since having my face slapped. Sherry was much sicker than either Lochton or I had appreciated. She was a borderline psychotic who could not tolerate the anxiety of probing psychotherapy. Borderlines are patients whose psychological state straddles the line between normal anxiety and psychosis. When under stress, they tend to distort reality and have delusions and hallucinations. All my delving into Sherry's past and not answering any of her direct questions about me had pushed her into a psychotic delusion that I was having sex with her by looking into her eyes. She didn't need probing; she needed support and nurturing.

Sandler suggested I take a closer look at Sherry's medical history. I looked up her old hospital medical records and found that her lab tests were all normal, but she had never had a head CT scan or an electroencephalogram (EEG). It was a long shot, but maybe Sherry had a brain tumor or some kind of neurological problem that was contributing to her psychosis and erotomania.

I knew Sherry needed help, and I got some referrals for her in case she wouldn't continue therapy with me. Despite my anxiety about working with her, I felt bolstered by my new supervision and wanted to try again.

After a week, I gave Sherry a call. I encouraged her to come back and talk about what happened. She was snippy at first but willing to listen. I told her that I really did want to help her and that a different approach might make sense at this point. But she would have to follow the rules—no hitting and no gifts. I told her that we would not need to explore her past so much but would look for ways to help her cope with the feelings that brought her to therapy in the first place—emptiness and loneliness. We could also slow things down and meet just once a week. I wanted her medical doctor to get some additional tests so we could possibly start her on some medication to help calm her nerves. Finally, I assured her I would not stare into her eyes and reiterated that I had not meant to make her uncomfortable. I think she sensed I was back in the driver's seat as her psychiatrist, and she agreed to come back.

Sherry returned to weekly therapy, and I started her on a low dose of an antipsychotic drug. It quickly dampened her eroticized transference delusion, and she also toned down her wardrobe.

"I don't know what I was thinking, Dr. Small," she said. "I was just stressed out because Eddie was traveling so much and you seemed to be interested in what I had to say."

"I'm just glad you're feeling better, Sherry."

"I can't believe how stupid I was going to that bar. I could have taken home an axe murderer or something."

"I think the medicine is helping you cope better with your anxiety," I said.

In the meantime, the results of her medical evaluation came back. Her EEG revealed no evidence of temporal-lobe epilepsy, a condition sometimes caused by a brain tumor under the temples, which can lead to personality changes and hypersexuality. Sherry did have a pattern of hypersexuality, but the scan ruled out a possible neurological explanation for her symptoms. A diagnosis of borderline personality disorder turned out to be the best explanation for her symptoms and her negative response to the insight-oriented psychotherapy Lochton had recommended.

Sherry continued to see me weekly for supportive psychotherapy and medication follow-up. In general, she was less anxious and seemed to have a good grip on reality. Whenever her husband would leave for an extended business trip, I would increase her dose of antipsychotic, and she didn't relapse into her old barhopping behavior—as far as I knew. In fact, she was progressing so well that I started to delve a bit into her past, and she revealed that her parents had separated when she was twelve— Lochton had been partly right about her having an early trauma. But at the next session, Sherry showed up wearing a miniskirt and pumps, so I backed off digging into her early childhood, and focused on helping her cope with her current anxieties and fears. After another year in therapy with me, she decided to switch to someone in the suburbs near her home.

Part of me was sorry to see Sherry go because her therapy was finally going well and her life seemed to be relatively stable. Another part of me was relieved. I never forgot that slap, and I always had lingering fears that the slightest misstep on my part could tip her from reality into another psychotic delusion.

I realize now that what most disturbed me about working with Sherry was that my initial diagnosis had been so off the mark, and my supervisor had been clueless too. Week after week I sat in a tiny office with someone I thought I knew, who turned out to be somebody completely different—an unpredictable, seriously disturbed, and potentially dangerous woman. I followed Lochton's advice and instructions even though they often felt wrong to me.

The "sexy stare" incident taught me a lot about trusting my own instincts as a therapist. The Loch Ness Monster had turned out to be partly right, but once I dropped him as a supervisor, I realized that nobody's perfect—not even know-it-all professors who treat celebrities and politicians. Sherry's slap in the face hurt, but it knocked the giggles out of me, and for the first time, I started to feel like a real psychiatrist.

CHAPTER TWO

The Naked Lady Who Stood on Her Head

Spring 1979

I WAS HALFWAY THROUGH A CROSSWORD puzzle during a break in the psych residents' coffee lounge. Mike Pierce had been the attending that day and was getting ready to head out. I had been on call for eleven hours and had thirteen more to go when we heard the familiar overhead page: "Psychiatry to room six." When the security officers considered a new arrival particularly rambunctious, they whisked the patient immediately to room 6, where the feisty newcomer could be locked in for observation.

"Room six. You're up, Small," Mike said.

"Oh boy, my favorite," I said.

"You may think room six is a bummer, but trust me, it is," Mike said with a smirk.

"This'll be a piece of cake," I said, gripped with apprehension.

"No one will wait up for you," Mike said as I left.

As I walked to the emergency room, several nurses raced by me. I passed a surgical resident bandaging the head of a crying teenage boy lying on one of several gurneys lining the hallway. Another doctor was yelling for a crash cart. The E.R. was a cacophony of wailing patients and on-call doctors shouting orders at nurses and attendants—typical for a Wednesday evening.

My heart was pounding. I was eager to meet this new patient, but I was scared too. Room 6 was sometimes horrifying, almost always challenging, but never boring. Responding to a room 6 page could mean anything—an agitated schizophrenic killer with a hidden barbecue skewer, a suicidal bipolar with a secret bottle of Valium, or a heroin addict going into withdrawal and about to projectile vomit on you. Thanks to an unfortunate but traditional rite of passage in medical training, the doctors with the least experience—me, for instance—had to grapple with the most challenging and difficult patients.

To deal with what seemed like impossible situations, I often fell back on my textbook knowledge and tended to treat patients in a stilted, clinical way. Freud would have said I used intellectualization as a defense mechanism to cope with my anxiety about wanting to help my patients and not harm them. Like any doctor, I had the daunting task of trying to translate a massive amount of information into a simple diagnosis and treatment plan. Whatever defenses I was using in those days, my human side managed to slip out on occasion, and I think those moments of empathy were the ones that helped my patients the most. Later in my career, as I gained more experience and confidence, I became better at listening and understanding my patients.

By the time I reached the nurses' station outside room 6, I was so anxious and worked up that Judy Nelson, the head nurse, gave me a tissue to wipe my brow. Judy had been an E.R. nurse for twelve years and had seen hundreds of green residents like me struggle with room 6. She was in her early thirties, divorced, and really pretty. She also had the perfect balance of poise and sarcasm. Whoever divorced her was an idiot.

Judy handed me the patient's chart. "She's a Jane Doe, around twenty. The cops picked her up babbling in the North End. I'll have to remember that babbling's a crime around here."

Judy's casual attitude calmed me down, and I scanned the chart. The police had found the patient disheveled and wandering the streets of Boston's North End, an Italian community less than a mile from the hospital. The emergency techs noted that she kept shrieking and pulling at her clothes during the ambulance ride over. Between screams she mumbled about how hot she was, although the outside temperature was in the forties. The techs had performed a brief examination and had found nothing abnormal, aside from her agitated and unusual behavior.

I walked down the hall to room 6. Unlike the other E.R. exam rooms, room 6 had a door with a window covered by a sliding wood panel so we could check on psych patients before entering. I slid back the panel and saw a petite girl who looked to be about nineteen or twenty, standing on her head, stark naked. It took a moment to register. I didn't know whether to laugh or run. Before I slammed closed the wood panel, I did notice that she was balancing herself rather well. I turned and stared at the gurneys and patients in the hallway, trying to process what I had just seen.

"Are you all right, Dr. Small?" Judy asked.

"Fine. I just want to check something in her chart here before I go in."

But I wasn't fine. What did this naked headstand mean? Was there some psychological significance to it that I wasn't getting? Was she trying to communicate something, or was she just completely out of her mind?

"Judy, could you call a couple of security guards down here in case I need them? Also, please grab a gown for the patient."

I slid open the little window again. The patient was still doing a headstand and had a blank expression on her face as she stared toward the door. "Hello. My name is Dr. Small. I'm the psychiatrist on call tonight."

No response.

"Can you hear me? I need to come in and ask you some questions," I said.

Again, no response.

Okay, I was afraid to go in the room, and Judy was watching. Jane Doe's bizarre behavior meant that anything could happen. She could become violent without warning. I imagined her lunging and trying to strangle me. On the other hand, her nakedness made her seem vulnerable, and she was probably scared too. I needed to interview her, but first I had to get into that room.

I took a few deep breaths and calmed down, recalling that sometimes simply showing a patient that the staff was in control helped avoid a scene. Finally, Judy came over with a gown and two security guards, Joe and Carl. Both were local guys who loved teasing the residents and giving us a hard time. Having them around made us feel safe if patients got out of control.

I spoke through the little window in the door. "I'm going to come into the room now with a nurse and some of our staff. I need you to stop standing on your head, please." She didn't move. I noticed her filthy, torn clothes in the corner of the room.

"We're going to place a hospital gown on the gurney. You have a choice to either put it on yourself or let the nurse help you." I had been taught that offering unpredictable psychotic patients a choice sometimes distracted them from their hallucinations or delusions, essentially tricking them into being more reasonable.

As Jane Doe continued to stare from her headstand, our troupe moved slowly into the room, which contained only a rolling stretcher and a metal chair. Judy led the way and placed the gown on the gurney. Carl and Joe took positions in the corners. I stood in front of the open door. Though I believed it was to block the patient from bolting from the room, I think now it was also, subconsciously, to allow me to make my own quick escape.

The strength-in-numbers tactic seemed to work. Judy moved toward the patient and gently helped her down from her headstand, as if she was spotting a gymnast. Judy spoke quietly as she assisted her with the gown, "You're so lucky to have those pretty blond curls." She escorted Ms. Doe to the gurney and said, "Sit down, sweetie, and get comfortable."

I pulled up a chair and took a moment to observe the patient. Her hair was matted and dirty, and she had a butterfly tattoo on her ankle. "Can you tell me your name?" I got no response, so I followed with, "Do you know how you got here?"

She mumbled something about how hot it was.

"You're right, it is warm in here," I said. "Would you like me to get a fan?"

Blank stare and no reply.

"Is there someone I can call for you?"

The patient twitched for a moment, and I thought she was finally going to say something real, but still nothing. Joe and Carl were clearly amused by my futile queries but stifled their laughter. I didn't dare look at Judy.

I was getting annoyed—I was trying to help this patient, not entertain the staff. After what seemed like an endless string of feeble attempts to get her to talk, I moved on to a physical exam and tentatively lifted her wrist to check her pulse. Her hand felt clammy. When I tapped her knees and ankles, her deep-tendon reflexes were normal. She wouldn't cooperate for me to test her arm and leg strength, but other than a slightly rapid heart rate and low-grade fever, I couldn't find anything physically wrong with her.

I had performed hundreds of physical exams, but this was the strangest one yet. Not only was I onstage for the staff, but my patient's mind was off somewhere else. Because I couldn't get her to walk for me, I wasn't able to check her gait, which might have revealed various brain problems—wide-based could mean hydrocephalus, shuffling could indicate Parkinson's disease—but I did know that she was neurologically quite capable of standing on her head. I knew she was out of touch with reality, but diagnostically, I was stumped.

People lose touch with reality for many reasons. Sometimes severe depression, stress, or trauma can push them over the edge and they escape into a distorted mental state that appears crazy to other people. But many mental symptoms, like psychosis, ultimately have a physical cause. In fact, many medical emergencies initially present themselves with *only* mental symptoms—delirium, confusion, depression, anxiety, psychosis, or panic attacks.

To help me remember the various physical causes of psychological symptoms, I had come up with my own mnemonic for some of the more common ones—"WHHIMP." Each letter was the first initial for a medical cause of delirium: *w* was for *W*ernicke's encephalopathy, due to brain damage from chronic alcohol abuse. The *h*'s stood for a *h*ypertensive crisis (extremely high blood pressure causing an acute drop in brain blood flow) or *h*ypoglycemia or *h*yperglycemia from an imbalance in blood sugar. *I* reminded me that *i*ntracranial lesions such as strokes, tumors, and bleeds could be the culprit. *M* was for *m*eningitis and related infections of the brain and meninges, which coat the brain; and *p* was for *p*oisons, certainly high on the list of possibilities in a young person who might be experimenting with recreational drugs.

Jane Doe coughed suddenly, and we all jumped. She was looking straight at me now but still wasn't talking. I moved my index finger from left to right in front of her face, but her eyes didn't track it. I snapped my fingers in front of her eyes and got no response. When I suddenly clapped my hands, she flinched and blinked, so I did get some reaction. I ordered a CT scan to rule out a brain tumor or hemorrhage.

Her low-grade temperature could mean an infection, but she lacked the neck rigidity that was typical of meningitis. Her complaints about the heat and her nudity suggested possible heat intolerance due to an overactive thyroid, which the blood-screening tests would rule out. We needed a urine sample for a toxicology screen, but no way was she going to pee in a cup. She would have to be catheterized. To spare her the humiliation of two burly security guards holding her down, Judy shuffled us guys out of the room and enlisted the help of two female interns to catheterize her. She also drew blood for screening laboratory tests to make sure the patient didn't have anemia, a thyroid disorder, or some other chemical imbalance that might be altering her mental state.

As I waited for the lab results, I decided to take another stab at an interview. The guards and I walked back into room 6, and I could tell that Joe and Carl were looking forward to seeing me get nowhere again. I tried to be casual with the patient and offered her a cup of orange juice. She finally seemed to respond to me. She slowly raised her hand for the cup. She took a small sip at first, then quickly gulped it all down.

"It looks like you were pretty thirsty," I said. The staff smirked, anticipating yet another useless round of questions, but the patient's demeanor seemed to change—her blank stare was replaced by an inquisitive look. She scanned the room; her body tensed; her brow furrowed.

I felt like maybe we were getting somewhere, so I continued in my light tone, "Maybe we can talk now."

Ms. Doe suddenly sat straight up and became aware of her scant attire. She wrapped her hospital gown tightly around her body and asked, "Where am I? Who are you? What the hell?"

I could sense that the team was impressed. I should have felt cocky that my astute, relentless, and well-timed interview skills had finally cracked this obstinate naked-lady case. I should have been proud that in my role as a psychiatrist, something I had said had actually gotten this delirious, mute woman to talk like a normal person. I mean, sure I had gone to school and read some books and aced some tests, but here I was in the real world, playing doctor, and I actually fixed somebody. Unfortunately, I had no idea what I had said that worked.

The patient held out her cup and said, "More."

In an instant I realized it was nothing I'd said but something I'd done that got her to talk. More precisely, it was the orange juice. And that cup of OJ was also the key to what caused her bizarre behavior. Her blood sugar had obviously crashed, and she had been suffering from acute hypoglycemia.

Responding to the patient's anxiety about her skimpy hospital gown, I asked Judy to get her a pair of scrubs to put on and escorted the security guards out of the room while Judy helped her change. I returned with another cup of orange juice and sat in the chair next to her gurney while she drank it. She was calmer now.

Again I told her I was Dr. Small and asked her about herself. Her name was Katie Genaro. She was nineteen and lived with her parents above their popular family bakery in the North End. She worked part-time as a waitress while taking acting classes and doing Equity theater whenever she could get a part.

I moved the conversation along to find out more about the cause of her delirium. "Katie, do you have any medical illnesses?" I asked.

"Why do you want to know?"

"Because you were brought to the hospital tonight, delirious. You'd been walking in the street babbling, and you only just now came out of your delirium when you drank some orange juice."

"Shit. It's my stupid diabetes again. I probably didn't eat enough breakfast before taking my insulin shot."

"So this has happened before?"

"Once or twice. I don't always get my insulin right, so sometimes I get light-headed and sweaty," she said.

"How long have you had diabetes?"

"I found out about a year ago."

Diabetics don't make enough of their own insulin—the body's natural hormone for moving sugar from the blood into the body's cells for energy. If somebody injects too much insulin after not ingesting enough sugar or carbohydrate from a meal, her blood glucose level can take a quick dive. Because sugar is the brain's main source of energy, Katie's low brain-sugar level plunged her into an amnesia-driven delirious state, which the orange juice instantly cured, making her sane once again. It wasn't a huge psychiatric achievement, but I had given her the right treatment—even though I didn't know it at the time.

"I couldn't believe it. I mean, I've always been such a health freak."

"Being a health freak is a good thing, but it won't help you control your diabetic symptoms if you don't stay on top of your blood-sugar levels. You're playing with fire, and if you're not careful, it can kill you."

"You sound like my mother. She's always accusing me of messing with my insulin so I can stay thin for acting parts. How ridiculous."

I noticed that she was very slender and wondered if it really was so ridiculous. "I certainly don't mean to sound like a parent. I just want to be sure you know the facts about diabetes. When you get it at your age, it's usually inherited," I said.

"Well, my aunt got diabetes when she was about forty, but she was overweight and worked in Dad's bakery."

Judy came in with a sandwich for Katie and handed me the lab results. As I suspected, Katie's blood-glucose level had been forty-five— well below the normal range.

"Katie, I want you to meet Judy; she's been taking care of you tonight. Judy, this is Katie Genaro. She lives with her parents in the North End. You know Genaro's? That's their family bakery."

"Oh my God." Judy swooned. "Your father's biscottis are my downfall."

"Thank you for the clothes and stuff. I'm sorry if I acted all crazy."

"Don't worry about it, sweetie. You came to the right place. I'm just outside if you need anything."

I hoped Judy would take my cue about Genaro's and get in touch with Katie's parents. They were probably worried sick over their daughter's whereabouts and would come pick her up.

"Katie, you were standing on your head when I first got here." I avoided mentioning the naked part so as not to embarrass her further.

She laughed. "Oh my God, I take yoga and sometimes I do headstands to relax."

Katie started eating her sandwich, and I stepped out to the hallway to write up my notes. Her headstand appeared to be psychologically insignificant, and I also thought she should have an endocrinologist and nutritionist consult on her diabetes management. Judy told me that Mr. and Mrs. Genaro were on their way. After about ten minutes, I checked back in on Katie, who was resting on the gurney with her hands covering her face.

"What's the matter, Katie?" I asked.

She wiped the tears from her face, "My whole life is a mess. I can't handle this diabetes thing. I'm trying to be an actress and pay for my own acting classes, but there's just no pleasing my mother."

"What do you mean?" I asked.

"What happened tonight will just be another disappointment to her. That's all I seem to do," she said. "She thinks being an actress is a joke, an excuse to skip college and be a waitress all my life. And it's ironic because she used to be an actress too."

My pager went off with my next emergency. I could see that Katie was going to be a much more complicated case than just an E.R. consult. I felt like moving on—I'd had my orange-juice victory, and if I stayed, I'd have to get involved and wrapped up in Katie's family and medical issues.

A part of me wanted to quit while I was ahead. I wasn't sure I could be the psychiatric hero in her next set of problems, and I already had a great story for the coffee room. But I knew at some level that to become a better psychiatrist, I needed to stay and face this challenge. So instead of dashing off, I muted my pager and said, "It must be really painful when your mother doesn't support your career."

My comment reopened her floodgate of tears. I handed her a tissue and let her cry for a while.

"It's true, Dr. Small. It's incredibly painful. Nobody ever seems to understand that."

"Katie, I think it would be helpful if you had someone to talk with about your feelings. Maybe you and I could meet later this week. Would you be willing to do that?" She nodded yes and the door suddenly swung open. A woman around forty and her tall, balding husband rushed in.

"Katie, we were so worried about you. We didn't know where you were or what happened to you." Mrs. Genaro threw her arms around her daughter, who looked annoyed and uncomfortable.

"Mom, I'm fine. I had another problem with my insulin, and this is Dr. Small. He helped figure it out . . . he's going to be my psychiatrist."

"What?" Katie's mother said. "You don't need a psychiatrist. You're not crazy." Mrs. Genaro looked at me. "What's going on? What is Katie doing here?"

I hesitated to respond. I had just established a doctor/patient relationship with Katie, and I wanted Katie to know that whatever she told me was in confidence. On the other hand, this had been a medical emergency and her parents were clearly worried. While I was mulling over my options, Katie rescued me.

"I'm here because my glucose got too low."

Mr. Genaro spoke for the first time. "But sweetheart, the emergency room again?"

"I didn't eat enough breakfast and got confused, so they brought in Dr. Small. I'm fine now."

Her mother wasn't satisfied. "But why didn't anyone call me?"

"We did, Mrs. Genaro, as soon as we could," I answered.

"Well, that wasn't soon enough. I ought to sue this hospital." She turned to Katie, "And you're grounded, young lady. You obviously can't handle your insulin and a silly waitress job at the same time."

Katie winced at her mother's criticism. "You can't ground me, Mother. I'm almost twenty."

"As long as you're under my roof, I can do whatever I want."

"Look, honey," Mr. Genaro said to his wife. "We found Katie and everybody's all right. Let's just go home and settle this tomorrow."

I handed Katie my card, and Mr. Genaro and I left room 6 as Katie's mother helped her change into the clothes she had brought. Outside the room he thanked me for my help. Before I left the E.R., I made sure that Judy gave Katie follow-up information about managing her diabetes.

As I headed back to the coffee room, I noticed that the E.R. was quiet now. I was exhausted and decided to lie down on the couch and rest my eyes for a moment.

"Small. Wake up. You look like shit." It was morning and Mike had just arrived for work. I had slept through the night, and my next shift was about to start.

"What time is it?" I asked.

"It's time for a shower, man. You're disgusting."

He handed me a cup of coffee, and I went off to the call room to shower and change. The rest of the day, I fought the chronic fatigue that always followed a busy night on call. If I kept moving, I was all right, but if I sat down too long, I had to focus on keeping my eyelids open or I'd nod off. Today, on-call hours are limited to ensure that residents don't experience this level of fatigue while dealing with patients.

My mind kept going back to Katie Genaro's unusual presentation in the E.R. The emotional issues she was struggling with were complex. I wasn't sure I had enough experience to really help.

FRIDAY WAS MY OUTPATIENT-CLINIC DAY, AND KATIE was scheduled for an afternoon appointment. I had finally graduated to my own assigned outpatient office. Even though it didn't have a window, there was a worn upholstered chair, two metal chairs, a small coffee table, and all the other necessary trimmings including desk, phone, and tissue box. I hung a few diplomas on the wall and put some psychiatry textbooks on the shelves behind my desk to make it look official.

I had already worked with a few psychotherapy cases, but I still felt awkward getting total strangers to trust me and open up about their innermost secrets in fifty-minute sessions. I wished I had a cheat sheet that fit in my palm so I could refer to it when I didn't know what to say.

The clinic's secretary buzzed me on the intercom to announce Katie's arrival, and I went out to meet her. She was wearing jeans and a sweater and looked like any other pretty, blond, nineteen-year-old struggling actress.

We sat down in my little office, and Katie began. "So how does this actually work? I see there's no couch, so do I sit here and talk while you take notes? Or do you ask me questions, or what?"

"Basically, we just talk about your feelings and discuss what's going on in your life."

"Okay," she said.

"Well, how's it going with your blood sugar?" I asked.

"Fine. I'm taking care of it, but my mom won't stop nagging me about the other night. She says I screwed up and almost killed myself. She actually thinks I did it to get attention."

"Well, you have ended up in the emergency room several times," I said.

"They were all accidents. I wasn't trying to get attention. And even if I was, it wouldn't matter."

"What do you mean?" I asked.

"All my life I've tried to please her. As a little girl I helped out in the bakery, I got straight A's in school, I took dance lessons twice a week, and she hardly even noticed. When I told her I wanted to be an actress, I thought she'd be happy for me."

"What happened?" I asked.

"She got hysterical. She said I was ruining my life by not going to college and getting a real job."

"But you told me your mother was an actress too."

"Yes, but she gave it up when she married my dad and got pregnant. Now she works in the bakery. I know she's not happy."

"That may well be, Katie, but whether it's accidental or intentional, when you don't take care of your diabetes, it definitely gets a rise out of your mother."

"So you're saying I do it on purpose too?" she asked.

"No, but sometimes we do things that feel accidental even though they serve a purpose."

"But it's such a bummer going to the emergency room," she said.

"True, but it sure gets your mom's attention." She didn't respond, so I continued. "How do you feel when your mother doesn't support your career?" I asked.

"Angry, misunderstood . . . She says I'm bound to fail as an actress just like she did and she's only trying to save me from the pain and rejection."

"Maybe that was her experience of it, and in her way she's trying to protect you."

Katie snapped, "What? Are you working for her? This is *my* life and she just won't see that. I think she's jealous of my career."

I was struck by how quickly Katie got angry and realized that she had taken my last comment as unsupportive of her. I went back to my imaginary cheat sheet. "Why do you think she's jealous?" The question seemed to bring her back to me.

Katie took a deep breath and said, "Last year I was in a big play at the Colonial Theater. We were doing Bram Stoker's *Dracula*. Even though I had a bit part, it was a major theater and I was really excited. I got tickets for my parents on opening night."

"Sounds great," I said.

"It was, but . . ." She appeared sad and looked away.

"But what, Katie?"

"Every time I came onstage, I could see my father sitting next to an empty seat. My mother claimed she had a headache and couldn't make it." Katie started to cry, and I pushed the box of tissues toward her. "She just couldn't stand to see me have any semblance of success." She blew her nose and cleared her throat. "Maybe I *am* getting sloppy with my diabetes to get her attention, who knows?"

I felt like we were getting somewhere, but I wasn't sure which direction to go in. Katie's relationship with her mother was the hot button here, so I had an idea, "How would you feel about your mother joining us for a session?"

"I don't think she'd come. She thinks shrinks are for psychos." She paused, looking thoughtful. "But you know, it's not a bad idea. She needs therapy more than I do. I'll let you know."

The following week the E.R. was remarkably quiet. On Tuesday afternoon, we had finished up with the morning walk-ins and there were no more patients. Mike Pierce and I went over to the corner sub shop for a sandwich. After paying, we took our lunches outside and found a bench.

"I heard about that naked headstand lady you saw last week. What happened with her?" Mike asked.

"I gave her a cup of orange juice and cured her. She had acute hypoglycemia."

"Way to go, Small," Mike said. "Any follow-up?"

"Yes, actually," I said. "I'm seeing her in the outpatient clinic. She's nineteen and has separation issues with her mother. She's bringing her mother to the next session."

"Oh man, good luck with that one. You better reserve a soundproof room."

"So you think it's a bad idea?" I asked. Mike's supervision and advice were usually pretty sound.

"It's not a bad idea. In fact, it can move the therapy along quickly. It's just that you've only known the patient a short time and haven't established a strong therapeutic alliance with her yet. It also can get kind of complicated working with your patient *and* the person who's stirring up her issues, but I'm all for taking off the training wheels as soon as possible."

▪   ▪   ▪

THE NEXT DAY, KATIE AND HER MOTHER were due at 3:00 P.M. I tidied up my little office and arranged it as best I could to accommodate the three of us. After all, this was my first family session. The intercom buzzed and I jumped. The secretary announced that they had arrived, and I asked her to send them in. As they opened the door, I invited Katie and her mother to take a seat.

Katie began. "Listen, I've got to leave early because I have an audition downtown."

"Of course you do," Mrs. Genaro snipped. "I made the time to be here, the doctor made the time to be here, but you've gotta go to your big audition. It's ridiculous. What are the chances?"

"Thank you for that show of support, Mother," Katie said and then turned to me. "You see what I'm talking about?"

"Oh," Mrs. Genaro said to me, "has Katie been talking about me? Did she tell you I was jealous of her famous theater career? How she's decided to put off her college education because acting comes first?"

Mike was right. I'd really stepped in it this time. I could see Katie seething as her mother continued to rant.

"Mrs. Genaro, Katie," I said. "Maybe today we can skip the . . . accusations and just talk about feelings."

"Well, I feel completely alone and misunderstood," Katie said, beginning to cry.

"What are those?" Mrs. Genaro asked. "Stage tears?"

Katie grabbed her purse, sobbing. "I've got to go to my audition. I'll see you next week, Dr. Small. Alone." She darted out of the office.

As the door closed behind Katie, her mother said, "That's her M.O. When things don't go her way, Katie either has a crying fit, runs away, or screws up her blood sugar and ends up in the hospital. One day she won't get there in time and will kill herself. I'm telling you, Dr. Small, I don't know what to do with that girl."

"Sounds like you've had your hands full, Mrs. Genaro," I said.

"Please, call me Ellen," she replied.

"I'm going to make a guess here. I think that underneath your anger and frustration, you really just want to protect your little girl."

"Of course I do. She's my baby."

"But Ellen, she isn't a baby anymore. She's a grown woman. She needs to make her own choices."

"Well, her choices are childish. Acting is just a lot of heartache," she said.

"And you learned that for yourself, right?"

"I sure did, but she can't even manage her diabetes."

"I know it's frustrating, but it doesn't seem like she wants to hear it from you. Maybe it's time to back off and let her take responsibility for herself. She's got to learn to deal with her illness *and* her career," I said.

"You know, I'm frightened for her every day. We worked so hard to save the money to send her to a good college, and now she's throwing it all away."

"Maybe you could use some of that money to help her with her acting classes so she wouldn't have to work so hard at her day job."

Ellen snapped back, "You're not listening to me. My daughter has a life-threatening disease that she doesn't take seriously. And she's living in a dream world about becoming a star."

At that moment, I got a glimpse of how Katie must have felt when her mother didn't take her seriously. "Ellen, all I'm saying is that it seems like the more you push Katie, the more she goes the other way. I think you're feeling scared for her, and understandably so."

"Listen, Dr. Small, I don't need you or anybody to tell me how I'm feeling or how to raise my daughter. I came here as a favor, and I think I've had just about enough of all this shrink talk." She gathered her things and left.

My first attempt at family therapy was a complete bust. My actual patient had bolted after just a few minutes, and then rather than let her mother talk, I *guessed* at what her problem was and *told* her what she was feeling. Why didn't I just listen as I had been taught to do? I must have been too nervous. I felt like a therapist imposter. Maybe I should put those training wheels back on.

As I halfway expected, Katie canceled her next therapy session. Then she left a message saying that she was taking six weeks off. She said she was in rehearsals for the part she had gotten the day she left my office early. I figured she just wanted to quit therapy but was afraid to tell me. I admit that I was partly relieved. I felt that my attempt to help might have just worsened the tension between her and her mother. Unfortunately, whatever psychological issues were eating at Katie had not begun to be resolved, and they were likely interfering with her ability to manage her diabetes. I didn't want her to end up in somebody else's emergency room naked and standing on her head again.

Six weeks later, Katie surprised me and showed up for an appointment. She looked different—more confident and poised. Smiling, she settled into her chair.

"It's good to see you, Katie. How are you?"

"I couldn't be better." She beamed.

"What's going on?" I asked.

"Well, that day when I came here with my mother, I was so emotional by the time I got to my audition, I forgot to be nervous. I landed a great part at the Wilbur in *Ain't Misbehavin'*." She handed me a playbill and said, "You should really come. It's a fantastic show and getting great reviews."

"And how has your blood sugar been doing through all this excitement?" I asked.

"It's funny, Dr. Small. Whenever I'm in a play, or really busy or excited about something, I'm more motivated to take care of myself."

"That's good to hear, Katie," I said. "How are things going with your mother?"

"Believe it or not, we're getting along pretty well. She's stopped nagging me about my career, and we've actually had a few real adult conversations."

"Really," I said. "What did you talk about?"

"Acting, of all things. She told me how tough it was for her to deal with the rejection and then to give up her dream of being on Broadway."

"And what did you say?"

"I told her how it's different for me. The rejections just spur me on and make me want to work harder."

"How does it feel to have these conversations with your mother?" I asked.

"It feels good. I don't feel so alone," Katie said. "It's like for the first time in my life, she really sees me." She started to tear up.

I pushed the tissues toward her and asked, "Are you sad, Katie?"

"No, really. I'm happy. I was just thinking about opening night."

"What about it?"

"The first time I had the guts to look out at the audience, I could see my father sitting there, and next to him was my mother, smiling up at me."

I realized that even though that first family session was a disaster, something had sunk in and their therapeutic work continued outside of my office, without me. I've kept that lesson in mind throughout my career. An hour is a brief but potentially powerful slice of a patient's week, and if that person's going to gain insight and change, it won't always happen right in front of me during that hour.

Katie continued in psychotherapy throughout the rest of my residency training. She had her ups and downs with her mother and her diabetes—ending up in the emergency room a couple more times. But her relationship with her mother improved. Katie got her own apartment, and Ellen came to grips with the fact that her daughter was an adult and had to live her own life.

When I was finishing my training and getting ready to leave Boston, Katie landed a part in her first Broadway play and moved to New York. She has remained a working Broadway actress, and occasionally she still sends me a postcard or playbill.

CHAPTER THREE

Take My Hand, Please

Winter 1980

I WAS FAST ASLEEP IN THE on-call room when the telephone woke me. It was just after 2:00 A.M. and the orthopedic surgical resident wanted me to come down to the E.R. and consult on a twenty-eight-year-old man who had fractured his wrist. I dragged myself out of bed and took the stairs down.

The emergency room was crowded with the usual accident victims, worried parents, really sick people, and others who would have been better off taking a Tylenol and staying home. I spotted the surgical resident, Dr. Neil Cooper, writing in a file at the nurses' station. A former tennis pro, tan, buff, and full of himself, Cooper was born to be a surgeon. It must be good to be king.

"So, Neil, since when do you need a shrink to set a fractured wrist?"

He glanced up and said, "Gary, I need your advice. There's something weird about this patient."

Cooper was actually an okay guy, and sometimes we hung out. To the outside world, he'd put on the usual I'm-too-sexy-for-my-scrubs attitude, but beneath the surface he was as insecure and overwhelmed as the rest of us. I suspected that he hung out more with the shrinks than the blades because his mother was a psychiatrist. He thought psychiatry and surgery were the two most intrusive specialties—he would cut into people while I looked into their minds—and that's why we were both feared and revered.

"What's so weird about him?" I asked.

"This is the third time he's been here with left upper-extremity injuries."

I yawned. "Maybe he's just a klutz."

"No really, the guy is strange. He keeps asking if he needs surgery—like he wants it or something. He gives me the creeps." Neil was one of the more psychologically savvy surgeons that I knew. He must have sensed something about this patient that made him worry about an imminent danger.

In an emergency setting, when an internist or surgeon requests a psychiatric consultation it's usually because of possible suicidal risk or agitated behaviors that disrupt and distract the medical team from their hectic routine. Busy E.R. doctors usually don't have the time to accurately assess their patient's subtle, complicated, or strange behaviors that might suggest a mental disturbance or emotional issue.

During my own medical internship, when I had to track up to twenty patients at a time, at any hint of weirdness or emotional agendas I paged psychiatry ASAP. I blocked out the possibility of exploring the subtleties of the mind—even though I had always harbored an interest in psychiatry. I knew from talking with my fellow medical interns that they felt the same way.

Later, during my psychiatry training, one of our professors, Ed Messner, helped me overcome this block. He taught a small seminar entitled "Autognosis," which helped us recognize our own emotional reactions to patients in order to improve our diagnostic skills. The course was based on the principle that our innate empathic abilities allow us to experience, to some degree, the emotional state of others. In other words, if we spend time with a depressed or angry person, that individual's mental state is "empathically contagious," and we might start feeling sad or irritable ourselves. Thus, when therapists can identify their emotional responses to patients, they can get clues to the patient's diagnosis. This strategy is particularly helpful when patients, consciously or unconsciously, attempt to mask or disguise their true emotional experiences.

Of course, a psychiatrist wouldn't want to go overboard and become depressed every time a depressed patient comes in for an evaluation. It helps to maintain "detached concern," a simultaneous emotional distance from and sensitivity toward the patient. Detachment protects the doctor from the emotional challenge of caring for patients who cannot get better or perhaps face imminent death. Detached concern and empathy can be taught, and those skills improve a doctor's ability to help her patients. Unfortunately, medical schools spend little time, if any, teaching these skills. It wasn't until my psychiatry residency that I became aware of them as effective techniques.

The patient, Kenny Miller, was brought to the emergency room by his mother, with a dorsal triquetrial avulsion fracture of his left wrist, a common injury that required only a brace and sling until it healed. He said that he had been building a cabinet in his parents' garage when his hammer slipped and hit his wrist. Neil's note documented the two previous E.R. visits for similar injuries to that same wrist and hand within the last year. I wondered what he was doing building cabinets in the middle of the night. The whole story was pretty weird.

I pushed back the curtain and saw Kenny sitting on the gurney with a middle-aged woman in a chair next to him. She seemed concerned and distressed. Kenny had long, sandy-colored hair and a closely trimmed beard. He wore an old Pendleton shirt and faded jeans and had a new brace and sling on his left arm.

"Hey, what happened to my surgeon?" Kenny was calm, almost cheerful.

"Dr. Cooper had to take care of an emergency," I said. "I'm Dr. Small. He asked me to stop by and get some more information. Can you tell me how you hurt your wrist, Kenny?"

"I already told the other doctor—I do carpentry for a living. I was putting the door on a cabinet when I must have got distracted and my hammer slipped. It was stupid."

As he spoke, the woman stood up and rubbed his back to comfort him, "Are you in pain, dear?"

"Nah, Mom, I'm fine, thanks."

"So you're a carpenter. You must get a lot of work. It says here that you've had two other injuries to your wrist this year," I said, trying to lead him to explain.

"Yeah, well, I'm pretty busy with a couple of contractors. And I guess I'm a little accident-prone."

His mother nodded sympathetically, "Poor baby. He works so hard and it's so dangerous."

Kenny was getting a lot of TLC from his mom, and she was starting to distract me. "Mrs. Miller? Would you mind giving us a few minutes to talk alone? The cafeteria is right down the hall."

"Is that okay, Kenny? You know where I'll be if you need me," she said.

"I'm fine, Mom. Don't worry."

She left the room, and I said, "Kenny, I'm a psychiatrist, and Dr. Cooper asked me to come by because he thinks your wrist injuries might not be entirely accidental."

He looked offended. "What are you saying? That I broke my wrist on purpose?"

"I'm not saying it was necessarily deliberate or planned. It's just that there could be something bothering you that you're not aware of."

"Look, Dr. Small, like I told the surgeon, it was just an accident. I don't know why you guys are so uptight about it."

As Kenny spoke, I silently ran through the possible reasons he might have "slipped" with his hammer. He could be after workers' comp, or maybe he liked all the attention from his mother. Perhaps he was a drug addict and was just after some pain medicine. Whatever the real story was, I doubted I was going to get to the bottom of it at this hour. I knew he was getting defensive in response to my relatively direct approach, so I lightened up a bit.

"You know, Kenny, sometimes stress can distract us and make us accident-prone. Is there anything stressful going on in your life?"

He was getting agitated. "Well, yeah, if you call separating from your wife and living back home with your parents stressful." He paused and collected himself. "I mean, it's a drag, but I can handle it."

"Have you and your wife tried counseling?" I asked.

"No, and I doubt she'd go for it," he said. "She's fed up with me."

"You know, Kenny, I have some time Tuesday or Wednesday afternoon. Why don't you see if your wife will come in with you next week? Even if she doesn't, you and I can look at ways to cut down on your stress."

"I don't know. I guess I can try to talk to her. We've been together for almost ten years. Maybe she'll come."

After completing my notes on Kenny, I skipped the stairs and walked toward the elevators. I kept wondering about what was really going on with Kenny. It made sense to bring the wife into the picture—he was upset about the break-up, and she might shed some light on the multiple wrist accidents.

The following Wednesday I was tidying up my office and arranging the chairs when Kenny and his wife showed up for their appointment. I shook Kenny's good hand, and he introduced me to Lauren Miller. She was blond and attractive in an outdoorsy way. They were dressed casually in T-shirts and jeans, and I could feel the tension between them.

"Nice to meet you, Lauren," I said.

She shook my hand stiffly, and I sensed her anger. I knew she didn't want to be there.

"Please sit down." I pointed to the empty chairs.

Their tension was making me feel insecure, and I realized I hadn't prepared any strategy for the session. My mind suddenly went blank, and I considered asking them if they thought the Celtics would go all the way that year.

Over the weekend, I had spent some time reading up on marital-therapy technique. Dealing with couples is often more complex for a therapist than treating an individual. Not only do you have to think about the psychological perspectives and motivations of two instead of one, you also often serve as a referee between them. If you focus your probing and interpretations too much on the husband, then the wife might sense you're on "her side" and her husband might feel like the two of you are ganging up on him. If you shift your support to the husband, then the wife might feel misunderstood and abandoned. At the same time that you're juggling these supportive and interpretative comments, you need to simultaneously pay attention to your own reactions to the situation and not let those bias you.

As the Millers sat uncomfortably in silence across from me, a cascade of questions flowed through my mind: What was Lauren so angry about? Did she know why Kenny kept injuring his left wrist? Why was Kenny being so quiet and deferential around her? What had originally brought these two together, and what was now driving them apart? I didn't know where to begin, and my weekend of reading wasn't helping much. I suspected they sensed my anxiety, so I blurted out, "I'm really glad you two could come in today."

"Look, Dr. Small," Lauren said. "There's no way we're getting back together, so just what is it you want to know?"

Kenny looked stung by her comment, and her directness threw me as well. We were barely out of the gate, and she had put me on the defensive.

"Lauren, I wanted you to come in today because I thought it might help us understand what's going on with Kenny," I said. "If either of you would like to talk about your feelings toward each other, we can do that too." She looked down and fidgeted with her purse. "Did you know Kenny has injured his wrist three times this year?" I asked.

Lauren laughed. "No shit. I'm not surprised that he banged it up again last week. He's been obsessed with his left arm for years. If he paid as much attention to me, I might not have kicked him out."

Kenny jumped in. "That's not fair. I give you plenty of attention, but nothing is ever enough for you."

Lauren rolled her eyes.

"So I've had a couple of accidents," Kenny said. "I've been working really hard, and I'm under a lot of stress."

"That's not the problem. You're *always* working, and even when you're not, your mind is somewhere else. And admit it. You've had this thing about your left hand way before all these injuries started."

"What kind of *thing* with his hand are you talking about?" I asked, thinking that if she directed her comments to me, it would take some of the heat off Kenny.

She turned toward me and said, "It seems like ever since I've known him, he's walked around with his hand in his back pocket."

"Lots of people do that," Kenny said. "What's the big deal?"

She glared at him, "It's not normal, Kenny. It's like a nervous tic for you. And it really bugs me."

"Fine," he said. "If that's your big problem, I'll stop."

She snapped back, "Don't try to make it my problem. What about Halloween?" She turned to me. "His costume was perfect. He went as the one-armed man from *The Fugitive*."

"I thought it was a funny costume," Kenny said. "It's ridiculous that you're even bringing that up."

As I watched the Millers' bickering escalate, I felt a need to calm the situation, but I also wanted to know more about this Halloween costume. "Kenny, let's give Lauren a chance to talk," I said.

"Thank you, Dr. Small." She looked smugly at Kenny. "I admit the costume was kind of funny at first. Kenny used to have a sense of humor. Anyway, the first time he wore it, that was fine."

"The first time?" I asked.

Kenny broke in. "Why are we talking about this?"

Lauren ignored him. "After Halloween, he started wearing the costume around the house, even when friends came over."

"It was just a joke," Kenny said in exasperation.

"Yeah, Kenny, real funny," Lauren said sarcastically. She looked at me. "He seemed pretty serious when he started going out of the house with this so-called costume on. He'd wear it to the movies, out to dinner. It wasn't funny; it was ridiculous."

I figured that the costume was a link to why Kenny kept injuring his left hand, but I hadn't pieced it together yet. Whether accidental or deliberate, his injuries were self-inflicted and at some level a cry for help. That brought up a short list of possible psychiatric diagnoses, which I began to check off in my mind. He didn't seem depressed, and his injuries weren't consistent with suicidal gestures. Sometimes people with borderline personality disorder will injure themselves to experience physical pain to replace the emotional pain they are trying to escape.

"Kenny, were you aware of how much your costume joke was irritating Lauren?" I asked.

"If I had known that," he said, "I would have cooled it."

"How could you *not* know?" she said, annoyed. "I told you ten times a day!" She looked at me and said, "It was embarrassing me."

"So Kenny wasn't hearing you. How would you like it to be with Kenny?" I asked.

"I'd like it to be the way it was when we first got married. We were always laughing, and when something was bothering me, he listened. He would comfort me and hold me." She paused and her eyes teared up. I handed her a box of tissues, but she waved them away.

"Kenny, do you remember those times?" I asked.

"I loved when we would just hang out and laugh." He turned to Lauren and said, "And I still want to hold you and comfort you."

Lauren looked like she was about to reach over and hug him, but instead she snapped, "But only with your right arm."

The fact that Lauren had come to the session suggested that she might be interested in giving the relationship another try, but she seemed too hurt to let Kenny in again. As the session continued, they seemed to get beyond their bickering. I learned that for the last few years they had been debating the idea of starting a family, but Kenny was less interested in it than Lauren. As the session ended, I got them to agree to come back for another appointment—a minor victory for me.

After they left, I made some notes. I could understand Lauren's frustration with Kenny's hand obsession and his reluctance to have a baby. Despite her anger and frustration, she still seemed to care about him. If we could bring back the old Kenny, the guy who made her laugh and knew how to comfort her, I suspected she might give him another chance.

▪ ▪ ▪

LATER THAT WEEK I HAD MY NOON supervision meeting with Dr. William Browning. I wanted to discuss Kenny's case with him because of his expertise in psychosomatic medicine—the subspecialty that interfaced mental and physical conditions. Will also had a fascination with Sherlock Holmes and solving mysteries. Among other peculiar talents, he could look at the details and design of a sailor's tattoo and figure out the person's original port of embarkation—something he picked up while in the navy.

Will's office was prime Harvard hospital real estate. Overlooking a grassy area just outside the Bullfinch Building, it was spacious, airy, and decorated with memorabilia from his world travels. I sat down in a comfortable chair, and he sat behind his desk.

"What's up?" he asked.

"I saw a twenty-eight-year-old carpenter in the E.R. last week," I answered. "The surgical resident asked me to step in because the patient had self-injured his left wrist three times in less than a year." I took a long sip of my orange juice.

"That's it?" Will asked.

"No. While they were putting on a brace, he asked the resident if he would need hand surgery. The resident said it seemed like the guy *wanted* surgery."

"Interesting," Will said. "What else did you get?"

"He agreed to come back to see me for a session with his soon-to-be ex-wife, and she said he's been obsessed with wearing a one-armed man costume since Halloween."

Will put down his sandwich and asked, "Does he have a tendency to neglect or hide his left hand or arm?" I was amazed. How did Will know that?

"Yes," I said emphatically. "For years he's had a habit of keeping his left hand in his back pocket."

Will said, "I wonder if this is a case of hemispatial neglect."

Hemispatial neglect commonly results from a right-hemisphere brain injury, which causes visual neglect of the body on the left side. It usually results in a sensory deficit, and it might cause a victim to pay less attention to sensory input. Kenny clearly had sensation on his left side, so this condition was ruled out.

"I don't think so," I answered. "His neurological exam was normal."

"This talk about surgery, though, could just mean he wants attention," Will said.

"He did get a lot of TLC in the E.R. from his mother and—"

Will interrupted, "Do you think there's a sexual component to this one-armed-man thing?" Will loved delving into possible sexual explanations when trying to understand and diagnose complicated cases.

"I don't think so," I said. "But I didn't really get a chance to go there. The two of them were arguing so much that I barely got them to agree to come back in again."

Will smiled. "So they still have feelings for each other."

"Yes," I replied, "but this hand thing is too much for her to take. Also, her biological clock is ticking, and he's reluctant to start a family."

"My guess is your patient's hand obsession is just a distraction to keep them from dealing with the real problems between them. Try and get them to talk about their underlying issues. Also, ask him directly what he'd like to see happen with his hand."

THE FOLLOWING WEEK, KENNY AND I WERE waiting in my office for Lauren, who was late. He was jumpy and kept checking his watch. "I don't think she's going to show up," he said angrily.

"That's okay. You and I can get started. How have you been feeling this week?"

"Like crap," he said. "I thought Lauren and I made a connection last week, but now she won't return my calls. My parents are driving me crazy—I can't live with them much longer . . ." As Kenny spoke he absently pulled his jacket downward to cover the sling on his arm.

"You know, when you were in the emergency room, you asked the doctor about surgery. Why did you bring that up?" I asked.

"I don't know," he said. "Sometimes they have to put in metal pins and stuff. They might even have to amputate for all I know."

Whoa. How did he get from a broken wrist to amputation? Was he kidding, or did he have some kind of unconscious wish to get his hand amputated? Maybe he was psychotic.

"Don't you think amputation is a little extreme for a wrist fracture?" I asked.

"How the hell should I know?" he snapped. "I'm not a doctor. Besides, I can work just fine without my left hand. I'm right-handed, you know."

Maybe his amputation wish was not so unconscious after all. At that moment, his face seemed to shift from anger to sadness. It was so apparent that I thought I should comment.

"You seem sad, Kenny."

He grunted and shrugged his shoulders.

"Tell me what's going on," I said.

He sighed. "I just feel alone. I always do. There's nobody I can talk to."

"You can talk to me," I replied. "Why don't you tell me what you really want to happen with your hand."

Kenny looked up at me, worried. "If I told you, you wouldn't understand. *I* don't even get it."

"Try me."

Kenny stood up and walked to the window. He stared outside for a few moments and then said, "I've never told this to anyone before. It's embarrassing, Dr. Small."

"Maybe you'd feel better if you told me," I said.

Kenny sat back down and said, "I get the craziest feelings sometimes. Like my hand isn't supposed to be part of my body—like it doesn't belong. I never told Lauren because she'd freak out, but she knows I have a secret and that drives her crazy."

Kenny's secret feelings helped explain his bizarre behavior. He could be psychotic, but it sounded more like he had a rare form of distorted body image. Kenny's feelings were similar to those of anorexics who starve themselves because their normal body size feels wrong to them. In Kenny's case, instead of a skinny body, he wanted one less hand. I felt an urgency to learn more about this condition before Kenny actually found a surgeon who would agree to cut off his hand.

"I can understand why it's hard to talk about these feelings," I said.

"Lauren would never understand. She'd think I was some kind of freak." Kenny got agitated again and kept nervously pushing his left arm back, away from him. "Sometimes these urges get so intense that I'm afraid I might go down to my table saw and chop it off myself."

That comment changed the whole situation, and I was suddenly concerned that he was in danger. "What keeps you from doing it, Kenny?" I asked, trying to remain calm.

"I always thought it would be safer if a surgeon did it. I don't want to die, I just want to get rid of this stupid hand—it shouldn't be there." He looked down at the floor and continued, "But I don't know. What does it matter? Lauren won't accept me either way."

At this point I was worried that Kenny was at risk of seriously hurting himself, and I knew I would have to hospitalize him—whether he liked it or not. To keep him from bolting, my next move was crucial. While Kenny was staring at the floor, I used the old make-your-own-beeper-go-off trick and paged myself. Kenny looked up as I checked my pager and said, "Will you excuse me a second, Kenny? This is an emergency." He shrugged and I left the office, shutting the door.

I quickly told the clinic secretary to page security because I had to put my patient on a seventy-two-hour hold over at Lindemann. She said she'd buzz me on the intercom as soon as they were stationed outside my door.

I went back into the office and sat down. "Sorry about that."

Kenny looked distracted and said, "Whatever. Look, Doc, I know I must sound crazy, but I've had these feelings a long time and I do just fine."

"You're not concerned that you might act impulsively at some point," I asked, "and maybe try it yourself?"

"They're just thoughts, Dr. Small, I haven't done anything yet, have I?" he said with an edgy tone. To my relief, the intercom buzzed. I picked up the phone and asked them to wait.

"But you're having a tough time right now, Kenny," I said. "Your marriage is in trouble, and living at home with your parents is driving you crazy. And you're talking about possibly cutting off your own hand. I think you might be better off going into the hospital for a little while until we sort this out."

"You mean the loony bin?" he sputtered. "Not a chance in France."

One of the difficult decisions a psychiatrist is sometimes forced to make is whether to hospitalize patients against their will. There are essentially three reasons for involuntary commitment: a patient is acutely suicidal, homicidal, or perceived in some way to be a danger to himself or others. Often it's a psychiatrist's judgment call as to whether self-destructive thoughts or feelings pose an imminent danger. Some people might feel chronically suicidal and talk about those feelings constantly but never act on them. Others engage in chronic suicidal behavior, destroying themselves at a gradual pace through starvation, drugs, alcohol abuse, or smoking. However, these people are not perceived as acutely dangerous; they are rarely committed.

Part of a psychiatrist's training involves putting together what a patient says, his history, and his current behavior to make this critical decision. The methods for potential self-harm that patients discuss will influence the doctor's decision. A man is more likely to shoot himself, whereas a woman would sooner opt for an overdose of pills. If a depressed and lonely woman mentions a large stash of sleeping pills at home, that would heighten a psychiatrist's concern. And if a carpenter who's obsessed with cutting off his hand mentions a table saw in his basement . . .

"I'm sorry, Kenny, but at this point it's not up to you," I said. "I'm going to have to admit you for observation to make sure you don't hurt yourself."

Kenny stood up suddenly. "No fucking way. I trusted you, you asshole." He swung open the door and stepped out as two burly security guards grabbed his arms. "Hey, easy on my sling, you jerk," he said.

THE NEXT DAY, WILL BROWNING WAS ABLE to squeeze me in for half an hour. He wasn't surprised by what had happened with Kenny. "You had to do it, Gary," Will said.

"I know. I just feel bad that I'm the first person he's ever trusted with his secret, and he thinks I've screwed him over."

"You probably saved his life, and now you have a chance to really help him." Will went to his file cabinet and pulled out some papers. "Check out this article."

I read the title out loud: "Apotemnophilia: Two Cases of Self-Demand Amputation as a Sexual Preference." I scanned the abstract describing these unusual cases of male patients who had a sexual obsession with their own amputated stump.

"Gary, I think you've stumbled upon a very rare condition. Kenny finally told you what he wants—amputation of his left upper extremity," Will said. "Did you find any sexual connection to his wish to amputate?"

"I don't think there is a sexual component to his obsession," I answered.

"Then it could be a form of dysmorphophobia, where the patient perceives himself or part of himself as grotesque, even though he looks perfectly normal."

"That sounds closer to what he's got," I said. "But I don't think he sees his hand as grotesque. He just feels it doesn't belong there—like he won't feel normal until it's gone."

Dysmorphophobia was first described by an Italian psychiatrist, Enrico Morselli, in 1886. Today we call it body dysmorphic disorder, which describes people who seek body modification to rectify some perceived physical imperfection. The condition has some similarities with obsessive-compulsive disorder, and patients often suffer from both illnesses simultaneously. Sometimes these people appear to be addicted to plastic surgery, and the results can be irreversibly grotesque. Usually they don't pose an immediate danger to themselves, unless their symptoms become extreme.

Kenny had some of these symptoms but actually suffered from a related and extremely rare condition that today we term body integrity identity disorder (BIID). Patients suffering from BIID believe their bodies don't match the image of themselves they have in their minds. They might feel their unwanted limb is not necessarily ugly but makes them incomplete or disabled. They're often jealous of actual amputees and experience such shame about their feelings that they rarely discuss them. They are typically not suicidal but just want the limb gone, so they seek out surgeons for elective amputation. Occasionally BIID victims will damage the unwanted limb to the extent that it requires amputation. In one reported case, a man rigged his car with automatic hand controls and then froze his unwanted legs in dry ice until they were unsalvageable. He then calmly drove himself to the hospital, where his legs had to be amputated.

For most BIID victims, the wish for self-mutilation begins in childhood or adolescence. Some experts think the condition results from a brain disorder that somehow disrupts body image, but a specific cause has not been pinpointed. Treatment involves both psychotherapy and medication, and though patients may continue to have thoughts of removing their extremity, they can be helped to improve their quality of life and find ways to function reasonably well *with* their unwanted body part. Antidepressants can reduce the obsessive thoughts, and an important aspect of therapy is helping the patient reveal his secret to people in his life who can offer support.

I WAS WALKING BETWEEN THE HOSPITAL CLINIC buildings and saw Neil Cooper in the distance, so I shouted "Neil!" but he didn't turn. I picked up my pace and shouted again, "Dr. Cooper!"

His walking slowed and he shouted back, "My God, I'm hearing voices. Get me a psychiatrist. Stat."

I caught up with Cooper and gave him an update on the Kenny Miller case.

"You know, Gary, this is an interesting situation. At what point do you say a person doesn't have the right to elective surgery? Lots of people don't like their appearance, so they change their hairstyle, get a nose job or maybe a face-lift. At what point do we call them crazy?"

"But you've got to admit, Neil, wanting your hand amputated is a bit over-the-top."

"Maybe, but where do you draw the line? Do you set a limit on how many nose jobs a person can get? No. Plastic surgeons often do multiple surgeries on the same body part. Are you going to commit somebody for wanting her eyes done a fifth time?"

"So you're saying you'd do an elective amputation for this guy if he asked you?"

"Well, it depends," Neil said.

"On what?" I asked.

"How good his insurance is. I gotta go. See you later."

I walked on to the Lindemann Mental Health Center. Lindemann was the lockdown inpatient unit affiliated with Harvard's Mass General Hospital. It was a modern concrete structure that from the outside could have been an art gallery but on the inside had the feel, smell, and tension of a typical psychiatric ward.

Dr. David Keller's office door was open. He was busy at his desk, which was cluttered with papers, files, and books. Keller was a resident in my year, with an engaging, self-effacing humor. He planned to be a psychoanalyst after residency, and he never missed an opportunity to make an analytic interpretation about nearly anything.

"Dave," I said, "I like the way you've gotten a handle on your office clutter."

He looked up and grinned. "Well, Dr. Small, you just can't see the intricate organization I've got going here."

"So how's my boy Kenny Miller?" I asked.

"He's a fascinating case. You were right on with the body dysmorphic diagnosis. And despite being in my care, he's doing quite well."

"He was pretty agitated when I sent him over here," I said. "Do you think he's still in danger of cutting off his hand?"

"Well, he claims his amputation thoughts have diminished," Dave said. "I started him on some clomipramine. It's been less than a week, but I think it's beginning to reduce the obsessive thinking. He's having a little dizziness, but I think he'll tolerate it."

Anafranil, the brand name for clomipramine, is a tricyclic antidepressant often used to alleviate obsessive-compulsive symptoms. It usually takes a couple of weeks for its full benefits to take hold. Unfortunately, many patients report troubling side effects including dizziness, headache, and fatigue. Today newer antidepressant drugs known as selective serotonin reuptake inhibitors (SSRIs) such as Prozac, Zoloft, or Paxil are used because they have fewer side effects.

Dave went on. "I think the separation from his wife really aggravated his condition. But now that she's been visiting here, he seems much calmer and definitely more accessible."

"Lauren's been here?" I asked.

"Every day," Dave answered. "And now that she's in on his secret world, they seem much closer."

"That's great," I said. "I'd like to see him."

"Be my guest. Room 212."

Kenny's room was in the low-security wing of the unit—a good sign that he was improving. As I approached his door, I heard talking. I knocked and entered. Lauren was sitting on the bed beside Kenny, and they both turned to me.

"Hi. It's good to see you two," I said.

"Hi, Dr. Small," they both said.

"How are you feeling, Kenny?" I asked.

"I'm sorry that I was so pissed off at you," he said. "I realize now that you had no choice about sending me here, and the truth is, I'm doing better."

Lauren jumped in. "*We're* doing better too."

"That's great," I said. "What do you think is helping?"

"I don't feel shut out anymore," Lauren answered. "Kenny's finally telling me what's really going on with him."

"I'm glad to hear that." I said.

Kenny smiled. "And when I get out of here, I'm moving back in." She added, "We're giving it another try."

Kenny was released from the hospital two weeks later. He and Lauren started seeing me for couples therapy on a weekly basis. It became clear that Kenny's symptoms had gotten worse when Lauren first brought up the idea of having a baby. Kenny was worried that amputation might ruin his carpentry career and he wouldn't be able to support a family. But instead of discussing it with Lauren, he allowed his shame to make him keep his feelings secret, so she never understood, which left her feeling shut out.

Thanks to Kenny's medication, he became less obsessive about his hand and better at communicating with Lauren. They even started talking about having a family again. After a few months, Lauren got pregnant and they decided to stop therapy. I tried to convince them otherwise, or that at least Kenny should continue on his own. But these two were on a second honeymoon and confident that they no longer needed my help.

At their final session, Kenny promised that if his amputation urges ever became obsessive again, he would call me right away. He never did call. When I think of Kenny, I hope that he's doing well and holding his children with both hands.

CHAPTER FOUR

Fainting Schoolgirls

Spring 1980

I WAS STUDYING CARL JUNG ESSAYS one May night in my chilly
Cambridge flat. I could hardly keep my eyes open when the sudden hiss-
ing of the steam heater going on shocked me fully awake. Had my landlord won the lottery and decided to share the wealth by actually heating
his tenants' apartments in the spring?

I was tired of Jung—too much theory and not enough action—so I
turned on the TV to watch the eleven o'clock news. I went to the kitchen
to make some tea, while listening to the headlines. A story caught my
attention—a bunch of grade-school kids in a nearby suburb had been hospitalized that day because of some mystery illness. I loved mysteries.

I ran back into the living room to watch the news coverage. A crowd of
young students milled about in their school yard looking frightened and
disoriented while their teachers tried to comfort them. Some of the kids
were crying, others were lying on mats, holding their stomachs, and a few
were being loaded into ambulances. A newsman on the scene described
the mysterious outbreak: "It began in the auditorium during a school

assembly. One teacher said the kids started dropping like flies. Most of the children who fell ill were taken to State Street Community Hospital and released within a few hours, perfectly well. Local health officials are still searching for a cause, and toxic fumes were among the lead culprits under investigation. However, nothing has been proven as yet."

I'd heard about mass hysteria—outbreaks of what seem to be physical illnesses but turn out to be group contagion of psychosomatic symptoms. This mystery illness might well fit in with that diagnosis. Even if the health inspectors found a physical cause, the events were pretty dramatic—lots of tearful children, frantic parents, and plenty of teachers and emergency technicians running about.

I stopped by the medical school library the next morning before clinic and found a few articles on mass hysteria. I learned that although these epidemics were pretty rare, they had been recorded as far back as the Middle Ages. Most often the outbreaks afflicted children and teenagers, girls more than boys, and fainting and hyperventilation were the most common symptoms. Occasionally the illness persisted for days; however, once the afflicted crowd dispersed, symptoms tended to disappear, because they were only contagious when new victims observed others falling ill. Rumors about the causes of the outbreaks tended to spring up throughout the communities.

Reading about these unusual events got me charged up. They had all the elements of a medical mystery and raised some fascinating psychological questions about the power of the group and the ability of the mind to control the body.

I had lost track of time and realized I was late for clinic. After quickly making copies of the articles, I raced off to the hospital. Fortunately, it was a light clinic day. I flew through the nearly empty waiting room and found my buddy Don Williams in the coffee area, drinking a diet soda while finishing up a note on his last patient. Don was one of my closest friends in our residency class and described himself as a tall, dark, and handsome version of Woody Allen.

"So nice of you to saunter in at this leisurely hour, Dr. Small. Dog eat your alarm clock?" Don asked.

"Always a comedian, never funny," I responded. "I was actually in the library."

He laughed. "And I'm playing shortstop for the Red Sox."

"Seriously, Don, did you catch the news story about those suburban kids who fainted and were rushed to the hospital yesterday?"

"Yeah, they're blaming it on some toxic leak or something. Everybody's so freaked out by the environment since that Three Mile Island thing."

"There's no proof of any toxin at the school. I think there might be a psychological spin here. The kids suddenly get sick and just as quickly get better—it sounds suspicious. That's why I was looking up mass hysteria at the library."

After a pause, Don said, "Could be . . . You know, Gary, *you* ought to go take a look into this. You keep threatening to get into research; here's your big chance."

"I'd actually love to go down there, but I've got clinic all day," I said.

"I'll cover for you. Go talk to the locals and find out what's going on. Maybe you could put together some kind of study or something. You could get published. If nothing else, I'm handing you a get-out-of-clinic-free pass." Don then went into his best Marlon Brando *Godfather* impression. "But one day, I may come to you for a favor . . ."

"So what are you saying? I just go down there and start asking questions? On whose authority?"

"You don't need any authority—you're on staff at the prestigious Harvard Medical School. Tell them you're an expert in epidemic illness and you're there to get to the bottom of this *disturbing* incident."

I was getting excited about the possibilities. I had dabbled in research during medical school but never had a chance to follow up on anything. Ever since I was a kid, I had loved solving puzzles. There was something about figuring out a strategy or solution to a problem that was tremendously satisfying to me. This was an opportunity to solve a real-life puzzle.

Don was right. Whether or not I played the Harvard-doc card, I could just go down there and try to find out what went on. I might not really be a mass-hysteria expert, but I had read two articles, and probably knew more about it than any of their local doctors. As I learned later, even the Centers for Disease Control tended to overlook mass hysteria as an explanation when searching for diagnoses of unexplained illness outbreaks.

I made a few phone calls and set up an appointment with the principal of the school where the outbreak had occurred. I typed up a one-page questionnaire for the parents and kids and made copies of it.

Driving down Boylston Street in my 1974 red Toyota Corolla, I watched as the scenery changed from buildings to foliage as I headed out to the suburbs. I figured I would just apply the psychotherapeutic investigative approaches I had been using on individual patients, although I would probably be talking to multiple individuals. I guessed that wouldn't be too hard as long as I was given access to the families. At the same time, I realized I would need to come up with a research hypothesis for a study.

There exists a general bias that studies of behavior and other psychiatric investigations are somehow less scientific than other kinds of medical studies. Many reasons exist for this: the mind seems nebulous and immeasurable; there is a persistent stigma about anything psychiatric; and many people are afraid of looking at their own underlying psychological issues.

I MADE PRETTY GOOD TIME OUT TO the suburbs and parked across the street from the school. I grabbed my notebook from the backseat. Seeing my white clinic coat there, I grabbed it and slipped it on— maybe I would try Don's concerned, Ivy League–expert angle to help pry the doors open here.

As I waited in Mr. Saxon's outer office, I could hear his tired, raspy voice on the telephone. It sounded like he was trying to reassure a parent that everything was fine. He hung up and came out to greet me. A tall, imposing man, he practically crushed my hand as he shook it. He invited me into his office, and I sat across from his desk. I had a momentary flash of being called into the principal's office in elementary school.

"So, Dr. Small, what brings you here from Harvard?" he asked.

"I wanted to talk about the incident they covered on the news last night." I took out my notebook and pen and asked permission to take notes.

"What do you want to know?" he asked.

"Well, several of the doctors at Harvard heard about the illnesses, and we've . . . I mean, I've . . . had some experience with this kind of thing." I *had* gone to the library, after all. "Could you tell me how the outbreak started?"

"Essentially, the sixth-graders were about halfway through their dress rehearsal for their spring performance," Saxon said. "The rest of the student body was in the auditorium watching when one of the boys onstage fainted and fell. He hit his chin against the riser and started to bleed. Everyone was startled, and the next thing we knew, other chorus members grabbed their stomachs and sank to the floor. Then it started getting out of hand, and it seemed like half the kids in the auditorium were getting nauseous, fainting, and having trouble catching their breath."

I was taking notes furiously. "Did you notice if more girls than boys got sick?" I asked.

"Actually, I think there were more girls who fainted."

"What happened next?" I asked.

"Well, the fire marshal got here pretty quickly—maybe less than half an hour. He thought he smelled fumes, so he evacuated the auditorium. The ambulances took about two dozen kids to the hospital, and I was just trying to calm everybody down," Saxon said. He stood up and walked to the window. "A lot of the students were crying, but when their parents showed up, they calmed down. I think our teachers and staff did a fantastic job of keeping things together."

I looked up from my notepad. "Sounds like you had quite a scene on your hands. What did they find at the hospital?"

"Not a thing. The lab results were normal. It was before lunch, and I think the kids were just hungry and tired. A couple may have started hyperventilating, and then everyone got scared. But there was nothing really wrong with our students physically, and the school followed all the correct protocols," Saxon said defensively as he sat back down behind his desk.

"So we still don't really know what caused this temporary illness."

"We're not worried about that, Dr. Small. They found no toxins in the auditorium, and the school is perfectly safe for the students and faculty. We have an outstanding record here and everything's fine."

It seemed to me that Saxon was not very interested in digging any further to find the true cause of the outbreak. In fact, he was describing typical features of mass hysteria: absence of laboratory evidence supporting a physical cause, hyperventilation, fainting, and rapid remission of symptoms once the students were separated from one another. His explanation alluded to a psychological cause, but I suspected that if I mentioned mass hysteria at that point, he'd get even more defensive. He clearly didn't want the school, or himself, blamed in any way for contributing to the incident, but if we didn't get to the bottom of this thing—whether it was a psychological cause, physical cause, or both—there was a risk of it happening again.

"Aren't you concerned about another outbreak?" I asked.

"Not at all. It's finished. Everybody just got overly excited. It's never happened before, and it's not going to happen again." He shifted in his seat and arranged the papers on his desk nervously. Was he trying to reassure himself or me?

That may be, I thought, but if it did recur, I wanted to see it for myself. "When are the kids doing the actual show for their parents?" I asked.

"The Spring Sing is on Friday night, and we should get a big crowd. Why don't you join us?"

The invitation seemed halfhearted. No doubt Saxon was getting tired of swatting away my questions. Sensing I'd outworn my welcome, I stood and said, "Thanks for the invitation, Mr. Saxon. I'll be here."

He didn't seem thrilled that I said I'd come, and looked relieved that I was on my way out. Just as I was about to leave, I turned back and said, "You know, Mr. Saxon, there is one more little thing . . ." My favorite TV detective, Columbo, would have been proud.

He looked at me, clearly annoyed. "What?"

"I wonder if it would be possible for me to speak with one or two of the families and maybe pass out a brief questionnaire so we can be absolutely sure this type of thing doesn't happen again. Because I know you wouldn't want that."

"Well, I don't know. I'll have to look into that," he said. "You know . . . we have to be *very* sensitive to the privacy of our families. Listen, I've got another meeting right now. Call me and we can discuss it." He stood and escorted me out of his office. He was clearly not interested in my little study and wanted things to go back to status quo.

I drove over to State Street Community Hospital and parked by the front entrance. I hoped to find some staff who had treated the fainting children. The lobby was crowded with families waiting and kids running around, and there was no one at the information booth. I walked down the hall looking for a nurses' station when an orderly practically knocked me over coming around a corner. He was pushing a patient on a gurney while steadying the IV pole. "Could you give me a hand, Doc? I've got to get this guy up to the O.R., and we're short-staffed."

I realized that I was still wearing my white coat, and I panicked. How short-staffed were they? Was I going to have to scrub up and do this man's surgery? I'd performed appendectomies in med school, but if this guy needed a heart transplant, he was in big trouble. To my relief, the surgical team was ready and waiting in the operating room, and I quickly retreated through a side door.

I walked down another hallway and spotted a nurse with a friendly face. I asked her about the fainting schoolgirls.

"Oh, that thing came and went. They never figured out what caused it." She looked down the hallway and pointed. "Right there are the parents of the last little girl who's getting discharged today." I thanked her and hurried over to the parents.

Dorothy and George Holland were talking quietly outside the door of their daughter's room. I introduced myself as a Harvard doctor and didn't mention that I was a psychiatrist because I didn't want them getting defensive right off the bat.

They were eager to talk to me about what had happened at the school.

They were frustrated because no one had figured out why their daughter had passed out. "Those kids were so sick," Dorothy said, "they could hardly breathe. I heard that our daughter Lindsey was twitching on the ground and practically paralyzed."

George jumped in. "The school botched the whole thing. No one brought in the CDC, and those health inspectors hardly looked anywhere. Something made all those kids sick. I think the school is pulling a cover-up."

I said, "It's true, we don't know what caused the outbreak, but I'd certainly like to find out too."

George smiled. "Thank you. It's nice to have a doctor agree with me."

I went on. "I heard there was a lot of anxiety and chaos going on. Do you think that might have made the symptoms worse?"

Dorothy glared at me. "What do you mean?"

"I mean, do you think the panic and hysteria may have made the kids get sicker?"

George looked puzzled, and Dorothy was angry. "Are you saying my daughter was faking her illness? Are you calling her a liar? She's been in the hospital for two days. What are you? Some kind of psychiatrist?"

"Well, yes, I am."

"I don't want to hear any more of this," George snapped. "We're done talking with you. Come on, Dorothy." She followed her husband into their daughter's room and shut the door. I guessed they wouldn't be filling out my questionnaire that day.

Their defensiveness was typical. When mass-hysteria victims and their families are approached about possible psychological causes for their very physical symptoms, they run the other way. Most people don't want to be told that their illness is "all in their heads."

In the years that followed, I studied several episodes of these strange outbreaks and learned to tread very gently when discussing any psychological underpinnings. It makes sense when you think about it from the victim's point of view. The physical symptoms are experienced as real, and when they strike, the victim is swept up by the excitement and anxiety of the crowd. How could real physical experiences—hyperventilation, fainting, nausea, stomach pains—be the result of anything but an actual physical illness?

Victims are more likely to endorse a far-fetched or outlandish cause for their illness than to cop to the mind-over-matter theory. Examples of bizarre explanations for mass hysteria have included a "mad gasser" that Mattoon, Illinois, residents believed was spraying poisonous mist into the bedroom windows of teenage girls, causing nausea, vomiting, and burning sensations in their mouths and throats. In the early 1950s, when people in the state of Washington were nervous about nuclear testing, many believed that cosmic rays or shifts in the earth's magnetic field were causing previously unnoticed windshield pits or dings. Some even blamed it on "supernatural gremlins." Although this was an example of collective delusion rather than mass hysteria, it shows how a worried group can overinterpret physical phenomena that were already there but went unnoticed before the spread of anxiety.

My Boston-suburb elementary school outbreak had its own set of rumors. Two priests arrived to attend to the families of the "deceased" because of a rumor that a dozen children had died of food poisoning. Another rumor circulated that the boy who cut his chin on the riser underwent open-heart surgery shortly after fainting. These and several other rumors about toxic fumes and poisonous water were all false.

When we face uncertainty, our minds crave explanations. If we have no way to account for symptoms, we feel out of control and our fear escalates. And if we learn that our own minds *caused* the very real symptoms, then we feel more anxiety about what our minds might do next. People might worry that their brains are possessed by some outside spirit, or perhaps a poltergeist has taken charge of their willpower. They'd rather latch on to something like the mysterious poisonous-water theory.

Psychosomatic specialists have come up with additional physiological explanations for some of the symptoms of mass-hysteria outbreaks. When people get excited and scared, they might hyperventilate or start breathing too quickly, thus exhaling too much carbon dioxide. Low carbon dioxide levels in the body cause muscles in the extremities to spasm, which can explain the numbness, tingling, and muscle twitching some victims experience. If the carbon dioxide depletion is treated by simply breathing into a paper bag, the symptoms rapidly disappear.

In a heightened state of anxiety, victims often notice and misinterpret normal physical sensations. A stomach gurgle can be mistaken for a sign of food poisoning. And if others around you grab their stomachs and fall to the floor, your fear level might heighten, your knees might buckle, and you might fall to the floor as well. The sheer force of group dynamics tends to take over, and people get swept up in the symptoms of the crowd. The social hierarchy of the group can also play out in the spread of symptoms. If the "popular" girls faint first, the less popular will likely follow their lead. In this Boston-suburb outbreak, the original boy who fell ill and cut his chin was one of the most well-liked kids in the school.

A decade later I studied a similar outbreak of illness that suddenly afflicted a group of student performers in Southern California. Our research team found that the *best* predictor of a child getting the symptoms of hysteria was when that child observed a friend become sick. An outbreak of mass hysteria is like a perfect storm, where all the necessary elements are lined up together: the crowd, heightened anxiety, physical stress such as heat, fatigue, or hunger, and influential social networking. One trigger, whether it's a chin cut on a riser or a friend's indigestion, can cascade into a full-blown outbreak of group hysteria. Today, when mass hysteria strikes, health officials are savvier in identifying both physical *and* psychological explanations. What people often don't realize is that even if the symptoms have a psychological cause, the victim is not making a "decision" to get sick. It's an unconscious process, and the physical symptoms are real.

I WAS BECOMING FAMILIAR WITH THE ROUTE to the suburbs as I drove back down to the elementary school for the Friday-evening performance. I parked a couple of blocks away from the school, and as I walked toward the auditorium, I started to worry about what I would do if there actually was another outbreak. Maybe I should have stopped at the market and brought a couple of hundred brown paper bags for people to breathe into. Then I wondered whether there might truly be a physical cause and I would get sick as well. Or worse, what if I fell victim to mass hysteria? Okay, I had to calm down. I was getting hysterical before I even got to the auditorium. Some big-shot Harvard psychiatrist I was.

I entered wearing an anonymous blue blazer rather than my white coat. The place was filling up with parents and siblings of kids in the show. I took a seat in the back, with my notepad in pocket, prepared to jot down any potentially important observations. I subtly sniffed in several directions to make sure I didn't detect any toxic fumes. I noticed Dorothy and George from the hospital, sitting toward the front of the auditorium. George was talking with some friends, but Dorothy was staring straight at me. Oh boy, she was probably still pissed. I nodded toward her, and to my surprise she nodded back in a friendly way.

Saxon welcomed the audience and introduced the chorus. I watched them perform while scanning the room for any signs of unusual behavior. After about twenty minutes, I was bored. Everything went along smoothly, without incident—no stomachaches, no fainting schoolgirls, no mass hysteria at all. I admit I was a little disappointed but also greatly relieved.

As I got up to leave after the show, I heard someone calling, "Dr. Small! Dr. Small! Please, wait." Seeing Dorothy rushing toward me, I braced myself.

"I'm glad to see you again. I'm sorry I was so short with you at the hospital. We were just worried about Lindsey."

"How is she doing?" I asked.

"Much better, thank you," Dorothy said. "But she's had some difficulties, and I wanted to talk to you about that. Do you have a moment?"

"Of course," I replied. "Let's step outside."

We sat down on a nearby bench, and Dorothy told me that she blamed the school for mishandling the whole affair, but she wasn't surprised that Lindsey got sicker than the other kids. "She's been getting sick a lot and having a hard time of it ever since I divorced her father two years ago. It's gotten even worse since I married George. She's missed a lot of school—

she plays up every little sniffle or stomachache and then refuses to go. I can't seem to lay down the law with her."

"Why do you think that is?" I asked.

"I guess I feel guilty about the divorce and then marrying George so soon."

"Have you talked to your doctor or a therapist about this?" I asked.

"No, I haven't . . . When you said you were a psychiatrist, at first I got mad, but you seemed like you really wanted to help, and Lindsey's only gotten worse since this school thing. Now she claims that if she goes to school, the other kids might get her sick again."

It sounded like Lindsey had been playing up her physical symptoms to cope with feelings about the divorce. This defense mechanism, known as somatization, allows people to express emotional pain as physical pain. If Lindsey coped with stress this way, it wasn't surprising that her mass-hysteria symptoms were more severe than those of the other children. Her mother's guilt about the divorce likely reinforced Lindsey's soma-tization. Dorothy would have been better off setting limits and insisting that her daughter go to school. It would also have been helpful if Dorothy had given her daughter an opportunity to talk about her feelings around the divorce. I guessed that there hadn't been much real communication going on in this family.

"Dorothy," I said, "I appreciate your telling me about Lindsey. It might be a good idea for the two of you, or at least Lindsey, to meet with a therapist to talk about what's been going on."

"Could we talk with you about it? You seem to understand," she said.

"I'd be happy to, but it would be a lot easier for you if I found you someone who's nearby. Lindsey's issues aren't going to disappear over-night, and you might want to schedule regular meetings with somebody more convenient." I told Dorothy that I would call her the next week with some names of local therapists. She thanked me and gave me her phone number. She said George would be relieved as well.

As I walked back to my car, I thought about Lindsey's situation. Perhaps some of the other kids had similar issues. Divorce was pretty common; maybe children whose parents had divorced would be more likely to get symptoms from mass hysteria. Also, the hysteria outbreak may have been partly triggered by the psychological stress of impending losses. The sixth-graders were graduating, the principal had recently announced that he was moving to another school, and many of the students were about to go on their first overnight trip. It was possible that anxiety about these impending separations and losses contributed to the episode of mass hysteria.

I could easily test the hypothesis that previous loss influenced a child's vulnerability to current loss, and predisposed that child to mass hysteria by using a questionnaire that simply asked whether these kids had experienced divorce or other losses, like the death of a close relative. Finally, I had a clear idea for my study. My old loss-obsessed supervisor, Professor Lochton, would have loved this spin. But I had to convince the principal first.

I called him after the weekend, and his secretary put me right through.

"Dr. Small, nice to hear from you," Saxon said.

"Thank you. I really enjoyed the Spring Sing on Friday night. The kids were great. And you were right—there was nothing to worry about, no more mystery illnesses."

"I'm not going to say I told you so, but I'm glad you enjoyed the show. How can I help you today?" he asked.

"I wanted to follow up on that questionnaire I mentioned. It would be a great opportunity for you to help other principals who might have to deal with this type of incident. It's just one page with a few questions for the parents. The kids don't have to be involved at all. You and your school would be helping a lot of other school systems." I tried to play down the idea that we'd be doing a research study and appeal to his sense of altruism, as well as his ego. It worked.

"I guess that sounds reasonable. It would be nice to help other schools, and since it won't involve the students directly, I think I can get it past the board. Can you get me a copy of the questionnaire?"

"No problem. I'll send one over today." Maybe there was a future for me in research after all. If not, perhaps I had a shot at elementary school politics.

With numerous phone calls and persistence, I eventually got an 80 percent response to my questionnaire. I had a statistician help me analyze the results, and my hypotheses proved to be true. The outbreak definitely had the characteristic features of mass hysteria. And early loss—a death within the family or parental divorce—was significantly more frequent in students who got sick than in those who did not.

I was thrilled. My first attempt to publish a study succeeded, and I got it into a fairly good journal.

It was interesting to note the reaction of the medical community itself to my findings. I remember presenting my paper to the medical staff at Harvard's Massachusetts General Hospital Research Symposium. When I reported that mass hysteria consistently affected girls more than boys, many of the scholars and clinicians actually hissed and chuckled. Whenever I described the gender differences in hysteria symptoms, it often seemed to stir up a charged response from both scholars and families of victims. Years later Harvard's Larry Summers lost his presidency there for suggesting, at an academic conference, that "innate sex differences" might explain why fewer women have successful careers in science. I made sure that when I talked about women being more prone to mass-hysteria symptoms I was merely reporting the news, not editorializing. The studies proved it so, but no one really knew why—perhaps it had to do with girls having closer friendships and tighter social networks, or maybe they were just more likely to talk to one another about their feelings than boys. Adolescent boys tend to hold their feelings inside and tough it out, the way they envision their fathers would behave.

Almost exactly two years after the mystery illness in the suburbs, a strikingly similar outbreak struck a different Boston suburb: another chorus rehearsal, kids fainting and being rushed to the hospital, and lots of worry about environmental toxins. Again the kids got better quickly, and before I could even get out there, the school decided to go ahead with the actual performance that very evening. However, soon after the kids began to sing, a new wave of nausea and fainting spread through the chorus. Ambulances and fire trucks stirred up the hysterical crowd of parents as the sickest kids were rushed to the hospital for the second time that day. Once again, all the children recovered in a few hours, and, like most mass-hysteria outbreaks, mostly girls were afflicted.

Before rushing down to another principal's office, I decided to get some advice from one of the top psychiatric researchers in the country. Gerald Klerman had returned to Harvard after a stint at the National Institute of Mental Health, and I was able to meet with him that afternoon. I summarized the current mystery school illness, as well as the events and study I'd conducted two years earlier. He told me to forget about dealing with the school this time and go straight to the local health department. Health officials have a mandate to get to the truth; the school system, on the other hand, is usually more interested in not making mistakes and covering its tracks. What Klerman said seemed so obvious to me now—I wished I'd had that conversation with him two years earlier.

The health department was delighted to have me join their team—a Harvard psychiatrist with real experience in this type of epidemic would be an asset to its investigation. They were happy to help me with any research study I wanted to do, as well. They made me an ad hoc health investigator, giving me full access to all school and hospital records.

I was able to meticulously review the health records of all the students afflicted, and this time I distributed study questionnaires to both the kids and parents. Thanks to the health department, the response was 100 percent. The study confirmed that all the typical characteristics of mass hysteria were present—fainting and hyperventilation, rapid onset and remission of illness, girls affected more than boys, and spread of symptoms by observing them in others—strongly arguing against a physical epidemic.

There was, however, an interesting twist to this outbreak. Two days after it occurred, the hospital's laboratory disclosed that urine samples from thirteen of the sick children contained a chemical compound found in insecticides, plastics, and disinfectants.

Despite the community anxiety about environmental contaminants, many parents were surprisingly relieved to learn about the laboratory reports of toxins in the urine of the children. They wanted to latch on to that explanation rather than consider the possibility that the kids' minds had made them sick. But weeks later, sheepish officials announced that no toxin had been found in or around the school. As I reported in the *New England Journal of Medicine* article describing the study, it was the plastic containers in which the urine samples had been stored that had leached the toxin into the samples. All the urine samples that were stored in glass containers were clean. This intermingling of physical *and* psychological evidence became typical of the dozens of mystery illnesses I studied over the years.

In all the mass-hysteria episodes I've studied and written about since then, the lingering question for me is why they don't happen more often. The essential ingredients—groups under psychological and physical stress, perhaps hungry, tired, or both—come together almost daily all around the world. So what is that ultimate trigger that pushes people over the edge and lets their minds take over their bodies en masse? I'm still searching for the answer.

CHAPTER FIVE

Baby Love

Winter 1981

DURING MY LAST YEAR AT HARVARD'S Mass General, I landed
the position of chief resident of the consultation service. I supervised
a group of less experienced residents in the day-to-day care of medical
patients with psychiatric problems. I quickly learned that just because I
had this fancy title and a larger office with a view of the Charles River,
my Ivy League trainees—only one year behind me—weren't convinced
that I had all that much to teach them. They saw me more as a big brother
than a supervisor.

The residents I got to know best were in my year of training. We
learned about one another, and about ourselves, in our notorious little
therapy/training group, or T-group. Led by a senior psychoanalyst, the
group, which met weekly, was meant to teach us group-psychotherapy
techniques by putting us through it. It wasn't really a therapy group per
se, but for most of us, it ended up being therapeutic.

One guy in my T-group who I hung out with a lot was Jim Schaeffer.
He was a few years older, since he had worked in a research lab before

coming back and doing his psychiatry residency. I admired his ability to be candid with his feelings about people in the group. If he didn't like somebody, he'd let that person know it. Jim came from big money but wasn't obnoxious about it. He was quick-witted and had a competitive streak that sometimes got out of control. He also had quite a reputation as a womanizer.

Our T-group had just ended and Jim and I were walking back to the clinic building. Jim said, "I can't believe what a moron Mike Calhoun is. His backstory is such bullshit that even he wasn't buying it."

"Are you saying you don't think he was a NASCAR driver after his rock band toured Europe and he gave it all up to be a psychiatrist? I can see all that happening," I said, laughing.

"And what about Arlene?" he asked, referring to our group leader. "Is it me, or does everybody want to go home with her and get tucked in at night?" He suddenly looked at me and said, "Gary, don't turn around, but Pam Sefton is walking toward us. God, she is one hot O.B. How's my hair?"

I turned to check her out, and before I could tell him she wasn't my type, Jim spoke up. "Hey, Pam, what's happening? Looking good."

She smiled, "Hi, Jim. Always good to see you. Gary, I'm glad I ran into you. I saw on the board that you're covering the O.B. clinic for psychiatry this afternoon."

"You dog," Jim muttered under his breath.

"In fact, Gary, could you walk with me for a few minutes? I want to discuss a patient with you."

"Sure, Pam," I said. "See you later, Jim."

"You two have fun now. Don't do anything I wouldn't do," he said as he walked away sulking.

Once out of Jim's earshot, Pam said, "Jeez, what's with that guy? He's all over me like a cheap suit, and he doesn't even know me."

"What can I say—he has a warped sense of self. So, tell me about this patient."

"Her name is Anne Drexler. She's in her mid-twenties and almost ten weeks pregnant, but I just got back a negative test result."

"So she miscarried?" I asked, stating the obvious.

"Yes, for the third time," Pam said.

"You must see a lot of these cases. Why do you need me?"

"She's so into having a baby that I'm concerned she's going to freak out when I break the news. I'd feel a lot better if you were there for backup. She's coming to my clinic in an hour."

Mass General's obstetrics clinic was in one of the new structures nestled among the potpourri of architectural styles that made up the medical center. During my hurried trek through the maze of corridors and shortcuts over to the clinic, I had to answer a page that tied me up for a few minutes. By the time I got to the exam room, it was obvious that Pam had already delivered the unpleasant news.

Anne Drexler was agitated. "That can't be! I've been through this too many times before. I just can't lose another baby." She started to cry, and Pam handed her a tissue box. Anne slapped it away.

I entered the room and said, "Hello, Anne. I'm Dr. Small, one of the hospital psychiatrists."

When Anne heard the word *psychiatrist,* she really started to wail. "I don't need a psychiatrist, I need an obstetrician who knows what the hell she's talking about!"

"Look," Pam said, fed up, "lab tests are lab tests. You can believe what you want. I have to see other patients. I suggest you talk with Dr. Small." Then she left abruptly.

So much for Pam's bedside manner.

Anne stood up and began collecting her things to leave.

"Please, Anne, don't go just yet. Let's talk for a minute."

She glared at me. "Talk about what? I look pregnant. I feel pregnant. Obviously there's something wrong with the doctors and labs in this hospital."

Anne was in denial. She was so wrapped up in the idea that she was pregnant that even the hard evidence of laboratory results indicating a miscarriage couldn't shake her conviction. I needed to make a quick maneuver to get through to her, so I tried to convey empathy and hoped she'd respond.

"I can understand how you feel, Anne, and I think you should definitely get another opinion."

"Thank you, Dr. Small. That's the first sensible thing I've heard around here." She sat back down on the exam table. "You know, my feet are so swollen, I could use a minute to rest." She rubbed her eyes, and I noticed how striking they were—large, piercing, and hazel.

"Sounds like you've had quite a day," I said.

"It actually was pretty good until this appointment. I can't believe how completely wrong Dr. Sefton is. I mean, in my family the women are so fertile, you just look at us and we get pregnant."

"Really," I said as I instinctively looked away.

"My mom was only nineteen when she had my oldest sister, Karen, and a year later Valerie was born. Karen had three kids right after she got married, and Valerie's twins are due any day now."

"So there are a lot of babies in your family," I said.

"Yeah. And now I'm having one too." She stood and stretched her lower back, emphasizing her protruding abdomen. "Look, Dr. Small, you're a nice guy, but I don't need a psychiatrist. I'm actually a therapist myself. I got my marriage and family counseling degree two years ago. What I need right now is an obstetrician who knows what she's doing."

I handed her my card and said, "If you ever just want to talk—about anything—give me a call."

As I headed back to my own clinic, I figured I would never hear from Anne. Though she was in denial now, she'd probably come to her senses after a second opinion confirmed Sefton's diagnosis. From what little Anne had told me about her life, I could understand why it was so difficult to face the pain of another miscarriage. Her older sister with her three kids was probably getting lots of attention, and now that her other sister was having twins, Anne's ovaries must have been feeling the competition to step up and deliver.

THAT NIGHT I MET JIM FOR DRINKS at the Harvest, a popular restaurant in Harvard Square. We managed to find two stools at the bar and ordered some beers. On the TV, the Celtics were playing the Lakers, and as an L.A. boy, I was completely outnumbered by Boston fans. Jim was taunting me because the Celtics were up by nine, but we could hardly hear the game anyway, since the music was blaring and so many people were jammed into the little space, milling around and scoping one another out.

Jim sipped his beer and asked, "So how did you make out with my true love, Pamela Sefton?"

"I think she really likes you, Jim. I could tell by how she ran the other way," I said with a smile.

"She just hasn't tried the Schaef-man." He laughed. "But what was this big case she needed you for?"

"Oh, some twenty-five-year-old who had her third miscarriage. Pam couldn't handle delivering the news herself," I said.

"So how did the patient take it?" Jim asked.

"Not well. In fact she didn't believe it and wants a second opinion," I said, taking a sip of my beer.

"So she was in denial?" he asked. I was beginning to get his attention.

"Completely, and I can understand her disappointment. To me she looked more than ten weeks pregnant—her stomach was bulging, she had that glow thing going on, and she looked so sad."

Jim leaned back and said, "Boy, are you clueless."

"What do you mean?" I asked.

"Ever heard of pseudocyesis, you moron?" he asked.

A lightbulb lit up in my tiny brain. "If you mean hysterical pregnancy, just say so."

"What were you thinking?" he asked, incredulous.

"Okay, so maybe I wasn't thinking and you're the psychiatric genius at this bar," I said, embarrassed. "I've got to get her old charts and check this out."

"I hope you got her to come back and start therapy," Jim said.

"Well, I gave her my card, but she told me she was an MFCC and didn't need a shrink."

Jim slammed his hand on the bar. "That's so rare. She was a real find—a mental health professional with pseudocyesis. I would have jumped all over that."

"You jump all over anything with a pulse."

"No, really, Gary. You have to be more aggressive, man. She'll never call you now." He laughed. "I may have to report you to the psychiatric police."

I laughed too but felt humiliated and realized that I had blown it with Anne Drexler. Anyway, maybe she really had been pregnant and Jim was wrong.

Pseudocyesis, also known as false or hysterical pregnancy, is an extremely rare condition but one that has been documented since antiquity. In 300 B.C., Hippocrates reported twelve cases, and in the sixteenth century, Queen Mary of England had several episodes. In hysterical pregnancy, all the typical signs and symptoms of a real pregnancy can occur: morning sickness, breast tenderness, sensations of fetal movements, and weight gain. The woman's abdomen might expand the same way it does during a normal pregnancy, so she really does look pregnant. The patient stops menstruating and becomes convinced that she is pregnant. Hormonal imbalances often contribute to the physical symptoms and result in false-positive pregnancy tests. Stress can sometimes alter pituitary gland function, resulting in an increase in the hormone prolactin, and as a result, the patient will produce breast milk even though she is not pregnant. In fact, the symptoms can be so convincing that an estimated one out of five women with pseudocyesis get diagnosed as pregnant at some point by a medical professional.

What I find most interesting about the condition is its underlying psychological causes. What could drive a woman who is not otherwise psychotic to make her body change to the point that she is convinced she's pregnant? Often she is desperate to become pregnant—her self-esteem and identity might be tied up in having a baby, or at least carrying one in her uterus, or it might help her to overcome loneliness or gain attention. For some infertile women, the sense of biological failure pushes their minds to trick them into a hysterical pregnancy.

And for others, pregnancy gives them power—the power to procreate or to keep a man.

The next couple of weeks went by quickly. I was busy attending seminars, seeing patients, and finishing a research paper. I was in my office preparing notes for my Thursday-afternoon teaching rounds when the phone rang; it was Anne. I was happy to hear from her, but she was sobbing so hard I could barely understand her. "Take a deep breath and slow down, Anne," I said.

"I got my period! I'm not pregnant! That bitch Sefton was right." She paused to blow her nose. "I have nothing to live for . . ." That definitely caught my attention.

"How soon can you come in? We need to talk." It crossed my mind that it would bring my oh-so-superior buddy Jim down a notch to know I'd gotten the patient back after all.

Two hours later, after my teaching rounds, Anne dragged herself into my office looking haggard and sad. She was thin and showed no signs of pregnancy.

"Please, Anne, sit down. Tell me what happened."

She sat on the sofa and looked at me. "Dr. Sefton was partly right, but I never *was* pregnant. I just wanted it so badly that my mind made me feel like it was really happening. I'm a therapist, for God's sakes. I should know better. I know how crazy people are when they want something they can't get."

"Go on," I urged her.

"But for me it was so bizarre. I could've sworn I felt the baby kicking. Now my new doctor says it must have been gas. How can that happen?"

"Sometimes we want something so much that our minds trick our bodies into believing it. Tell me why you want to be pregnant so much."

"I've always wanted to be a mother, and it's just not fair that there are so many babies in my family and I don't have one."

"I remember you mentioned your sister was going to have twins. Did that happen yet?" I asked.

Anne burst into tears. "Yes—a boy *and* a girl. And they're adorable. Valerie's so lucky, I hate her." I handed Anne a tissue. She blew her nose and continued, "And I can't stand Karen and her three perfect little angels, either."

"Sounds like there's friction between you and your sisters," I said.

"No kidding. But they're so blissed out that they don't even notice it. Nobody notices me anymore."

We were really getting into something here. Anne had finally accepted the reality of her situation and was willing to explore what might be driving it.

"When did you start feeling like this?" I asked.

"I don't know. I guess when we were little, I was the baby and I got treated special—everybody thought I was so cute and precocious. I always felt like I was Mom's favorite. And my sisters would fight over who got to babysit me."

"When did that change?"

"It was gradual. I guess by the time I got into middle school, I wasn't the cute little baby anymore. Karen was 'the pretty one,' Valerie was 'the funny one,' and I didn't know what I was."

"So you no longer felt special. How did you cope with that?" I asked.

"I worked really hard in school and became 'the smart one.' But it turns out nobody cared—especially when my sisters got married straight out of high school and started popping out babies. My parents couldn't have been happier with that. Then they started worrying about me, their poor spinster daughter, going to college to be a therapist."

"Did you ever get married?"

"Gordon and I have been living together for five years. We don't believe that a piece of paper will make us any more committed to each other, and frankly, I resent that my family is more concerned about that piece of paper than they are about me."

"If Gordon wanted to get married, would you?" I asked.

She started crying again. "I don't know, maybe. But it would just be to get my mom off my back. Or maybe I do want it. I don't know! But I want a baby more, and we can't seem to have one."

Anne went on to tell me about her miscarriages and how she hadn't told her parents after the first one because they were so disappointed—not for her, of course, but because they were denied another grandchild. Despite her problems with infertility and concerns about Gordon possibly leaving her if she couldn't have a baby, she still managed to keep a busy psychotherapy practice specializing in adolescents. It struck me that it was during Anne's adolescence that her insecurities about her identity emerged. It was probably no coincidence that she chose to specialize in treating adolescents.

Many mental health professionals are drawn to the field in part to resolve their own personal struggles. I've known anorexic-looking psychiatrists who focus on patients with eating disorders, hypomanic psychologists who run mood-disorder clinics, and obsessive therapists who focus on treating obsessive-compulsive disorders. Some of these individuals, especially those who have overcome their personal struggles, are better therapists for it, because they have more empathy for their patients who are going through what they themselves have experienced. Other therapists, still grappling with their issues, might find that their patients' problems are too close to their own, and it can interfere with their ability to help.

For Anne to come to terms with her insecurities and competitive feelings with her sisters, she needed to give up her adolescent need to be "the baby" and instead appreciate who she had become—an educated adult, a successful therapist, and a partner in a long-term relationship. Today's session was a big step for her—admitting that she had not been pregnant, talking about how becoming a mother was fundamental to her sense of self, and openly expressing the competition she felt with her sisters. I suspected that this competitive drive was so fierce that it had forced her unconscious mind to trick her body into a false pregnancy. For all I knew, her two previous miscarriages had been hysterical pregnancies as well.

At a biological level, women are genetically primed to procreate. If a woman discovers that she is infertile, she might feel like a physiological failure, and the psychological consequences of that can be devastating.

Each infertile woman copes with this challenge in her own way, and her partner, of course, plays a large part in how well she copes. Some couples eventually adopt children, while others invest in high-tech fertility procedures that have no guarantee of success. The stress of infertility can be overwhelming, and many couples break up as a consequence. Infertility has been known to drive some women mad. They can't stand to look at a pregnant woman or a baby; they might become psychotically depressed each month when they menstruate. Pseudocyesis is an extremely rare, though temporary, solution to what is an unacceptable reality for many women.

THE NEXT WEEK I WAS HAVING LUNCH with Jim in the hospital cafeteria. We grabbed an empty table by the wall, and I barely had a chance to bite into my sandwich when Jim said, "Check out the brunette nurse at the cash register, eleven o'clock."

"Eat your lunch, Jim," I said. "This isn't a singles bar."

"Yeah, but she's cute and she's smiling right at me. Do you think I slept with her?"

I looked over at her. She was beautiful—way out of Jim's league. "I sincerely doubt it. Hey, remember that therapist patient Pam Sefton referred to me?"

He laughed. "You mean the awesome one with pseudocyesis that you let slip through your moronic fingers?"

"Whatever," I said. "I'm seeing her weekly now. And I think there might be a really great paper in this."

Jim stopped eating and looked at me, trying to hide his shock. "That's great, Gary. Good luck with that." He looked at his watch and said, "Oh shit, I gotta go." He stood and wrapped up his sandwich. "See you later."

I had enjoyed one-upping him, but now, as I watched him leave, I felt sort of bad. It seemed like he could dish it out but couldn't take it. Our competitive banter was fine when Jim had the upper hand, but when he didn't, he took off. Sadly, as my career trajectory rose, my friendship with Jim essentially ended. I've always wondered how much my own competitive issues contributed, but I realized later that a lot of it came from Jim. He had two very successful brothers—one a Wall Street financier, the other a powerful Boston litigator—both of whom Jim hadn't spoken to in years.

As I reflected on the competition I had felt with Jim, I thought about how Anne was just beginning to acknowledge her competitive issues with her sisters. Over the next few months of therapy, we explored her need for attention through either being the baby or having a baby. She also came to realize that her position on not getting married was a defense against her fear that Gordon might not really want to marry her.

Eventually, as Anne became more secure, her relationship with Gordon solidified and he proposed. As I expected, she was thrilled and accepted. He told her that he loved her whether or not they could have their own kids, and they started to seriously discuss adoption.

I hadn't seen Anne for over a month while she and Gordon were in Europe on their honeymoon. She walked into my office looking very tan and wore a white tunic with a turquoise necklace. Her large green eyes sparkled, and she had put back on a few pounds.

"Dr. Small, it's so great to see you. Gordon and I had a wonderful time in Greece. The water is so blue and clear."

"That's wonderful, Anne. You needed a break."

She sat on the sofa and grinned. "You know, neither of my sisters went to Europe for their honeymoons. In fact, I don't think either one has ever left the Northeast except maybe to go to Florida once or twice."

"Really," I said.

"And Gordon and I have gotten so close, we're like best friends *and* lovers. I don't think my sisters have that kind of relationship with their husbands."

"Anne, I'm hearing an old theme here today that we've discussed before."

"Really? What?" she asked.

"Your competitive feelings toward your sisters. But now it's about relationships and honeymoons, instead of babies."

"Babies! You haven't heard the best part!"

"What's that?" I asked, growing concerned.

"I'm pregnant!"

Oh brother, I thought. Was she having a full-on relapse? I needed to tread lightly here. I said hesitatingly, "That's good news."

"*Good* news? Are you kidding? It's *fantastic* news," she said. "Why the hell aren't you excited for me?"

"When did you find out?"

She laughed and said, "I did three more home pregnancy tests this morning, and they were all positive. Look at my stomach!" She lifted her tunic, and her tanned belly was protruding the way it had been with her last hysterical pregnancy. She went on. "You know how it is with all those couples who can't get pregnant. They finally decide to adopt and suddenly they get pregnant? Well, ta-da!" She raised her arms in a victory sign.

"I know you're excited, Anne, but have you seen an obstetrician?" I asked.

"What's your problem, Dr. Small? I thought you'd be happy for me. Seven months ago I was ready to leave Gordon, and thanks to you, I'm happily married and having a baby."

I supposed it was possible that Anne was pregnant, but the reemergence of her competitive issues with her sisters seemed like a regression, and I knew that pseudocyesis often recurs. I felt that the sooner it was proven true or false by a blood test from a real lab, the better off she would be psychologically. And I suspected that her avoidance of even discussing an obstetrician was another indication that she was in denial again. During our previous months of therapy, I felt she had gained insight and had begun to form an alliance with me as her therapist. If I pushed harder with Anne to help her face reality or at least get an official blood test, I might be able to break through her denial.

"Anne, I really hope you are pregnant, but it is possible that your mind is tricking your body again. When do you plan on getting a blood test?"

"What do you mean? You think I'm not really pregnant again?" she asked.

"I didn't say that, Anne. But right now it seems very important to you that I get excited about your baby, just like your family gets excited about babies. And as we've discussed over the last few months, that's been a major source of self-esteem for you throughout your life."

"You know, I hear you, Dr. Small, and I get what you're trying to say, but I don't really care. I know I'm pregnant. My breasts are swollen and sore, and I'm nauseous every morning. And I don't need this negative talk. In fact, I don't think I need therapy right now at all."

Despite my efforts to get Anne to stay, she wouldn't be swayed. She thanked me for helping her get over her problems and promised to keep me posted on how things went. But now that she was really pregnant, she didn't want any negativity in her life—she wanted to stay in a positive place. When I told her that sounded like denial, she just laughed and said, "See what I mean?"

In retrospect, I had probably pushed Anne too hard, and I should have given her more support at that point. I recalled that when I first reined her in as a patient, it was by embracing her point of view and agreeing that she should get a second opinion outside of the hospital. But I also knew that she very well might have been planning to leave therapy anyway.

I have found that most patients need to be motivated to want to do the work of psychotherapy. And Anne didn't appear to feel she had any problems to work on at that moment. Ironically, when patients are not in emotional pain or crisis, it can be the best time to do the deepest and most beneficial therapeutic work. It's then that patients have the serenity and perspective to truly explore their psychological world.

Over the next few months, I received several phone messages from Anne, mostly after work hours. She probably didn't really want to speak with me directly. Her messages told me how wonderful her pregnancy was going, that she and Gordon were painting the nursery and her sisters were planning her baby shower. She didn't mention any medical documentation of the pregnancy. I called her back but always got her answering machine.

I continued to read up on pseudocyesis and started drafting the review paper I was planning to write about it. I learned of several case reports of women convinced of false pregnancies for up to eight months. I worried that Anne might become one of those.

Her phone messages eventually stopped, but I did get a note from her about six months later. It was a handwritten card with two photos inside. The first photo was a black-and-white grainy amniocentesis snapshot of a large fetus—obviously a boy. My mind raced to the possibility that her pseudocyesis had progressed to a psychotic delusion of motherhood and that she was stealing photos from a neonatal clinic. But the second photo quelled my fears. It was of Anne and a man in his early thirties, presumably Gordon, holding a beautiful baby boy. His eyes were large, piercing, and hazel. In the note, she said that she wanted me to have copies of the first two pictures of her son. I was thrilled for Anne but a little embarrassed for myself. I had never really given her the benefit of the doubt.

As I walked into my apartment that evening, I kept thinking about Anne. I was amazed by the way her competitiveness with her sisters had driven her to believe she was pregnant when she wasn't. But I also thought about how her rivalries mirrored my competitiveness with my friend Jim. Did my own issues interfere with my ability to help Anne with hers? Or did it make me more empathic because I was going through a similar situation?

When does healthy competition cross the line and become unhealthy rivalry that drives people to behave in psychotic ways? For my patient, it had been a lifelong struggle, and I wondered whether her having a baby would continue to quiet her demons or simply stir them back up.

I flipped on the TV. The Celtics were playing the Lakers again. Thankfully there were no Celtics fans around, so I could root for the winning Lakers out loud. I got a cold beer from the kitchen and watched as Kareem Abdul-Jabbar posted up Larry Bird and dunked over him. But Kareem was fouled on the play and fell. Larry turned and offered his hand to help him up off the floor. Those two had mastered the art of friendly competition.

CHAPTER SIX

Silent Treatment

Fall 1984

I STEADIED MY MUG OF COFFEE and fiddled with the radio while waiting to turn left onto the 405 freeway south. I was commuting to work, and it was already bumper-to-bumper traffic at 7:00 A.M. As I reached the top of the hill near the Mulholland Drive overpass, I checked my rear-view mirror and saw the San Fernando Valley behind me. The Santa Ana winds had blown away the usual smog and haze, and the vista was as beautiful as it had been when I was a kid—except there were fewer farms and more buildings.

I loved being back in Los Angeles after my psychiatry residency in Boston. It was great reconnecting with old friends and family. I had taken a position in geriatric psychiatry at my alma mater, UCLA. Psychiatry for older people was just getting started there, and I saw a real need for it. Few young psychiatrists were looking to work with seniors, who were often confused and neglected, and whose cases tended to be complicated because of their multiple medical conditions.

I began building my clinical research in the geriatric area while my general outpatient and consultation practice slowly grew, but it wasn't as easy a transition for me as I thought it would be. During my three years at Harvard, I was one of an elite group of trainees who were handpicked from the top applicants throughout the country. I had established myself there and had a good reputation. UCLA was also an outstanding institution, but it was huge and I was once again a small, unknown fish in a big pond. It would take a while to get to know my colleagues and gain their trust.

UCLA Medical Center was as busy as Harvard's Mass General Hospital, but like Los Angeles, it was more spread out. Built in 1953, it was considered a landmark of early modern architecture. The eleven-story brick structure of the main hospital and school had half a dozen intersecting wings that created a tic-tac-toe layout. The horizontal stainless-steel louvers over the windows protected us from the heat and direct sunlight, but from the inside they resembled bars and, depending on the direction of the sun, sometimes made it look and feel like we were working in a prison.

I was jotting down my morning consultation notes at the nurses' station on the fourth floor when I heard a blaring voice coming toward me from the long east-west hallway. I saw a group of neurology residents following their attending doctor, Ralph Porter, out of a patient's room as they did their morning rounds. Porter was pontificating about the patient's stroke and hematoma. It was hard to concentrate on my notes because he was one of those loudmouthed know-it-alls who liked to humiliate the residents by asking questions he knew they couldn't answer.

The group crowded together next to the nurses' station, and Porter called on a shy first-year neurology resident, who had to present the patient they were about to see next. She hesitated as she began. Her insecurity was palpable—perfect fodder for Porter to chew up and spit out.

She described Heather Phillips, a young painter from Venice, the lively and artsy beach town south of Los Angeles. Heather had come down with the flu a month earlier, and her sister had checked her in to the community hospital, where she presented mute and unresponsive. A spinal tap turned up some white blood cells in her cerebral spinal fluid, suggesting meningitis, encephalitis, or some other type of brain infection. They treated her with intravenous antibiotics, but her symptoms persisted, so the doctors figured it was viral. She remained unresponsive, and they transferred her to UCLA. Heather's neurological exam was normal except that she still had no verbal or physical responses to questions or directions.

Something about this case didn't sound right to me. If the patient had a brain infection, why did she go mute so rapidly and for so long? Why wasn't she in a delirious state with episodes of clarity and confusion? Also, why was her neurological exam otherwise normal? Meningitis patients generally have severe neck rigidity.

As the team walked across the hall toward Heather's room, I caught up with Dr. Porter and asked if I could join them on their rounds. He looked at my name tag and smirked. "A psychiatrist? Sure. Maybe we can figure out what trauma in this patient's childhood made her catch encephalitis."

I ignored his sarcasm. "I'll do my best, Dr. Porter."

We crowded into Heather's room. She was lying on the bed by the window with her head propped up; the other bed was empty. A slim, pale brunette, possibly in her early thirties, she had a vacant expression. Porter moved beside her and introduced himself. He asked her what her name was and got nothing. He asked if she knew where she was; again no response. He tried a couple more orientation questions and then proceeded with a cursory neurological exam.

He pulled out his percussion hammer and checked Heather's reflexes, which were brisk and symmetric. He then held her upper arm steady while moving her forearm back and forth to check range of motion and flexibility. He turned to the residents and asked for a volunteer to summarize the case. As one of the nervous young neurologists began describing the differential diagnosis of encephalitis, I observed something strange— Heather's arm was still up in the air where Porter had left it. No one else seemed to notice. As the resident rambled on trying to impress Porter, I watched Heather's arm slowly, almost imperceptibly, ease down toward her side.

Was I imagining this? Why didn't anyone else see it? If I mentioned it now, would they think I was nuts? Porter suddenly turned to me. "Dr.

Small. You seem rapt by this presentation. Have you figured out the unconscious motivation for this patient's condition?"

This guy didn't like psychiatrists—that was for sure. I wondered what bizarre personal issues *he* was hiding. I said, "Not quite yet, Doctor. But I would like to do a formal consultation, if you don't mind."

Porter laughed. "Be my guest. In fact, maybe we should call in dental and see what they can come up with." He got a few snickers from the group as I felt my face redden—I hated when that happened.

Porter wasn't alone in his antipsychiatry attitudes. In the early 1980s, many internists and surgeons found little value in psychiatry. They didn't understand it, and their patients feared the stigma of being labeled mentally ill. While I was in medical school, I would hear an occasional student or professor take a poke at psychiatry, insinuating that it was an ineffective specialty based more on speculation than science.

In residency, I learned more about the reasons for these prejudices. Scottish psychiatrist R. D. Laing had questioned whether mental illness should be considered an illness at all, since it had no proven physical cause. He argued that the concept of madness stemmed from political and interpersonal influences.

In 1973, Stanford psychologist David Rosenhan published "On Being Sane in Insane Places," which described how university students pretending to be psychotic gained entrance into psychiatric facilities. Once admitted, these pseudo patients stopped feigning their madness, yet the hospital staff perceived their normal behavior as symptoms of psychosis. Interestingly, the actual inpatients knew better.

After World War II, psychoanalysis—a theory of mind investigation and treatment—dominated many medical school psychiatry departments. In Freudian psychoanalysis, patients verbalize their free associations, fantasies, and dreams to their analyst, who then interprets the unconscious conflicts he assumes are causing the patient's symptoms or problems. When the patient gains insight from the analyst's interpretations, the symptoms often improve, but it can take years of nearly daily treatment, which is expensive and obviously time-consuming.

Psychoanalysis has helped many people with their neuroses and personal problems, but it's difficult to prove scientifically that it works any better than just talking with someone who is empathic and supportive, although systematic studies have demonstrated the effectiveness of a similar treatment approach, psychodynamic psychotherapy. Also, psychoanalysis is not for everyone, particularly patients with severe depression or psychosis. With the development of antidepressant and antipsychotic medicines that often improve mental symptoms more rapidly, the medical community seemed to warm up to psychiatry. And many psychiatrists turned away from pure psychoanalytic approaches and took a more eclectic strategy combining both talk therapy and medication. This medicalization of psychiatry gave the field more credibility and acceptance by other medical disciplines; however, antipsychiatry sentiments persisted, particularly among older physicians.

For many doctors and laypeople, fear drives their prejudice against psychiatry. Sometimes in denial about their own mental struggles, people avoid or attack psychiatrists in an attempt to keep them from somehow recognizing their secret psychological issues—as if the psychiatrist had some magical powers to do so.

But with Ralph Porter, the antipsychiatry jabs felt personal. I was just starting out as a card-carrying psychiatrist and wanted to be taken seriously. He had a way of making me feel instantly insecure. When he directed his antipsychiatry barbs at me, I admit I even momentarily doubted my career choice. Luckily, my anger toward this jerk overtook my insecurities and spurred me to prove my worth to him. Public humiliation does have its upside—it can motivate people to push themselves to prove a point.

THE NEXT MORNING I RETURNED TO HEATHER'S room to begin my formal consult. The TV was on, and Heather was staring blankly at the screen. I introduced myself and sat down in a chair next to her bed. She didn't acknowledge me in any way, and the only reaction I could get was an eye blink when I clapped my hands in front of her face.

I did another neurological exam. Her reflexes were still symmetrical and brisk. I gently lifted her head off the pillow and flexed her neck—

there was no stiffness there at all. Finally I got around to what I had really come to do—I lifted her arm above her head and let go. I let it stay there for about five seconds, then I gently moved her arm to a horizontal position and it stayed there as well. After nearly thirty seconds, it slowly floated down to her side.

I tried her other arm and got the same result. I felt like one of those hypnotists in a Las Vegas lounge act who gets audience volunteers to freeze in weird postures while in a hypnotic trance. This whole time Heather had been staring at the TV. It was eerie.

I had never witnessed waxy flexibility before, but I had read about it in medical school. It was defined as a lowered physical response to stimuli and a tendency to maintain an immobile posture. When you move the arm of someone with this condition, he keeps it in that position until you move it again. In other words, the extremity responds as if it was made of wax. It was originally described in patients with catatonic schizophrenia, who have extensive loss of their motor skills and sometimes hold rigid poses for hours. In rare, untreated cases, victims have been known to die from exhaustion.

I was about to check Heather's pulse when someone entered the room, "Excuse me, are you a *real* doctor or just another med student?"

I turned and saw a slightly older version of Heather standing in the doorway.

She went on. "I'm sick of this teaching hospital. Are you even old enough to be in here?"

I had no gray hair in those days, and even though I was approaching thirty, I looked young for my age. I stood and extended my hand, "I'm Dr. Gary Small. I'm a psychiatrist consulting on Heather's case." She didn't shake my hand, so I let it drop.

"Oh, great, a shrink," she said. "Are you doing some kind of silent treatment therapy? Have you *noticed* that my sister's not talking?" She put her purse and coat down and started tidying up the room.

"I know the medical doctors have diagnosed your sister with encephalitis," I said. "But sometimes a psychiatrist can help when a patient stops talking or doesn't respond."

She sighed and began brushing Heather's hair. Her anger shifted to resignation. "Why not a psychiatrist? We've seen just about every other specialist in this hospital."

"What's your name?" I asked.

"Andrea. I'm Heather's older sister, and I'm the one who could use therapy. This whole thing with Heather has been a nightmare."

"I'm sure it's been tough on you," I said.

"It was unbelievable how fast this thing happened. One day Heather had the flu; the next thing you know, she's like this."

"Have you noticed any improvement at all in the last month?"

"Not really," Andrea said. "I mean, some days she seems a little more with it—I think she enjoys it when I brush her hair—but most of the time she's completely out of it."

Even though Heather seemed unaware of our conversation, there was an outside chance that she was listening to us. I asked Andrea to please step into the hall with me. We walked to a couple of chairs at the end of the hallway and sat down.

"What was Heather like before she got sick?" I asked.

"She's an amazing artist. Mom always said she got the talent in the family and I got the brains." She laughed bitterly.

Normally I would use that as an opening to delve into their sibling rivalries, but I decided not to go there. I needed more background on Heather.

"I understand she paints. What kind of paintings does she do?" I asked.

"It depends on her mood," Andrea answered. "When she's really energized, she'll go for weeks doing incredible, colorful abstract canvases, one after the other—they're huge. I don't know how she can be so productive and still find time to sleep."

"Really," I said.

Andrea went on. "But other times she locks herself in her studio for days and does these dark, moody self-portraits. It's almost like someone else is painting them."

It sounded like Heather was suffering from classic manic depression, also known as bipolar affective disorder. The illness afflicts about 1 percent of the population and is characterized by episodes of elevated mood or mania, interspersed with periods of depression. When in a manic state, bipolar patients don't require much sleep; they are productive, energetic, often euphoric, and fun to be around. However, if the mania escalates, their grandiosity can get them into trouble. They can also develop rapid speech, hallucinations, delusions, and aggressive behavior.

When bipolars switch to a depressed state, they are usually lethargic and often sleep through the day. Sometimes people have a mild form of the condition and rather than full-blown manic episodes, they have hypomania—they experience euphoria and productivity without the irritability and psychosis. And their depressed states are less severe or barely present at all. Because of the seductiveness of this hypomanic state, many bipolar patients "forget" to take their lithium, a drug that can stabilize their mood and reduce the frequency and intensity of the swings.

During their hypomanic and manic episodes, people with bipolar disorder often have bursts of extraordinary creativity. It's no surprise that some of our most famous artists, writers, and musicians have suffered from this illness, including Vincent van Gogh, Paul Gauguin, Jackson Pollock, Mark Twain, Ernest Hemingway, William Faulkner, Ludwig van Beethoven, Robert Schumann, and Brian Wilson.

"It sounds like Heather has mood swings. Has she ever seen a doctor or therapist to help her with that?" I asked.

"Why? Everybody has mood swings. And Heather's an artist. That's just how she expresses herself," Andrea answered defensively.

"Anyone else in your family have mood swings?"

She shook her head.

"Do you know if any relatives have ever seen a psychiatrist or perhaps taken lithium?" I asked.

Andrea thought for a moment. "Our parents died in a car accident when we were in college. But I remember my grandmother telling me about a sister of hers who spent years in some mental institution on the East Coast. I don't know what was wrong with her or if she took anything."

I wondered if this maternal great-aunt was a manic-depressive. She might have spent years in an inpatient facility without ever receiving medication. The FDA didn't approve lithium as a treatment for mania until 1969. Until then, a variety of treatments had been used, ranging from insulin shock therapy to psychoanalysis. Because manic-depressive illness tends to run in families, Heather's possible family history supported my hunch that she had an undiagnosed bipolar illness.

"Andrea, as far as you know, have any of your relatives ever had problems with alcohol or drugs?" Sometimes bipolar patients self-medicate by abusing substances, especially alcohol.

"Look, Dr. Small, you're obviously searching for some psycho answer to my sister's encephalitis. She needs an infectious-disease specialist, not a shrink, okay?"

"I agree with you—input from an infectious-disease specialist is critical. But Heather's condition has stumped all the doctors so far, and I think we should keep our minds open to all the possibilities."

Andrea slumped into a chair. "I guess so. I mean, she's the only family I have." She suddenly appeared very sad. Was it possible that Andrea too had manic-depressive tendencies? Sometimes the condition cycles up and down rapidly, from moment to moment.

"It must be tough for you to see Heather like this," I said.

She looked at me tearfully. "Heather's always been tough. I love her but I never know which Heather I'm going to find—the reclusive, moody one or the bubbly, creative one. And now she's like this."

"I can see it's painful for you," I said.

"Yeah," Andrea said. "But it's not about me, it's about my sister. She's just got to get better."

I could see Andrea wasn't ready to go any deeper into her own feelings at this point, and I wanted to follow up on my theory about Heather's illness. "Let's give all the specialists some time to put the pieces together," I said. "I'll let you go back to your sister, and I'm going to speak with Heather's other doctors. I hope that we can talk some more later."

The next day I knocked on the door of Dr. Porter's seventh-floor office.

"It's open," he said gruffly.

I entered the spacious, standard-issue, metal-desk-and-file-cabinet office with a view of the 405 freeway. The walls were covered with Perma Plaqued diplomas and awards—documentation to back up his oversized ego. He looked up from the slides he was sorting, "What is it, Small? I'm busy."

Although I had walked in prepared with my articles and arguments, it only took a moment for him to make me feel like an insecure idiot. Fortunately, I had already learned how to push on despite momentary humiliation.

I blurted out my thesis, "I've had a chance to examine your mute patient on Four North, and I think her encephalitis is complicated by a catatonic syndrome brought on by manic-depressive disorder."

Porter looked up from his desk and laughed. "Really? Did she suddenly snap out of it and tell you all this?"

My anger kicked in and spurred me on. "The patient's sister gave me a lot of background. Heather Phillips has a clear history of mood swings and a family member who may have had bipolar affective disorder. Also, when I examined her, she demonstrated classic waxy flexibility—"

Porter interrupted, "Waxy what? The woman has viral encephalitis for God's sake. Didn't you see the labs? She has elevated white cells in her cerebrospinal fluid. What's clear about this case is your naïve insistence that there's something mental going on here. Now could you please leave?"

I was seething. The patient needed to be treated for bipolar disorder, and this jerk was blinded by his antipsychiatry bias and stubborn arrogance. I wanted to pull one of his stupid plaques off the wall and hit him over the head with it. "Dr. Porter, I'm not saying she doesn't have encephalitis, but she might also need to be treated for bipolar disorder."

"That's absurd," he said. "And what would you suggest we do, anyway? Force-feed her lithium?"

"No. At this point, the safest and most effective treatment would be electroconvulsive therapy—ECT," I answered.

"Look, Small, I'm not going to give shock treatments to a patient with a brain infection."

"Could you just take a look at these articles I copied for you?" I asked.

"Leave them on the table there. I'm giving a lecture in ten minutes, and I have to get my slides together." He went back to the slide carousel on his desk as if I no longer existed. I dropped the articles on the table and left the office.

One of the articles was Alan Gelenberg's classic "The Catatonic Syndrome," which describes both waxy flexibility and the psychiatric differential diagnosis for catatonia. Gelenberg showed that mania was a more common cause of catatonia than any other psychiatric condition—even schizophrenia. The other articles described the safety and benefits of modern ECT, debunking the old perception from the media and movies like *One Flew Over the Cuckoo's Nest,* which depicted ECT as a punitive rather than a therapeutic intervention.

After leaving Porter's office, I headed back to my own cubbyhole. My office had a window as well, but the view was of the medical-center trash bins. Fortunately the window was paint-sealed shut.

It was frustrating that here I was, already an assistant professor, and still not taken seriously by guys like Porter. Being ignored felt worse than being ridiculed. There was an outside chance that Porter might glance at the articles I left, but it was unlikely that he'd come around to seeing things my way. I needed an ally at his level or higher, and I knew just the guy.

Dr. Larry Klein was an icon of American psychiatry, and I had sought him out as a mentor as soon as I arrived at UCLA. He was five feet five inches tall, but with his booming voice, insightful wit, and political savvy, he dominated any room he entered. As I waited in his office for our meeting, I stared at his infamous and incomprehensible blackboard, trying to decipher his scribbles. They were either genius or madness, which also described the man's charm.

The door flew open as Larry whisked by me. He simultaneously sat in his chair, lit a cigar, and plopped his feet on his desk. "Gary, I like the new haircut—very Steve McQueen."

"Thanks, Larry," I said. "I see you're still into bow ties."

"Always, Gary. Can never be too formal," he said. "Now, what's this urgent matter that couldn't wait?"

I filled Larry in on Heather's case and Porter's resistance to my diagnosis and treatment recommendation. Larry listened as he puffed his cigar. He was not only a world-class psychopharmacologist but a card-carrying analyst as well.

"I know this character Porter," Larry said. "He's an insecure, obsessive internist—probably compensating for inadequacies stemming from an overbearing mother. And I know just how to handle this schmuck. By the way, your assessment sounds right on the money. You did good, kid."

I felt a wave of pride—here was the idealized father figure praising my work. My own father would have asked why I hadn't made the diagnosis sooner. I knew that Larry would get Porter to fall into line now, but I also felt a bit infantilized. At this stage of my career, I would have liked to have handled this case on my own. But at least the patient was going to get the proper care.

Larry put his cigar down in his giant ashtray. "Let me get this idiot on the phone right now." He shouted into the other room, "Janet, can you page Dr. Ralph Porter, please?"

We wasted no time taking the stairs up to the patient's room. As Larry performed a neurological examination on Heather, Ralph Porter entered. Larry turned and said, "Ralph, that editorial you wrote for the *Archives* was brilliant." I was impressed by Larry's seamless political savvy.

Ralph beamed. "You're too kind, Larry. And Dr. Small, thank you for bringing Dr. Klein in on this most interesting case of mine."

What a kiss-ass, I thought. "My pleasure," I said.

I demonstrated Heather's waxy flexibility for them, and Larry quickly piped in, "Fascinating, isn't it, Ralph?"

Ralph said, "Yes. It certainly fits in with my original suspicion that something besides encephalitis is going on here." How full of crap could he get?

Larry smiled knowingly at me. "So we're all in agreement that this catatonic syndrome may be complicating her encephalitis?"

I nodded and Ralph said, "I guess so."

Larry went on. "The way I see it, we've got nothing to lose by buzzing her with a little electricity. Gary, how quickly can we get her on the list for a therapeutic trial of ECT?"

"If her sister signs the consent today, I'll get her on the schedule for the morning," I said.

"So you think that's the best course to take at this point, Larry?" Ralph asked.

"Absolutely. There's enough in her history to point to bipolar disorder, and even if we don't get a response after a few ECT sessions, we can stop it and just let the infection run its course. The ECT won't affect it."

"Then I completely agree," Ralph said officiously. It was hard to keep from laughing.

"Great," Larry said. "Gary will follow up on the details."

Although I had been relegated to errand boy, I got some satisfaction watching Porter kiss Larry's ass.

As Larry turned to leave the room he winked at me and said, "By the way, Ralph, I recall reading that one or two percent of the population has unexplained white cells in their spinal fluid. Do you think it's possible that this encephalitis is just a red herring?"

Ralph took his foot out of his mouth and said, "Anything's possible, Larry." I'm not sure Larry heard him—he was already halfway down the hall.

The ECT suite was a large converted conference room on the first floor of the medical center. It contained four gurneys separated by curtains at one end, while the other side of the room had a crash cart, two ECT machines with paddle electrodes, an electrocardiograph, medication bottles, and anesthesia equipment. The ECT attending physician, Tom Reynolds, was a stocky, muscle-bound psychiatrist who was rumored to use steroids to augment the effects of his weekend-warrior workouts at Gold's Gym.

Real-life ECT is very different from the so-called shock treatments seen in the movies where helpless, screaming patients are strapped down, hooked up to electrodes, and thrown into frightening grand mal seizures. In fact, the curative element of ECT is not muscular spasms at all but instead the seizure that results from the electrical stimulation of the nerves that control those muscles. To avoid the potential dangers of a full muscular seizure, the unconscious, anesthetized patient is injected with succinyl choline, a drug that temporarily paralyzes the muscles.

Heather was being prepared for her treatment, and I was there to observe and assist as needed. After she was injected with a short-acting anesthetic, Tom pumped a blood-pressure cuff around her opposite arm to cut off the circulation to her forearm. In this way the succinyl choline would not reach her forearm, and we could observe it shaking, to ensure the rest of her body was experiencing a neural seizure.

He placed one electrode on Heather's forehead and the other on her right temporal area. The nurse then set off the electrical impulse, which lasted only a second, and Tom pulled away the electrodes. We watched Heather's left forearm and hand shake for about thirty seconds. Tom took off her blood-pressure cuff and we wheeled her gurney to the other side of the room. I pulled the curtain around her and stayed, waiting for the anesthesia to wear off. I was jotting down notes in Heather's chart as Tom started to prepare the next patient.

As I finished my charting, I heard someone say, "What's going on?" I looked outside the curtain to see if somebody needed help.

"Where am I? Who are you?"

I quickly turned and saw Heather sitting up as if she had awakened from the dead. She was *really* looking at me for the first time.

"You're in the hospital, Heather," I said, "at UCLA."

She lay back down, weakened by her ordeal. "I'm really thirsty."

I was ecstatic. "Let me get you some ice chips."

For the next half hour, while in the ECT recovery area, Heather remained relatively clearheaded and responsive. I was able to fill her in on some of what had happened to her over the previous month and how she had gotten here. She asked to see her sister but then drifted off to sleep. By the time she got back to her room, she was again in her unresponsive, catatonic state.

After each subsequent ECT treatment, Heather's episodes of clarity lasted longer, and by the sixth treatment, the catatonia was gone. Her successful response to ECT confirmed that the cause of her altered mental state was acute mania, not encephalitis. She was transferred from her medical ward to a psychiatric inpatient unit. We started Heather on lithium to stabilize her mood and discontinued ECT after twelve treatments.

I found an outpatient psychiatrist in Santa Monica who could see her for therapy and medication monitoring once she got home.

The morning of Heather's discharge from the hospital, I took the stairway up to her ward to say good-bye. She was on 2 South, along with the other low-risk, high-functioning inpatients. As I walked down the hallway, I passed the ward's dayroom, where a few patients were watching TV and playing cards. I continued on and saw Heather's door open. Her sister, Andrea, was inside helping her pack. I knocked and said hello.

Andrea turned to me. "Dr. Small, you're our hero. You brought my Heather back to me." Before I could say anything, she threw her arms around me and gave me a bear hug.

Heather laughed. "Whoa guys, get a room." I felt myself blushing, that reflex of mine I hate.

Andrea continued. "Really, if it wasn't for you, they'd still be pushing antibiotics, waiting for Heather's 'brain infection' to clear up."

I felt like scuffing my shoe and saying, "Aw shucks," but instead I said, "I'm just glad you're feeling better. Anyway, there was a whole team of doctors that helped with your case."

Andrea laughed. "Wow, Doc, you're not so comfortable with compliments, are you? Maybe you should see someone about that."

I grinned and said, "Yeah, maybe I should."

As I walked back to my office, I thought about what Andrea had said. I had mixed feelings about the case and how I had handled it. A part of me felt like a hero for correctly diagnosing Heather. But I also knew that my diagnosis would not have been taken seriously without my mentor, Larry Klein, stepping in and supporting me. I harbored some guilt, too, that my anger at Porter was a big part of what motivated me to solve the case. What I didn't grasp at the time was that even a seasoned clinician knows when it's necessary to bring in a Larry Klein to do his bidding. At that point in my career, I was learning when to ask for help from others and who to go to. It just took me a while longer to get comfortable with accepting that help.

CHAPTER SEVEN

The Shrinking Penis

Spring 1985

I WAS BUYING GROCERIES AT THE corner market near my house in Sherman Oaks, a half-hour drive over the foothills from UCLA. In the four years since I'd returned to Los Angeles, I'd been so busy with my clinical practice and building my research program that I usually didn't get to the market until eight or nine in the evening. I was in the fruit section, searching for a perfectly ripe, sweet-smelling cantaloupe, when I heard a familiar southern twang: "Well, Dr. Gary Small, what're you doin' shoppin' over here in the Valley?"

I turned to see my friend and colleague Dr. Pete Carter. He pulled up next to me with a full shopping cart.

"Well, if it ain't Pete Carter," I said, mocking his accent.

Pete grinned broadly as he towered over me from his six-foot-four height. He was an internist from Tulane University who had moved his young family out West to take a position as an assistant professor at UCLA. "You need to work on that accent, Gary." He reached out and grabbed any old cantaloupe and went on, "You know, it's great timing running into you like this. It saves me a call. I've got a couple I want to refer to you."

"Sure. What's their story?" I asked as we strolled down the aisle with our shopping carts like a couple of gossiping housewives.

Pete lowered his voice. "The husband is my patient—he's a lawyer at one of those large firms downtown. They've got three young kids, and he's completely stressed out about making partner. His wife is fed up, and I think the marriage is in trouble."

I noticed the diapers and Froot Loops in Pete's cart and realized why he might be sensitive to this patient's issues. "What are you treating him for?" I asked.

"Nothing exciting, just regular physicals. Our practice group does all the medical care for his firm."

"I've got some times open. Have them call me," I said as I started toward the checkout counter.

Pete looked down at his shopping list, "Oh, shit, I forgot the Tub O Peanut Butter." He looked at my cart and laughed. "God, I miss those days when I could just buy a couple of bananas and some soda and be done with it."

When I got home, the house was quiet and dark. I usually liked being alone, but that night I felt lonely. I was about the same age as Pete, and he was already married with a family. And though I had been dating my girlfriend, Linda, for a couple of months, it didn't feel like a serious commitment for either of us. I wondered when I'd ever get around to settling down. The idea of diapers and Froot Loops didn't really do it for me then, but having someone I cared about sounded good. I started putting away my groceries and realized that Pete had distracted me from my quest for the perfect cantaloupe. The one I picked was not quite ripe, so I left it out on the counter.

Two days later I listened to the message from Pete's patient. "Yeah, hi, this is Steve Ackerman. Dr. Carter suggested I call you." He sounded brusque and businesslike. After exchanging a few messages, we finally arranged a time when Steve and his wife, Sharon, could come in for an appointment.

I'd been at UCLA long enough to start feeling more at home there. Including my time as a psychiatry resident, I had already chalked up half a dozen years of psychotherapy experience. I had moved into a slightly larger office with a view of the Jules Stein Eye Institute. Besides my desk and some file cabinets, I had three chairs, a small green sofa, and a coffee table in it.

I was catching up on some articles when the Ackermans knocked on my open door. "Are you Dr. Small?" Sharon asked.

She was around forty, thin and wiry with curly brown hair; she wore faded jeans and a tank top. Steve looked about the same age, dressed in a pin-striped suit. As he stood by the door, his body language told me he was in a hurry and wanted to get on with it. I guessed he had rushed over from his office and wasn't pleased about it.

"You must be Sharon and Steve," I said. "Please, come in and sit down." I got up to shut the door as they sat at opposite ends of the sofa.

Before I could get back to my chair, Sharon started talking at a rapid clip. "We had a tough time finding your office, Dr. Small. This place is like a maze—you go down a hallway and it just keeps going, but when you turn a corner the office numbers change. We finally figured out that the *C* in front of the number stood for the floor, but it didn't say that on the elevator, so we had to keep going back to the information desk in the lobby and—"

Steve cut her off. "None of that matters, Sharon. Let's get to the point. The man bills by the hour, just like I do." I was surprised that Sharon didn't seem bothered by his patronizing tone.

They made me feel anxious, which was a clue that they felt anxious too. Sharon's pressured speech had a manic flavor to it, but it was linear and logical. I suspected that this Chatty Cathy persona was how she expressed her anxiety. Steve appeared to be working hard to keep his anxiety in check, and his impatience also suggested an undercurrent of anger—he seemed to be seething inside and ready to explode at any moment.

"So, how can I help you two today?" I asked.

Sharon jumped in. "Well, I worked as a pharmacist before we had kids, and Steve is an attorney who graduated top of his class at USC. We have three kids—Lisa, our six-year-old, was planned, but our three-year-old twins, Jackson and Robby, were sort of a surprise. That's why I'm not working anymore." As Sharon continued at lightning speed, Steve looked both exasperated and bored. He stared out the window as she rambled on. "We live in Benedict Canyon. You know, the place where the Manson murders happened in the seventies?"

Steve snapped, "That's enough, Sharon. It's amazing how you can talk so much yet say so little."

"I'm just giving him some background, honey. And I was about to tell him about the stress you've been under while you make partner at the firm. I mean, you hardly sleep at night, and you seem pissed off all the time, sweets."

She remained composed despite Steve's biting remarks. I could also understand his frustration with her nonstop chattering. I turned to him, "Tell me about this stress, Steve."

"Everybody goes through it. I'm working around eighty hours a week, but it's not that big of a deal. Sharon's the one who can't handle it."

"That's not true, hon. I can handle it. I'm just worried about you," she said.

I intercepted. "Let me see if I've got this straight. Steve, you're up for partner and working long hours. Sharon, you're concerned that it's affecting Steve's mood and stressing him out. But Steve, you say you're handling it. Sounds like you disagree whether there's a problem here at all."

"Oh, there's a problem, all right," Steve said. "I'm out trying to support my family, I'm working for our future, and she never shuts up about how I'm not doing enough at home."

He had finally provoked Sharon—she tensed up and replied at a higher pitch, "I'm not asking for much, Steve. I just want you to be there for the kids sometimes. I do everything around the house while you're either working or staring off into space. And I don't ask for any help."

Steve spoke slowly, in a controlled rage. "I've told you a million times, Sharon. We can afford a nanny. You could have some free time to yourself to do your yoga or Pilates or whatever you do." He shook his head and turned to me. "She's too controlling to hire anyone to help her with the kids or the house."

Steve's long hours at the office kept him away from the kids and the house, and he didn't seem to mind that they also kept him away from Sharon. I figured he was no picnic to live with either. His constant criticisms must have been hard for Sharon to take. I could see what Pete Carter meant about things being rocky with the Ackermans.

Despite my attempts to mediate, they squabbled through most of the session. I was becoming impatient with Sharon's nonstop commentary, yet Steve's cruel quips made me want to protect her. They were definitely a provocative pair. Sometimes when Sharon spoke, Steve would just tune out, as if he was having a private conversation in his head. And the more silent and withdrawn he became, the faster she spoke.

I tried to keep her on topic so I could eke out more history about their relationship. "So you two dated in high school?"

Steve rolled his eyes as Sharon snapped at the bait. "Yes. Steve was a basketball jock and I was a cheerleader. In college we moved in together and got married in our senior year. I went on to pharmacy school and Steve got his law degree. But I stopped working when I was pregnant with the twins."

I learned that there was no family history of psychiatric illness, and neither of them reported ever being depressed or seeing a mental health professional. They drank alcohol socially on weekends, and during college they had experimented with recreational drugs, mostly marijuana.

With about twenty minutes left in the session, I wanted to get beyond basic history; during a rare moment when Sharon stopped talking, I asked, "So how is your sex life?"

They answered at the same time.

"It's fine," he said.

"It could be better," she said.

Steve glared at Sharon and she shrugged.

Steve suddenly stood up. "You know what? I'm late for a meeting. You two can talk about whatever you want."

Before I could say anything, he was out the door. Apparently, sex was not a topic Steve wanted to discuss.

Sharon started to cry. I handed her a box of tissues. "Are you all right?"

She blew her nose and nodded.

"So you two disagree about what's going on in the bedroom."

"*Nothing's* going on in the bedroom. That's the problem. We haven't had any real sex in almost a year."

"What do you mean by *real* sex?" I asked.

"Intercourse," she said. "For a while, we were still fooling around, but he wouldn't let me touch him—down there. He said he had some kind of crotch rash that he got at the gym, and he didn't want me to get it. But how long does that last? The rest of our lives? For all I know, he's having an affair."

"What do you think is going on?" I asked.

"I don't know, but whenever I ask him about it, he changes the subject," she said. "About a week ago, he got out of the shower and when I asked to see the rash, he flipped out and got all paranoid, like I was going to pull the towel off him. Then he disappeared into the other room to get dressed."

"Before this rash thing started, how was your sex life?" I asked.

"Great," she answered. "We couldn't keep our hands off each other. Now he's always got some lame excuse to avoid sex—he's got too much work, or he's too tired or stressed out, or he just put his ointment on the rash. It's always something."

"Ointment?" I wondered aloud.

"Yeah, some cream he got from Dr. Carter when the rash first started." She paused, then said, "I don't know how long I can take this, Dr. Small."

I made a mental note to follow up with Pete about Steve's rash and ointment. "Sharon, I appreciate your candor. I think it will be helpful to talk more about this, but right now we've got to stop. I can meet with you and Steve next week at the same time."

That Saturday night, Linda and I were driving back to my house after seeing a movie. She was staying over, and I had already stocked the house with snacks and breakfast food.

As we got into bed, I reached over to kiss her, and she announced that she had just gotten her period and didn't feel like making love. I hid my disappointment and kissed her on the forehead. She rolled over to go to sleep. I picked up my Ken Follett novel and started reading.

My mind wandered from *Eye of the Needle* to Linda's preemptive rebuff. Then I thought about Steve and Sharon's sexless marriage. In their case, it was Steve putting on the brakes, and his crotch-rash alibi seemed pretty weak. Also, it didn't explain why he got so paranoid when his wife wanted to see his rash. What was he hiding under that towel? How bad could his pubic irritation be, and why did he still have it after a year?

I had a sense that Steve might have deeper psychological issues that Sharon knew nothing about. The guy was wound tight as a watch and looked like he might bust his springs at any moment. He could be a closet obsessive-compulsive or an enraged depressive, or perhaps this towel episode was a clue to something even more serious. I wondered what was going on in his mind while he spaced out during our session. When we started talking about their sex life, he bolted from the office.

Sex is a big issue in therapy for many people. Freud viewed sex as our primary social activity and defined it as much more than merely intercourse. Sexuality can be a symbol of power, and powerful people—billionaires, politicians, celebrities—are often perceived as sexy, even though they might not be physically attractive. In loving, intimate relationships, sex can be an expression of that love, even though one or both partners might be having humiliation, bondage, or other fetish fantasies involving other people.

There are plenty of reasons why sex can decline in a relationship; job or money stress, children or family obligations, and health problems can diminish libido and lead to a pattern of asexuality for some couples. Depression can also decrease a person's sex drive, and many antidepressants will boost mood and improve libido, but ironically they can also reduce the ability to reach an orgasm.

I wasn't sure what was going on with Sharon and Steve, but I was determined to find out and try to help them. I gazed over at my girlfriend, who was snoring, which helped dampen my own libido. I tried to get back into my book but started nodding off, so I turned out the light and went to sleep.

▪   ▪   ▪

MONDAY MORNING I STARTED PLAYING PHONE TAG with Pete Carter, and we finally spoke in the afternoon. When I asked about Steve's rash and ointment, Pete was surprised. "He's still using those creams I prescribed? That was like a year ago when he came in with that rash."

"Do you remember the details?" I asked.

"Sure do," Pete replied in his usual drawl. "He had tinea cruris, better known as jock itch. I gave him an antifungal cream for his pubic area and a corticosteroid cream to help stop the itchiness for a few days."

"Sounds like he's still using it," I said.

"That could cause some problems," Pete said. "It's pretty rare, but occasionally people absorb enough of the steroid in their blood for it to shut down their pituitary gland and their blood sugar shoots up. More likely, if he's really usin' it a lot, it'll just make his itching and rash worse."

"Thanks for the info, Pete. They're coming back in later this week."

"Good," Pete replied. "I'd like to see him again too and check out what the heck's goin' on down there."

"Better you than me," I said as we hung up. I never did like that dermatology rotation in medical school. Skin eruptions made me gag.

It was Thursday afternoon and Steve showed up at two o'clock on the dot. Before I could even say hello, he sat down and began. "She's late, huh? Typical."

"We can get started anyway," I said.

Ignoring me, he went on. "Sharon has nothing to do all day except drop those kids off at my mother's and get over here, and still she's late. She always does this."

"I'm sure it's frustrating, but it gives us a chance to talk alone for a few minutes, and I wanted to follow up on something." That seemed to get his attention.

"Oh yeah? What?"

"After you left last week, Sharon and I discussed some of your medical history. She mentioned that you'd been using a cream for a rash," I said.

"Yeah? So?" he asked defensively.

"Are you still using it?" I asked.

"Once in a while when I need to," he said. "I mean, you go to the gym, don't you? Everybody gets jock itch at some point. Why does it matter?"

"Because Sharon thinks it's affecting your sex life," I said hesitantly, hoping he wouldn't bolt at the mention of the word *sex*.

"Sex again? Sex, sex, sex. Sharon never shuts up about it. That's all I hear—voices talking about sex." He was becoming agitated and started rambling as if there was someone else in the room.

"Voices?" I asked. Could this guy be psychotic, having auditory hallucinations?

He didn't answer. He just stared out the window as if in another world.

I raised my voice. "Steve! You said you were hearing voices?"

He snapped out of it. "Huh? What did you say?"

"Voices . . . Are you hearing voices in your head?" I asked.

"Well . . . not really voices. You know what I mean, she just never shuts up." He looked toward the window again. I remembered Sharon's comment that he seemed paranoid when she saw him in the bathroom and wanted to check out his rash. And now he just let it slip that he heard voices talking about sex and seemed to be hallucinating right in front of me. If he was having some type of psychotic experience, he was covering it up pretty well because most of the time he just seemed like an obsessive, angry, intelligent lawyer—pretty much like a lot of lawyers I knew.

I tried again to reach him. "What are you looking at, Steve?"

"Huh? Nothing," he said. "I thought I saw something . . ."

Sharon suddenly came barreling into the office, "I'm so sorry I'm late, but there was a traffic nightmare on Wilshire. Some kind of protest at the Federal Building and then I had to try and park here—it's insane! But I did finally get a space like a mile away and then ran back—"

Sharon's incessant chatter seemed to pull Steve back from his private world, and he was able to focus his full irritation on her. "That's enough, Sharon. You're already late. Let's try to salvage what time we have left."

Sharon looked hurt. "I said I was sorry, Steve." She started crying,

"I'm doing the best I can. I just get overwhelmed."

Steve seemed to soften with her tears. "I'm sorry, Sharon. I'm so busy and stressed out that sometimes I just snap." He moved over on the sofa and put his arm around her to comfort her.

Though he'd snapped a moment ago, I liked the direction in which this was going now. I wanted to help them move beyond the squabbling match of the last session so we could discover what was really going on between them.

"Sharon, how do you feel when Steve comforts you?" I asked.

She sniffed. "I feel good . . . closer to him."

"What about you, Steve?"

"I guess I'm a sucker for her tears," he said. "And when we hold each other, I don't think so much."

She smiled. "You know, honey, it reminds me of when we used to spoon each other to fall asleep."

"Yeah, so?" Steve asked, pulling away from her.

She went on. "So we never do that anymore."

"And why do you think that is?" he asked.

"Because you never fall asleep," she shot back at him. "You're either up working in the other room or reading files in bed. And when you finally do turn off the light, you toss and turn all night and we never have sex."

"You know, Sharon, I've got a lot on my mind right now. I don't really need that much sleep, and I definitely don't need to be nagged about sex."

I tried to steer the conversation away from sex. "How many hours of sleep are you getting, Steve?"

"I don't know, maybe four or five," he mumbled.

I knew that wasn't enough sleep for someone Steve's age. I didn't know what was keeping him up at night—it could have been depression, stress, or any number of things, but his behavior was pointing to an underlying psychosis. And like many psychotic individuals, he was too defensive to open up and tell me what was going on in his head.

Psychosis is defined as a loss of touch with reality. Psychotic people might hallucinate, which means they hear voices or see things when there's really nothing there. They might also have delusions or false fixed beliefs, which come in many flavors, ranging from paranoid beliefs that Martians are monitoring their thoughts to grandiose ideas that they're a famous rock star, say, or even Jesus Christ.

A lot of things can make a person psychotic. A psychiatrist usually rules out medical illness first, then considers various psychiatric conditions such as acute mania, psychotic depression, or schizophrenia. The nature of a patient's delusions can help differentiate these illnesses. Depressed patients often have somatic delusions, meaning that they believe that their body is somehow diseased, abnormal, or altered. Sometimes they have exaggerated feelings of remorse, as if they have committed some horrible crime and should be punished severely. By contrast, psychotic schizophrenics have more bizarre experiences and might believe that their thoughts are being broadcast on the radio. Sometimes they'll hear running conversations in their head between two or more people.

If Steve was in the beginning stages of psychosis, I doubted that a medical problem was the cause—Pete Carter was a thorough internist. Since Steve was in his early forties, schizophrenia was less likely because its psychotic features usually become apparent at a younger age, in a person's late teens or early twenties. Steve's lack of sleep could be consistent with a manic episode, but he didn't have the pressured speech and euphoria typical of bipolar patients when they're in an upswing. He did show the irritability, anger, and withdrawal that can point to depression. But at the same time, his paranoia and strange behavior in my office reminded me of someone on the verge of schizophrenia. I needed to know more about what Steve was experiencing and thinking to nail down his diagnosis.

Many times a therapeutic trial of an antipsychotic medication can clear up some of the defensiveness, paranoia, and hallucinations of psychosis. It can also help people sleep better at night. I saw Steve's sleep problem as an opportunity to prescribe an antipsychotic drug to improve his symptoms and hopefully make him more accessible in therapy.

"Steve," I said, "a guy your age needs to sleep at least seven hours a night. I'm going to give you a low dose of a medicine that will help you sleep better. You'll probably feel more rested during the day and less stressed out."

I wrote him a prescription for two-milligram Haldol tablets. "Try taking one of these about a half hour before you to go to bed. If you still can't sleep, take a second one."

As I handed him the prescription, Sharon said, "He hates taking medicine."

"It's a very low dose, and it's not the type of sleeping pill that you can get dependent on," I reassured them. "It also helps reduce stress."

"It's fine, Sharon," Steve said. "I'll try it."

"Good," I replied. "Call me in a few days and let me know how it's going."

I didn't hear from Steve the entire week and figured he was either doing well on the medication, or he never filled the prescription at all. I hoped I'd find out at their scheduled appointment.

The phone rang, and it was Steve. He said that they wouldn't be able to make it in later because the twins had fevers and Sharon didn't feel comfortable leaving them with his mother.

"I'm sorry to hear they're sick," I said. "But why don't you come in alone, Steve? We both booked out the hour, and we could talk some more."

He thought about it a moment. "I guess so. Why not?" I was surprised to hear his upbeat tone.

"By the way, Steve, how's that medication working for you?"

"Not bad. I'm sleeping better."

"What about during the day? Are you noticing anything?" I asked.

"Well, I'm not as tired, and Sharon says my mood's better." Often, the initial benefits of psychiatric medicines are noticed only by people close to the patient, rather than the patient himself. This was a good sign that the Haldol was working.

"That's great, Steve. And listen, I have a staff meeting right before our appointment, so in case I'm running a few minutes late, just let yourself in. I won't be long."

"No problem," he said.

As I walked toward the elevator on my way to the staff meeting, I started to worry about Steve. Even though he sounded better, I knew that a low dose of Haldol wasn't going to cure him overnight. At least he was cooperating, and I was encouraged that he was flexible enough to come in on his own.

As I had expected, the staff meeting went long and I was ten minutes late for Steve's session. Too impatient to wait for the elevator, I raced up three flights of stairs to my office. As I walked briskly down the hall, I wondered whether I had prescribed a high enough dose of antipsychotic for Steve. Maybe he needed an antidepressant as well. I wondered if his psychosis would resurface if I asked too many probing questions.

I got to my office and opened the door. I couldn't conceal my shock when I saw Steve on the sofa. I stared at the scene in disbelief, unable to move.

Steve's pants were down around his ankles. He was holding his penis with one hand and rubbing a cream on it with the other. He had a small, round makeup mirror wedged between his thighs so he could watch what he was doing. An open condom sat nearby on the sofa. He was so absorbed in his procedure that he didn't even notice that I had entered the room. Was he masturbating? Perhaps he was an exhibitionist and I had missed the diagnosis completely. Was this some form of psychotic ritual? Or was there some other unthinkable yet logical explanation for his bizarre performance? I was stunned but curious, and I didn't quite know how to proceed.

I finally blurted out, "What the hell are you doing, Steve? I'm going to wait outside while you get yourself together."

Startled and embarrassed, Steve said, "Oh, Dr. Small, just turn around for a second, I'm almost done with my treatment."

In a daze, I followed his instructions and turned around. I could hear him put the rubber on and zip up his pants.

"Okay, I'm finished," he said.

I turned back and saw Steve putting the cream and mirror into his briefcase. I stumbled to my chair as I tried to regain my composure. I've always found that therapy sessions go more smoothly when everybody's penis stays in their pants.

"What's going on, Steve? I mean, the door was unlocked and anyone could have walked in."

Steve looked at the floor, ashamed. "You know we talked about my crotch rash. Well, it was itching like crazy and I had to do a treatment."

"But it looked like you were rubbing something on your penis, not your crotch."

"I know," Steve said defensively. "But it's spread to my penis. It's been like this for months. When I apply the ointment directly on the rash, it feels better. And the condom keeps the ointment from rubbing off."

"Did Dr. Carter recommend this?" I asked.

"He knows about the pubic rash, but I haven't told him about it spreading to my penis."

I suspected that he hadn't told anyone, especially Sharon. That could explain why he didn't want her to see him naked or have sex with him. Perhaps the antipsychotic had helped him to open up and share this secret with me. The fact that I had caught him in the act might have helped as well.

"Anything else you haven't told anyone?" I asked. "I want to help you, Steve, but I can only do that if you're honest with me."

Steve slowly got up and walked toward the window. As he stared at the building across the way, I hoped that the Haldol had put enough of a lid on his psychosis to help him organize his thinking and allow me into his private world.

Still staring out the window, he said, "Well, there is something . . ." I waited. Eventually, he went on, "I know this will sound crazy . . . but ever since the rash spread to my penis, it's been getting smaller."

"The rash?" I asked.

"No, my penis. I can see it shrinking," he said.

He was finally letting me into his private world, but I wasn't so sure I wanted to go there.

Steve continued, "It seems like the only thing that keeps my dick from shrinking is that ointment."

I wanted to tell him to flip the mirror over to the magnifying side where objects appear larger than they really are. As soon as that tasteless joke entered my mind, I knew that it was an expression of my own anxiety about this awkward situation. Freud believed that humor was an effective defense mechanism for diminishing anxiety and repressed impulses. In a sense, laughter transforms these uncomfortable feelings into pleasant ones. In medical settings, gallows humor is common and helps physicians cope with overwhelming tragedy and illness. As long as patients and family members are out of earshot, most experts agree it is not only harmless but allows medical personnel to let off steam. As a result, doctors can be more accessible to and effective with their patients.

I also couldn't help but think about the symbolic nature of Steve's concern about his shrinking penis. He was trying to make partner at the firm, provide for a family of five, and satisfy his wife in the bedroom—all challenges to his potency and sense of self as a man. At an unconscious level, he probably wished for a large, virile penis, rather than a shrunken, itching one.

"Steve," I said, "I appreciate your telling me about this. I know you're convinced that this is happening, and I'm going to work with Dr. Carter to help you get rid of this rash and feel better."

"But can you stop my penis from shrinking? Is there a stronger medicine you can prescribe?"

I knew he meant stronger ointments, but I was thinking a higher dose of antipsychotic. "I'm going to discuss the situation with Dr. Carter. In the meantime, I want you to double your Haldol dose—I think it will help with the itching and make you less worried about it."

We made an appointment for a few days later so I could speak with Pete and try to get a better handle on what was going on. Steve promised that he'd keep the door locked the next time he felt the need for a midday treatment.

I got Pete Carter on the phone that afternoon and filled him in on Steve's situation. He was amazed that this apparently normal lawyer was pretty much "bonkers," as he put it. As far as Steve's rash was concerned, Pete wanted to see it again and consult with a dermatologist ASAP. He suspected that the long-term use of the steroid cream was sustaining the problem, causing skin irritation and itchiness, and the condoms kept the area moist instead of letting it dry out and heal. Also, some people develop a contact dermatitis from condoms, especially latex ones. As far as the penile shrinkage was concerned, Pete said there was no physiological way that Steve's penis was shrinking—not from the rash, the creams, the condoms or anything else he might be doing.

Without a medical cause for Steve's belief that his penis was shrinking, that left a short list of psychiatric conditions. The nature of Steve's delusion was consistent with schizophrenia, and occasionally patients did show their first symptoms later in life. Steve also had some features of depression—trouble sleeping, anxiety, and ruminations.

Although most schizophrenics tend to be so disorganized that they are unable to hold down jobs and relationships, there are exceptions. When schizophrenics are highly intelligent, their superior cognitive abilities help them control their psychotic thoughts so they can maintain seemingly normal lives, at least most of the time. One of the most well-known examples is the mathematician John Nash, portrayed by Russell Crowe in the film *A Beautiful Mind*. Nash's extraordinary intelligence allowed him to excel at MIT and other top academic institutions, and he won the Nobel Prize in 1994. However, he spent many periods of his life in mental hospitals, succumbing to his paranoid schizophrenia and intermittent depressions.

Like Nash, Steve Ackerman excelled in his legal practice, yet suffered from depression and psychosis. Many patients with both mood and psychotic symptoms fall into a diagnostic category known as schizoaffective disorder. Patients with this diagnosis usually have a better prognosis than schizophrenics without mood symptoms. Regardless of what I called his condition, I realized he needed both antipsychotic and antidepressant medications. Also, he would benefit from his own psychotherapy in addition to the sessions with his wife.

A few days later, Steve returned to my office. The higher dose of Haldol was the right way to go—he seemed more organized, less spaced out, and less obsessed about his penis. I also prescribed the antidepressant doxepin, which helped him sleep at night as well.

For the next few months, I continued to see Steve alone every week, while seeing Sharon and Steve together every other week. As his medications continued to kick in, things got better between them. Pete Carter helped Steve give up his steroid-cream habit and the rash cleared up, along with Steve's delusions about his shrinking penis. As Steve's psychotic symptoms diminished, Sharon calmed down. Although I would still classify her as a fast talker, she became bearable. They even began having sex again.

Steve eventually did make partner, and not long after that, his firm transferred him to their Chicago branch, and the family had to move. Knowing that schizophrenic symptoms tend to recur, I gave him a list of several good psychiatrists he could contact there.

I never heard from Steve again, but Sharon called me every couple of months for a while to give me updates. Steve was taking his meds and seeing one of the psychiatrists from my list. Sharon had hired a nanny and gone back to work part-time. I also noticed that her speech had slowed to a normal pace. I felt that my couples therapy with them had been a success. At least I had helped them with the two symptoms that seemed most disruptive to their marriage—her fast talking and his shrinking penis.

CHAPTER EIGHT

Worried Sick

Spring 1988

IT HAD BEEN ABOUT SEVEN YEARS since I had begun working at UCLA. I was just starting to get on track to become an associate professor with tenure, but I still had a way to go. First I'd have to convince an ad hoc review committee that my research was innovative and had a logical trajectory. I'd also have to demonstrate that I had become independent from my mentors. It was becoming clear to me that academic advancement wasn't just about science—politics came into play. I had to consider who would be writing my support letters and make sure that I impressed them with my scholarly accomplishments. At the same time, my practice was growing, colleagues were gaining confidence in my clinical abilities, and I was getting steady referrals.

It was a warm Sunday afternoon and I was lounging by my pool, relaxing. Life was good. I had all my weekend accessories outside with me—iced tea, crossword puzzle, and cordless phone—very high-tech back then. I dialed the number of a girl named Gigi whom I'd met at a Memorial Day party, and again got an answering service for some talent agency. I left a second message and hung up. It was frustrating—she still hadn't returned my message from a week earlier. I wanted to connect with her—she was attractive, funny, and smart, and best of all, she had seemed interested in me.

But Gigi wasn't calling me back. Maybe she wasn't that interested after all, or maybe I'd gotten the wrong number from my sister, who had called her friend who threw the party, who had called *her* friend who had brought Gigi to the party, who had then called Gigi to see if it was okay to give out her number. It had been a lot of freaking calls to set up a date.

I dove into the pool and swam a few laps, plopped back down on the lounge chair, and let the sun dry me off. I was almost asleep when the phone rang. It wasn't Gigi; oddly, it was my ex-analyst, Charles Reidel. I wondered why he was calling me, especially at home on a Sunday. I had completed my psychoanalysis years ago. Was he having issues letting go?

It turned out that Reidel had taken over a mental health program for doctors in training and wanted to refer a patient to me—the mother of a first-year medical student. He had evaluated the student for insomnia and anxiety and thought the young man's symptoms were complicated by his overbearing, intrusive mother.

"I've spoken to her and she's already willing to come in and talk to you," Reidel said. "In fact, she seems eager."

"Sure. Have her call me next week. I have some openings," I replied.

After an uncomfortable silence he asked, "So how are you, Gary?"

That simple question transported me back to his office couch during the years when I was in psychoanalysis, preparing for my career as a psychiatrist. A major part of any insight-oriented therapy, particularly psychoanalysis, involves developing transference to the therapist, then coming to understand it and eventually resolving it. In other words, the patient learns how he *transfers* feelings he's had about people earlier in life—often his parents—to the therapist. Ideally when therapy ends, the patient moves on. However, transference feelings are powerful and can linger for a lifetime. After analysis, if one bumps into his ex-therapist, it can be just as uncomfortable as when those chance encounters occur during treatment.

My reaction to Reidel's question probably stemmed from some unresolved issues. At an unconscious level, I must have still experienced him as powerful and all-knowing, and now he was asking me to see one of his patients. How cool was that?

I pulled myself together and responded to his question with a simple answer, "I'm terrific, thanks. I appreciate the referral."

Later in the week my assistant, Jackie, buzzed me and said I had a call from a Mrs. Carol Wilson, referred by Dr. Reidel. I was just about to start a conference call, so I asked Jackie to get her number. She told me Mrs. Wilson was calling from inside the hospital, room 632.

"Really," I said. "I'll call her back, but please get me the name of her internist and find out why she's in the hospital."

Jackie had learned that Dr. Lisa Chung had admitted Mrs. Wilson the day before for evaluation of back pain. After my appointments, I headed up to room 632.

I stood at the open door of the four-bed ward and observed a woman with bright red hair holding court as three other female patients listened. I checked the list of names on the side of the door to figure out which was Mrs. Wilson's bed, then hesitated in order to eavesdrop for a few moments.

Carol Wilson, the redhead, continued with her lecture. "Shirley," she said to the woman across from her, "I know you think your doctor is right, but I'm telling you, your symptoms suggest it's more than simple arthritis. You could very well have lupus, too. Has anyone thought to get a sed rate?" She was referring to the erythrocyte sedimentation rate, a nonspecific screening test that quantifies inflammation in the body and can be useful in detecting and monitoring a variety of diseases causing vague symptoms, ranging from tuberculosis to autoimmune disorders.

Shirley looked dumbfounded, and I made my entrance. "Good morning, ladies. Sorry to interrupt. I'm Dr. Small, and I'm here to see Carol Wilson."

Carol chirped, "That's me, Doctor. I called you."

I pushed a chair up to Carol's bed and pulled the curtain around us to create a semblance of privacy.

"I'm so glad you came up to see me, Dr. Small," she said. "You're much younger than I expected. You know, you remind me of my son,

Michael. He's a medical student here at UCLA." She raised both hands as if to stave off my congratulatory remarks. "I know, I know, I'm very proud of my little genius. He's my whole life."

She paused to take a sip of water and groaned in a spasm of pain. She leaned forward and grimaced, pushing her palms into her back. "Please, call for the nurse. I need something for pain."

She struck me as histrionic, so I wasn't sure how much pain she was really feeling and how much she was just performing for me. Maybe she was addicted to pain medications and putting on a show to get the doctor to prescribe them. I rang for the nurse and urged Carol to breathe deeply and slowly. After the nurse gave her a shot in the hip, Carol calmed down and seemed comfortable again.

"That really came on suddenly, Mrs. Wilson," I said.

"Yes, I know. It's a kidney stone," she said, "but Dr. Chung seems skeptical. I don't know why. I've had trace red cells in my urine, and the mid-back location of the pain is consistent with my diagnosis."

"You know a lot about medicine," I said. "Are you a physician?"

She laughed. "No, but aren't you sweet. I do have a Ph.D. in languages, and I'm an avid reader. In fact, did you catch that recent *JAMA* article linking Epstein-Barr virus and chronic fatigue syndrome? Or maybe I read that in the *New Yorker*. I read so much that sometimes I forget where I've seen things."

I barely had the time to read the abstracts in my medical journals, and I couldn't remember the last time I'd picked up a *New Yorker*. "No, I didn't catch that article. But let's talk about you. Dr. Reidel thought I might be able to help."

"I hope so, Doctor," she said quietly. "It's my son. I'm worried that he's overwhelmed with all the studying and competition in medical school. Sure, he's brilliant, but he's so sensitive and not willing to talk to me about what's going on."

"Did he used to talk to you?" I asked.

"We were best friends. His father died when he was five, and I became his confidante. I could always sense when something was bothering him, and I would advise him. But now he's so busy, I hardly ever see him."

"The first year of medical school can be hectic," I said.

"I know, but now he's getting these headaches—they're so bad that he gets nauseous, and he can't even come over on weekends. I'm really worried about him."

Dr. Reidel's suspicions about a doting and overbearing mother seemed accurate. Carol was sharp and articulate, but I suspected she might be missing the message her son appeared to be sending—that he needed some space. This could be a classic enmeshed mother-son relationship. Carol just said he was her whole life, but maybe Michael wanted his own life.

One of the challenges of consultation psychiatry is the lack of privacy in hospital settings. I didn't want to delve too much into Carol's personal issues while her roommates listened in. And she seemed more comfortable talking about her son than about herself, so I went with that.

"So what worries you about Michael's headaches?" I asked.

She lowered her voice. "I don't think he's telling me the whole story. I'm sure he's playing down his symptoms, and I believe his vision may be affected too. Lately, every time I see him, he's wearing dark sunglasses." She paused and looked down.

"What is it?" I asked.

"I haven't told this to his doctor yet, but I suspect a brain tumor." She leaned forward, "Malignant."

I barely kept from laughing. Since when had sunglasses and a headache become the diagnostic criteria for brain cancer? "Really? What makes you think he has a malignant tumor?"

"God willing I'm wrong, but all his symptoms point to it."

"Carol," I said, "lots of people get headaches and wear sunglasses."

"But this is new for Michael. Light sensitivity, headaches—both could be indications of cerebral edema from a tumor. In fact, for all I know, he could have a glioblastoma impinging on his optic nerve."

Boy, this woman knew her medical jargon and liked to throw it around. You'd think *she* was the one in medical school. Before I could reassure her that gliobastomas were almost never found in people under age thirty-five, Michael walked in wearing black jeans, a gray T-shirt, and dark sunglasses.

"Michael!" Carol exclaimed. "I'm so glad you stopped by. This is Dr. Small, the one you told me about." She patted the bed beside her for him to sit down.

"Nice to meet you, Dr. Small. I liked that lecture you gave on geriatrics a couple of weeks ago," he said as he pushed his sunglasses to the top of his head. "I see you've met Mother."

"Yes," I answered. "We were just getting to know each—"

Carol interrupted, "It's so nice to see you, sweetheart. I was just telling Dr. Small what a genius you are."

Michael looked annoyed and stood up. "Look, Mother, I just stopped by to say hello, but I can't stay. I have a study group." I figured this was my chance to get a few minutes alone with Michael.

"You know, I have to head out too," I said. "I'll be back later to talk some more, Carol. Michael, I'll walk downstairs with you."

Carol replied, "Lovely. You two boys get to know each other. Ta-ta!" As we headed out the door, Carol went back to holding court with the ladies, "Now Shirley, lupus is nothing to screw around with . . ."

We took the stairs down to the sunny courtyard below. Michael confessed, "I don't really have a study group, Dr. Small, I just wasn't in the mood to spend an hour with my mother while she diagnoses every move I make." He took off his sunglasses to clean them and continued, "She never stops with the questions—How did you sleep? What did you eat for breakfast? Are you still dating *that Mia*?"

"So she really gets under your skin," I said.

He laughed. "That's the understatement of the year."

"Your mother seems to be a very intelligent but intense woman. It must be exhausting being the center of her life," I said.

"She has way too much time on her hands, and she focuses it on me," Michael said. "If I ask for a sandwich, she makes a Thanksgiving dinner. If I cough, she's convinced I've got pneumonia. And it's getting worse."

We bought coffees and grabbed a table in the courtyard. "What do you think is making it worse?" I asked.

"She can't handle my moving in with my girlfriend. I lived at home all through college, but when I started med school, Mia and I finally got our own place. At first Mom acted like she was happy for me, but then things got a little weird. She sold our family house in Encino and bought herself a condo around the corner from UCLA. She claimed the house was too big for her alone, but I know she just wanted to be closer to me."

"Sounds like she's having a hard time separating," I said.

"You think? Mia keeps telling me that I need to set limits with Mom, but it's tough. She can't stand Mia, even though she's never really given her a chance. I mean, *no* girl will ever be good enough for her *little genius*. Mia's fantastic, and I want to make it work, but it's difficult for me to upset my mother." I could see that as much as Carol was struggling with Michael's perceived abandonment, Michael was having his own issues separating from his mother.

"You've met with Dr. Reidel," I said. "Are you going to continue seeing him?"

"We've got an appointment next week, and believe me, I can use it. I can't deal with all my mother's guilt trips—I never stay long enough, I don't call her enough, I'm too thin . . . It's keeping me up at night."

"I'm sure Dr. Reidel can help you with that, but I think your mother could use some help too," I said.

"That's where he thought you might come in."

As I headed back to my office, I thought about Michael's attempts to extricate himself from his mother's clutches. I speculated that Carol had never resolved her grief over the loss of her husband and held tightly to her son to fill that void. An emotionally mature, nurturing mother would be able to express her love for her son by allowing him to grow, make his own mistakes, and eventually become independent. Carol appeared to love her son and seemed to want the best for him, but she was having difficulty letting him live his own life.

The next day I went back up to Carol's four-bed ward to see her, but her bed was empty. The nurse told me she had been transferred to a private room. I paged Dr. Lisa Chung to find out what was going on, and she met me at the nurses' station.

Lisa smiled when she saw me. "Hey, Gary. Nice to see you."

"You look good, Lisa," I said. "I guess internal medicine agrees with you." After completing a psychiatry residency, Lisa had switched to internal medicine, and now she was chief resident.

"Thanks, I'm really enjoying it. Instead of having to listen to patients whine for fifty minutes, I only have to deal with them for ten minutes at a time."

"So what about this patient Mrs. Wilson? What's up with her?" I asked.

"She presented with acute mid-back pain, insisting it was a kidney stone about to pass," Lisa said. "We did find some red cells in her urine, but she also had a urinary tract infection, which explains that."

"What about an IVP?" I asked. An intravenous pylogram is an X-ray test that allows the doctor to see kidney stones after injecting an iodine-based contrast dye.

"Negative," Lisa said, "but I have a hunch about what's really going on with her—at least physically."

"What's that?" I wondered aloud.

"Whenever she swallows, it exacerbates her back pain. I think the pain is coming from her upper GI tract. She's been taking eight hundred milligrams of Motrin for pain, without food, for several months. She probably has gastritis or an ulcer from the antiinflammatory."

"So you think her back pain is referred from her esophagus or stomach," I said.

"Yes, and we've stopped the ibuprofen. I ordered an upper GI series for this afternoon."

"What do you think about all this medical meddling of hers?"

"My God, I've never met anyone—not even a surgeon—who is so opinionated and convinced of their diagnostic abilities," Lisa said with a laugh. "She does have a fair amount of lay medical knowledge, but she's so pushy that it's irritating."

"Have you met the son?" I asked.

"Yes, once. He's a little intense like his mother, but he seems like a normal guy," she said. "His mother talks about him nonstop, and she's really anxious."

"Maybe her anxiety is contributing to the gastritis," I said.

"Definitely. I'm convinced that most GI disorders have a psychological component."

Colitis and irritable bowel syndrome are classic examples of psychosomatic illnesses—true physical disorders that are influenced or aggravated by psychological factors. Many people share the misconception that physical symptoms resulting from stress are not serious or *real*. However, the emotional stress contributing to a psychosomatic illness can exacerbate physical symptoms that are just as real and potentially dangerous as those from any physical cause.

The interplay of psychological and physical components of psychosomatic illnesses in the GI tract is complex. For years, doctors believed that caffeine, antiinflammatory drugs, alcohol, and stress caused stomach ulcers. Although stress and diet can contribute to ulcer symptoms, in 2005 Barry Marshall and Robin Warren won the Nobel Prize in Physiology or Medicine for their discovery that the bacterium *Helicobacter pylori* can cause gastritis and peptic ulcer disease. Now, instead of taking months or years of dietary and other symptomatic treatments to heal an ulcer, a simple course of antibiotics often does the trick.

In the late 1980s, the antibiotic treatment for gastritis and ulcer disease had not yet been discovered. However, we did know that antiinflammatory medicines like Motrin could irritate the stomach lining and cause bleeding and discomfort, essentially an ulcer.

"It's fascinating how the mind can make the body sick," I said. "It's nice that you seem to be using both your psychiatric and medical training."

"If only I could double-bill for it." She smiled. "I'll let you know the results of her GI series as soon as I get them."

"Thanks," I said. "And why did Mrs. Wilson ask to be transferred to a private room?"

"*She* didn't. Her roommates did."

Carol Wilson's upper GI series came back positive for an esophageal ulcer, and she was started on antacids and an ulcer-friendly diet. Although forced to give up her conviction that she had a kidney stone, she was thrilled to receive a new, official diagnosis—one that Michael would have to take seriously. She had an appointment to come back and meet with me after she was discharged.

A week later Carol walked into my office wearing a tailored suit and coifed hair. Wedged under her arm was a folded *New York Times*. She sat on the sofa and smiled. "Dr. Small, it's a delight to see you again." She looked around the office, "I love the ambience, so UCLA."

I laughed and said, "I'm glad you're here, Carol. How are you feeling?"

"I'm happy to report that my ulcer is completely gone." She leaned in. "Don't tell Dr. Chung, but I've been sneaking an occasional cigarette with my morning coffee, and it hasn't hurt a bit."

"I'm glad you're feeling better, but take it easy on the caffeine, and you have to stop smoking. Have you been using the antacids?" I asked.

"Of course. You sound like my mother." She pulled out a roll of Tums and popped one into her mouth. She offered me one, but I declined. She crossed her legs and winced in pain.

"Are you okay?" I asked.

She changed her position on the sofa to get more comfortable, "I'm fine, I just have this ruptured L4-L5 disc in my spine. There is a new procedure at the Mayo Clinic that I've been considering, but I refuse to be a guinea pig. Once you start messing with your back . . . oh, I don't want to get into it."

I was seeing a pattern. For Carol, every new day brought a new symptom, injury, or disease, and I suspected that each problem got a rise out of Michael. She could have Munchausen's syndrome, where one fabricates illness to get attention. She also had a classic histrionic personality, which is essentially a long-term pattern of chronic attention seeking and emotional excitability.

She tried to put on a brave face but seemed distracted by her back pain. I changed the subject, "What's been going on since you left the hospital?"

"I'm very concerned about Michael. At first I was worried that he might have a serious ailment because of his headaches and nausea, but now I'm not so sure."

"What do you mean?" I asked.

"I think it may be psychosomatic," she said.

That's certainly the pot calling the kettle black, I thought to myself, sounding just like my father. Instead I said, "Psychosomatic?"

"You must have heard of medical studentitis," she said.

"You mean when medical students imagine they have every horrible disease they read about in their textbooks?" I asked.

"Yes. These kids get obsessed with all the illnesses they're learning about, and I think that could be what's happening to Michael. He's always been very sensitive and susceptible to suggestion."

Medical studentitis, also known as medical student disease, is believed to affect nearly 60 percent of all doctors at some point in their training. The condition is a form of hypochondriasis, or excessive preoccupation and worry about having a serious illness. It's no surprise that the voluminous and morbid details of medical training can trigger this kind of worry and anxiety. Although it's usually short-lived, some students get into a vicious cycle of maladaptive behavior—they frequently check their body for lesions and pore over their medical books for clues to the suspected malignant nature of their everyday bodily sensations. A transient ache in the groin becomes testicular cancer; craving liquids on a hot day turns into a sign of adult-onset diabetes; and writer's cramp from taking notes is evidence of incipient rheumatoid arthritis. The particular disease or organ under study in class is often the student's focus for his hypochondriacal concerns. As medical students gain more experience and knowledge, they usually become less anxious and their studentitis tends to disappear.

Michael was a first-year student, so he was at risk for this common syndrome. He originally went to the student health service because of anxiety, but he didn't strike me as particularly anxious. And he had already told me at the hospital that he was playing up his symptoms to get out of being around his mother.

"It's possible that Michael has this student disorder, but—"

Carol interrupted, "It's more than possible, it's highly likely. I think it would be extremely helpful if you could meet with us together. Then we could get to the bottom of what's going on."

It sounded like Carol was again trying to avoid dealing with her own issues by focusing our therapy on her son, but I also thought it might be helpful to observe more of the dynamic between them. "I could meet with the two of you. Let me give you some times so you can both check your schedules."

"Can't you just stop by my place tomorrow around five? Michael promised to come over after class and stay for dinner. My condo is right here in Westwood, just down the street. I'd really appreciate it if you'd make a house call."

Unlike most doctors, geriatric psychiatrists did make house calls on occasion because some of their patients were housebound. Although this wasn't a geriatric case, I felt it would be interesting to observe Carol on her own turf, especially with her son there. People reveal quite a bit about themselves in the comfort of their own home, and their surroundings tell even more.

I checked my calendar and said, "Fine. Why don't you let Michael know, and I'll be at your place tomorrow around five-thirty."

Carol lived just five minutes from UCLA on Wilshire Boulevard, the main east-west thoroughfare in Los Angeles. Her building was among a cluster of high-rises that offered views of the ocean, mountains, and downtown skyline, in one of the most desirable residential areas on the West Coast.

I pulled up to Carol's building, and the valet took my car. As I entered the elegant, high-ceilinged foyer, a doorman welcomed me and phoned up to Carol, announcing my arrival before he'd allow me on the elevators.

My ears popped as I approached the twenty-second floor. The elevator was covered in gold-plated mirrors, so I checked myself out—I looked pretty frumpy after a long day. I straightened my tie, tucked in my shirt, and ran my fingers through my hair, going for that casual but professional house-call look.

The elevator opened directly into Carol's apartment. I stepped in and was impressed by the view of West Los Angeles and the Pacific Ocean beyond. Carol ran up to greet me holding a martini and wearing a neck brace. "Please come in, Dr. Small. What are you drinking?" She leaned in and whispered, "You could have a cocktail and I won't tell . . ."

"Perrier, please, straight up," I said. "What happened to your neck, Carol?"

"Well, it's silly, but I've had this intermittent hacking cough—which I told Dr. Chung could be the onset of emphysema, and the cough upset my C4-C5 whiplash disc protrusion."

I thought to myself that this seemed too over-the-top to be Munchausen's and perhaps she was just a hypochondriac with a histrionic personality. I decided not to nag her about the martini and her ulcer, but if she lit a cigarette, I'd have to speak up . . . especially now that she had self-diagnosed emphysema.

"Michael's not here yet," she said, "but I wanted to talk to you alone for a few minutes anyway. I think we should do couples therapy."

"With who?" I asked.

"Michael and me, of course."

"Carol, couples therapy usually involves a couple, like a husband and wife."

"Not according to the eminent family therapist Salvador Minuchin. He's used his structural family therapy model to resolve many parent/child difficulties."

Carol was right. Minuchin often worked with nuclear families, as well as subsets of family members, to help them understand what was dysfunctional in the way they interacted. His methods were especially helpful for enmeshed relationships, where he would show family members how to define healthier boundaries. He believed that therapeutic change could only occur when the family members recognized the patterns in their relationships and were willing to modify them. Minuchin's approach could help Carol and Michael, but behind her request I suspected yet another ploy to spend more time with Michael.

"You know, Carol, both parties have to want couples therapy, and Michael is not a child."

"No, I'm not," Michael said as he stepped off the elevator. "And what's wrong with you now, Mother? Your whiplash kicking up again?"

"It's nothing, sweetie. Let me get you a glass of that merlot you love. You two sit down in the living room."

We walked to the step-down living room as Carol headed for the kitchen and called out, "Luticia? Could you please open a bottle of the merlot and help me with the hors d'oeuvres?"

Michael and I sat across from each other on Carol's white couches. "I didn't know doctors still made house calls." He shook his head and said, "I don't think I like that."

"Don't worry, most doctors don't." Luticia brought out a plate of hot hors d'oeuvres. I sipped my Perrier and noticed a volume of *Harrison's Principles of Internal Medicine* on the coffee table. It was the standard textbook for medical students and practicing physicians. "I see you've been studying over here."

"No way."

Carol came in, handed Michael a glass of wine, and sat next to him on the couch. "Mother, did you sneak into my apartment and borrow my volume one of *Harrison's*?" he asked.

She laughed, "Don't be silly, dear. You know how much I love to read nonfiction. And this was on sale at Dutton's."

"But this isn't just nonfiction, Mother," he said. "It's a medical textbook."

"I find it interesting," she said. "Besides, I want to be able to talk to you about what you're learning."

As I watched them interact, I realized how Carol had manipulated the scene. I was seated across from the two of them, who were sharing a sofa, perfectly poised for couples therapy.

"Look, Mom, we can talk about this later. I want to know what you and Dr. Small were discussing when I came in," Michael said.

"I was saying how worried I am about you lately," she said.

"Tell me something I don't know. Every time I sneeze you act like I'm dying."

"That's absurd!" Carol exclaimed. "I'm simply concerned, darling."

"About what, Mother?"

"That you have medical studentitis."

Michael laughed and shook his head. "Maybe you should stop reading *Harrison's* and stick to biographies."

"Think what you like, dear, but it's extremely common in first-year medical students, and there's nothing to be ashamed of." She winced in pain again, "Ouch, I get this throbbing headache whenever my neck acts up."

I noticed that when Michael didn't buy her studentitis diagnosis, she changed the subject to her own pain.

"You know, Mother, the most common cause of headache is muscle tension and stress. So don't start thinking you have a brain tumor."

Carol started crying.

"Are you okay, Mom?"

"What's the matter, Carol?" I asked.

"Nothing, it's just this headache." Michael put his arm around her to comfort her. Carol continued, "Dr. Small, could you ask Luticia for some Tylenol?" It seemed like Michael's sarcastic comment about the brain tumor triggered Carol's tears, and now she was once again in control.

I walked to the kitchen and couldn't find Luticia, so I headed down the hall to the bathroom. I found some Tylenol in the medicine cabinet and started back to the living room, but as I passed the library, I noticed a large stack of medical books. I was intrigued—Carol had nearly every first-year medical text piled on the desk. I thumbed through one of them and found the pages covered with yellow highlighting. This was more than casual nonfiction reading—Carol appeared to be studying them, as if *she* was going to medical school.

I returned to the living room and handed Carol two Tylenols. She washed them down with her martini.

"Are you okay, Mom?" Michael asked.

"Yes, honey. It's so comforting to have you home."

"I'm glad you're feeling better, Carol," I said. "You know, when I passed the library, I noticed that you have a lot of first-year medical texts."

Michael pulled away. "What? What are you talking about?" He dashed down the hall.

Carol hissed at me, "I didn't take you for a snoop."

Michael yelled from the library, "I can't believe this, Mother! So now you're my classmate? Why don't you just move into the apartment with Mia and me?"

I called to him, "Michael, please come back. Let's talk about it."

As Michael marched down the hall carrying a pile of the books, Carol glared at me and said, "He'll never talk to me now."

"Don't be so sure," I said.

Michael dropped the heavy books on the coffee table and sat back down. "So who's the med student here, you or me?"

Carol said sheepishly, "I just wanted to stay close to you." She looked at me. "Is that so bad?"

"Well, I don't want you that close!" Michael yelled. "I want to have my own life."

I realized that I'd better grab the reins of this session before it got totally out of hand. I stood up. "Let's slow down and try to understand what's going on here." They looked up at me, seeming to respond to the authority in my voice. "Carol, you're having a tough time dealing with your grown son moving out. And Michael, you can't please your mother completely and have your own separate life. I think you both need to set some boundaries in your relationship."

Carol spoke up. "I can deal with boundaries. But he's in denial, and that Mia supports it."

"You always call her 'that Mia' like she's a car or something. She's my girlfriend for God's sake, and I love her. Why can't you accept that? Why can't you accept me?"

Carol started crying again. "I really do want you to be happy, Michael. I just don't know if she's right for you."

"Well, how are you ever going to get to know her if you don't give her a chance?" Michael asked.

"I'm willing to give her a chance, but I'm worried that she buys into your studentitis."

I sat on a chair next to them. "Carol, I'm glad you're going to try to get to know Mia, but I think you should also focus less on Michael's symptoms and look more honestly at your own. I'm sorry, but if anybody has medical studentitis, it's you."

They were staring at me in silence. Had I said too much? I felt they both needed a dose of truth.

Carol broke the silence. "How could I have studentitis? I don't go to medical school."

"But you're reading every one of my textbooks. It's like you want to be one of my classmates."

"I don't know why I got the books, Michael. I just wanted to feel closer to you."

"By studying my medical texts?" he asked. "No wonder I always feel like we're competing when we talk about school."

I interrupted them. "Carol, regardless of why you're reading these books, it's certainly possible that they're feeding into your worries about your own medical problems." I was trying to soften my earlier interpretation.

"I just wanted to be able to discuss what was going on in Michael's life," she said.

"But Mother, school isn't my whole life."

"I know. Maybe I did get carried away."

"It's okay, Mom," Michael said. "You seem tired."

I stood up. "It's getting late. We can talk about this next time." I excused myself and took the elevator back down to the valet parking.

As I drove home, I reflected on Carol and her son; they had made some progress that evening, but there was still a lot of work to be done. Carol needed to understand why she was so threatened by Michael's girlfriend. It would also help them both if Michael admitted that he was exaggerating his headaches and other symptoms to avoid seeing Carol. Michael seemed to love his mother but was irritated by her indirect ways of trying to remain close to him. Carol's manipulations had not only backfired and pushed him farther away, but they had created a bizarre and neurotic mother-son relationship fueled by her hypochondriasis and their common physical symptoms. I was hopeful that therapy could offer them insight into their enmeshed and complicated relationship and bring them closer, yet allow them more autonomy.

When I got home, my answering machine was flashing; I had three messages. The first was from my buddy Ross, the second was from my sister, and the third was from Gigi—finally. I opened a bottle of cabernet, poured a glass, and called her back.

It rang three times, then she said, "Hello?"

"Hi, it's Gary from Nancy's Memorial Day party. Remember me?"

"Oh, sure. It's been a couple of weeks, and I was giving up on hearing from you. How are you?"

"I'm really sorry, but somehow I must have gotten the number wrong and I left two messages, but it was some kind of agency and I—"

She laughed. "I know. Your sister called Nancy who called Shelly who called me and told me what happened. So I decided to call you before we involve all those people again."

"Well, it's good to finally connect." There was an awkward silence, which I couldn't stand. "So, you're an actress?"

"Yeah, I have been. But I'm writing now and just sold my first screenplay."

"That's great," I said. "Congratulations."

"Thanks. I heard that you're a psychiatrist. How's that going?"

I took a sip of cabernet. "I think it's going well, but I'm not sure why." That was the first of many conversations I would have with Gigi over the years.

I saw Carol and Michael together a few more times. Michael's struggle to separate from his mother, and her difficulty letting go, were not that different from what many adult children and their parents experience. What was unusual in their situation was that Carol's preoccupation with being part of Michael's life had developed into a case of medical studentitis by proxy. Cases of Munchausen's by proxy have often been reported, where parents fabricate their child's illness in order to get attention. Proxy medical student disease was a new one on me.

I continued to treat Carol for the next six months. Both her anxiety and her physical symptoms improved, I suspect in part because of the therapy but also because of a low dose of antidepressant. Often when people get depressed, they experience physical symptoms that can be a manifestation of an underlying mood disorder. As Carol gradually came to grips with the loss of her husband, she had less need to cling to Michael as well as her real and imagined physical illnesses. She was still a hypochondriac, but her aches and pains no longer indicated mortal illness. She gifted her medical books to the school library and went back to reading biographies and fiction.

Carol eventually grew to love Mia, and her relationship with Michael improved. Two years after her therapy with me ended, I received an announcement of Carol's wedding to a well-known Westside internist. I was glad that she had moved forward with her life, and if her symptoms kicked up again, at least she'd have someone there for a house call every night.

CHAPTER NINE

Eyes Wide Shut

Winter 1989

JASON RILEY WALKED INTO MY OFFICE at exactly 2:00 P.M. Wearing a button-down shirt, striped tie, and gray slacks, he looked more like an accountant than a twenty-two-year-old philosophy major about to graduate with honors from UCLA. He began the session as he always did—by emptying his pockets and lining up his date book, wallet, glasses, keys, and mints in a neat row on the table beside the sofa. He brushed off the bottom and back cushion before sitting down.

In his soft voice, he said, "Today I'd like to explore the true meaning of why I'm coming here." Jason might have come off as stilted, obsessive, and controlling, but at least he knew what he wanted out of a session.

"As I recall, you were trying to decide on what to do when you graduate." I sipped my coffee and waited for a response.

He adjusted his tie and thought for a moment. "But that's only part of it."

"Last week it sounded like your father was putting pressure on you to attend his alma mater, Loyola Law."

"Yes, but I think what's best for me is to get my Ph.D. in philosophy at Berkeley," he said.

"If that's what you think is best, Jason, why even consider going to law school?"

"That's a completely different subject, Dr. Small. Today I'm looking to understand a very profound issue." He straightened his row of items on the side table. "I don't know if you are familiar with Wittgenstein's writings."

"I read some of his works when I was in college."

"Then you may recall his argument that many of our problems stem from the misuse of language. If we're going to come up with a logical analysis to solve my dilemma, we first need to answer the most basic question: Do I really have the free will to make this decision at all?"

For some reason, Jason's mini-lecture made me think about lunch. I usually enjoyed philosophical discussions, but Jason's need to control everyone and everything around him made his therapy sessions feel more like a power struggle than an exploration of his inner life. It reminded me of sitting through a long, boring speech, feeling desperate to escape. During Jason's first month of treatment, I had suggested an antidepressant to help with his obsessive-compulsive tendencies, but he didn't want to be controlled by a medication.

"All of us have free will, Jason. We make choices every day."

"You haven't met my father."

Now we were getting somewhere. "Tell me about him."

"Growing up in my house, there wasn't any free will, only my father's will. And he would let us know it all the time. Be friends with this person, take that class, don't eat so fast, go to UCLA—the greatest public education you can get."

"Sounds like a controlling guy, your dad," I said. "He must have really pissed you off." I thought by using the word *pissed* instead of *angry*, I might loosen Jason up a bit and help him acknowledge his feelings.

"Dad was firm, and I imagine I had a modicum of antipathy toward him." Oh brother, I thought; if he kept going on like this I'd have to sneak a crossword puzzle out of my desk to get through the session.

"How did you cope with your father telling you what to do all the time?"

"I listened, I agreed, and then I ignored him."

"Is that how you usually deal with authority figures?"

"I don't think so," he said. "Just my father."

"How do you ignore an overbearing father?"

"I never said he was overbearing," Jason snipped. "I just realized at a young age that there was no reasoning with him. He saw the world in only one way. California was the only decent place to live, except for the Democrats and the immigrants of course. Professional school was a given, and becoming a lawyer in Dad's firm was the only job option. But that's not why I'm here to consult with you, Doctor. I want to understand the basic decision-making process before I move forward."

"Perhaps understanding how you feel about your father will help you decide."

"That's an interesting hypothesis, Dr. Small, but it still doesn't address my original question."

Jason was using a classic Freudian defense mechanism, intellectualization, to avoid talking about his feelings. Freud believed that all memories have both conscious and unconscious components, and by focusing on the conscious aspects of our memories, intellectualization allows us to logically analyze an event and avoid any anxiety, sadness, or other uncomfortable feelings associated with it. By focusing on the facts, we can deal with any emotionally charged situation as merely an interesting problem and remain detached from our feelings.

Intellectualization is different from another common defense mechanism, denial, wherein we refuse to even acknowledge the existence of the problem or event. Intellectualization gives the impression that one is dealing with an issue, but the feelings and emotions underlying it are ignored and the root of the problem is never addressed. Jason had probably been intellectualizing away his problems for so long that it had become an automatic reaction for him.

For the rest of the session, I kept trying to bring him back to his feelings, but he kept avoiding them with his theoretical lectures and debates.

At exactly fifty minutes past the hour, Jason put his items back into his pockets and stood. "I'll see you next week, Dr. Small."

As I watched him leave I felt relief. It had been exhausting trying to keep up with his incessant intellectualizing. I knew he used it to keep me at bay and protect himself from his feelings, but he was starting to wear me down. I needed to rethink my strategy and find a way to break through his rigid defenses. My goal was to help him experience his feelings and make the decision he was avoiding.

That evening I met Gigi for dinner at our favorite Italian restaurant. Since we'd gotten married six months earlier, dining at La Loggia had become our Thursday-night ritual. When I arrived, the maître d' greeted me warmly and said that Gigi had called and was running a few minutes late.

As I put my pager on the table, I thought about Jason lining up his date book, wallet, mints, and other things. I realized that my frustration with him was getting worse—he'd been in therapy for almost two months, and it seemed like we had made little progress.

The waiter brought bread and asked if I wanted a drink. I ordered two Diet Cokes as I spotted Gigi's curly red hair. She was smiling as she entered the restaurant. The maître d' hugged her and pointed me out.

"Sorry I'm late, honey," she said as she kissed me.

"No problem. I ordered you a Diet Coke."

"Thanks, I'm starving," she said as she ravaged the bread and scanned the menu. "So how was your day?"

"Pretty good, but I keep thinking about this patient I saw today. He's about to graduate college and not sure what to do next."

The waiter brought the sodas and some bruschetta. "What are his options?" Gigi asked.

"He wants to get a Ph.D., but his father is pressuring him to go into the family business."

"I suppose he could get a Ph.D. *and* go into the family business. That way everybody's happy," she said as she beat me to the last bruschetta.

I liked talking to Gigi about my cases sometimes. It was helpful bouncing ideas off someone who was completely outside my field, and she had great instincts. I made sure that I avoided names and specifics to protect my patients' confidentiality.

"So what do you think your patient is going to do?" Gigi asked.

"I don't know, but I'm concerned that he's going to make the wrong decision because he's so out of touch with his feelings, and I can't seem to break through his defenses."

Gigi took a sip of soda. "Remember that supervisor in residency you told me about? What did you guys call him . . . the Loch Ness Monster?"

I laughed. "I'll never forget him."

"You told me he was obsessed with early loss and trauma. Didn't he say, if you wanted to get to the bottom of somebody's problem, find out what happened to him as a kid?"

"I know that my patient's brother died when he was young, but every time I try to ask him about it, he changes the subject. You may be right. I think I'm going to push harder on his past."

"Sounds good," she said as she waved over the busboy. "Can we get some more bread, please?"

THE FOLLOWING THURSDAY, AFTER JASON ARRIVED AT my office precisely on the hour, I watched him line up his possessions on the side table before brushing off the cushions and sitting on the sofa. He appeared more tense than usual, but I knew better than to say anything before *he* began the session.

"Dr. Small, we're going to have to put aside the profound question I asked you last week, because I have to make my decision about graduate school by tomorrow." Jason had been accepted to both Berkeley and Loyola Law School.

This was good—a deadline could help us make progress. Maybe by forgoing the usual intellectual chitchat and getting right down to the heart of something important, we'd actually move forward.

"I didn't realize you had to decide so soon."

He sounded annoyed, "As I recall, I mentioned the deadline to you several times last month. I guess you chose to ignore it."

Jason seemed to bristle at the possibility that I might be ignoring him. I thought it might be a hot button because his major psychological defense, intellectualization, was a form of ignoring his own inner life. I would share that interpretation with him if the timing was ever right, but I didn't want to spend today's session in a debate over what he might perceive as semantic details. I recalled Gigi's advice from last week and decided to go for his past instead. "Jason, I think it's important that we spend a few moments talking about your childhood."

"We've been through this before, Dr. Small. I don't see the relevance," he said.

"I'm wondering if it's too painful for you to talk or even think about it," I said.

"It's not that," Jason protested. "I just don't see how it matters."

"Humor me. It may help us understand why it's difficult for you to make this decision."

"Fine. What do you want to know?"

"You mentioned your older brother had passed away when you were young. What was his name?" I asked.

"Robert," he said as he took a mint and returned the roll to its spot on the table.

"What do you remember about him?"

"He was five years older and really smart. Robert was everything my father wanted in a son."

"What do you mean?"

Jason answered with disdain. "He couldn't wait to be a lawyer. I remember when I was about ten—he must have been fifteen, the year before he died—he would go to work with Dad on weekends. Then he'd come home and we'd set up a mock courthouse in our room. I was always the bad guy, and Robert was my lawyer who would defend me and keep me out of jail."

"Did he defend you or protect you in other ways?"

"As I said, Dad was firm—he had a bad temper. I don't remember him ever hitting us, but when he got *really* mad, especially at me, Robert could always calm him down."

"So it sounds like Robert had your back."

Jason shrugged.

"I don't think you mentioned how he died," I said gently.

Jason looked at me, expressionless. "Dad bought him a car for his sixteenth birthday, and some drunk driver killed him."

"That must have been horrible for all of you," I said.

"It was, especially for my parents—they lost their perfect son. I was just the spare."

With Robert's death, Jason lost his benevolent father figure, who protected him from his real father, a demanding and explosive control freak who Jason could never please. Any attention Robert received must have made Jason feel more like the spare, making it difficult for Jason to tolerate his parents' grief over Robert's death. Jason's ambivalence toward his brother must have made it difficult for him to grieve as well.

"It must have been hard for you to lose your brother at that age," I said.

Jason said nothing and looked down.

"Did your parents comfort you?" I asked.

"I was pretty much ignored. Dad did make a big speech about me having to step up and take on more of Robert's responsibilities."

"Like being a lawyer?"

Jason seemed irritated. "I think we're wasting time with all this talk about the past. You're ignoring the fact that I need help with a big decision."

"I think you've already made your decision to get your philosophy degree, and you're afraid to tell your father," I said.

"You're wrong. I just haven't made up my mind. Sure I want to do philosophy, but there are plenty of arguments for going into law."

"Jason, I believe you've learned to survive by ignoring your feelings. I don't think you've ever really grieved your brother's death or acknowledged your fear of disappointing your father. Until you understand those feelings, any major decision will be difficult."

"I'm not afraid of my father, Dr. Small, and I know more about my feelings than you think. In fact, I think I've just made my decision. I'm getting my Ph.D. in philosophy, and I don't think all this talk about the past has helped at all."

He began putting his things back into his pockets. "Our time is up for today," he said as he abruptly left the office. I guess I had pushed him too hard.

IT WAS ABOUT 11:30 P.M., AND I was awakened by the ringing telephone. Gigi slept right through it, hogging the blankets as usual.

"Dr. Small? This is the UCLA page operator. I have Tarzana Medical Center on the line."

"Okay," I said quietly, so as not to wake the sleeping princess next to me.

"Hi, I'm John Peterson, the E.R. attending at Tarzana. We have one of your patients here, Jason Riley. He was admitted this evening for sudden-onset blindness. He's about to get a CT scan and LP, and he keeps asking for you to come in. His parents are here, and the whole family is pretty hysterical."

Tarzana Medical Center wasn't far from my place in Sherman Oaks. "Tell them I'll be there in half an hour."

Not since my residency in Boston had I experienced the joys of waking up at night and heading down to an emergency room. I didn't miss it. I threw on some jeans and a shirt, grabbed a white coat, and left a note for Gigi.

As I drove down the deserted Ventura Boulevard at midnight, I worried about Jason. He'd been fine that afternoon, and now he was blind? He was too young for a stroke, but it could have been a bilateral retinal detachment. Maybe he'd hit his head or had some other accident. If Peterson was getting an LP and CT, he must have suspected an infection or tumor. I was surprised that Jason had asked for me, given the way our session had ended. I pulled into the E.R. parking area and walked quickly through the ambulance entrance.

In the waiting room I saw an elderly couple, the man in a wheelchair with apparent paralysis on his right side, perhaps from a stroke. His wife was offering him something to drink. Another family was comforting a little girl who was wincing in pain and holding her arm. In the back I spotted a middle-aged couple arguing. The man looked like an older version of Jason; the woman was brunette and petite, crying and wiping her eyes with a handkerchief.

I went directly to the nurses' station down the hall, and Dr. Peterson approached me. He was young, probably a physician resident in training, moonlighting in this community-hospital E.R. "Thanks for coming down. Your patient was pretty upset, but his mother was even worse," he said. "I thought she was about to hyperventilate, so I gave her five milligrams of Valium to calm her down."

"How's Jason doing?"

"Actually, we can't find anything organically wrong with him that would impair his vision, so we're thinking it's got to be psychological. He's in the room at the end of the hall." Peterson handed me the chart and headed toward the waiting room to call his next patient.

I walked toward Jason's room, skimming the chart. It was true that all of Jason's tests had come back negative. As I read the brief chart, it struck me how little E.R. doctors knew about the patients they were treating, yet so often they were able to save them in life-threatening situations.

I saw Jason lying on a gurney, wearing a hospital gown. His eyes were shut.

"Jason. It's Dr. Small."

"Thank God," he said. "Finally, someone who will believe me. I can't see and no one will tell me why. One minute I could see perfectly, and a second later I was blind."

"Jason, why are you keeping your eyes closed?"

"It doesn't matter. Open or closed, I still can't see a thing."

"Let me try something," I said. "Take a deep breath and relax. I'm just going to pull your eyelids up." I placed my thumbs on his eyebrows and pulled up gently on his lids. As I pulled, he squeezed his eyes shut so tightly that his whole face scrunched up.

This was bizarre. The more I tried to open his eyes, the more tightly he closed them. Peterson's conclusion was probably right—Jason's sudden blindness didn't appear to have an organic cause. Why else would he be resisting my efforts to open his eyes?

"Jason, do you remember what was going on right before you lost your vision?"

"Yeah, I told my father I had decided to go to Berkeley and get my philosophy Ph.D. See? I wasn't afraid of confronting him."

"What did he say?" I asked.

"I don't remember exactly. All I know is, suddenly I couldn't see and I panicked. Then everybody started yelling. Dad accused me of faking it, but Mom insisted they take me to the hospital."

"How are you feeling now, Jason?"

"Scared. I mean, I can't see. The doctors can't find anything wrong with me, and I don't think this Dr. Peterson even believes me. You believe me, don't you, Dr. Small?"

"Jason, I believe that you can't see, and I'm going to help you. I'm going to go talk with the doctor and your parents for a few minutes, and then I'll be back."

I went to the waiting room, which was empty now except for the couple sitting anxiously in the back. "Mr. and Mrs. Riley?"

They looked up expectantly. "Yes?" Mrs. Riley asked.

"I'm Dr. Small, your son's psychiatrist."

Mr. Riley stood and shook my hand, "Thanks for coming down here. I knew the moment this started that it was all in Jason's head."

"How did you know that?" Ruth Riley asked.

He turned to her. "He's got his eyes closed, for Christ's sake. He's faking it."

"Alan, you can't know that for sure," Ruth said.

"Don't defend him, Ruth. Let's see what his psychiatrist thinks."

"I'm not sure yet," I said. "But it would help me to know what happened just before he lost his vision."

Alan Riley sat back down. "Jason had come into my study to talk. It turned into a heated discussion about what he planned to do after graduation."

"How heated was it?" I asked.

"Jason started the argument: he was all puffed up, telling me that *he* had decided about graduate school. Since when is it *his* decision? Is he paying? Besides, we had already made a deal—Loyola Law."

Ruth spoke slowly. "Alan, it *is* his decision. You can't run his life forever. He's not Robert."

Alan slammed his hand down on the arm of his chair. "Why are you bringing Robert into this? He has nothing to do with it—"

I interrupted. "What might help is if you could tell me what happened in the very moments before Jason lost his sight."

Alan took a deep breath while gripping the arms of his chair. "I told him I wasn't going to send him to some hippie school to study philosophy so he could sit on his ass and teach for forty grand a year." Despite his efforts to remain calm, Alan's voice was rising and his face was getting red.

Ruth rubbed his arm. "Alan, calm down, it's not good for your heart." Turning to me, she said, "Doctor, they were arguing so loudly that I came running in from the kitchen. I'd never seen my son that angry. He held up his fists and was about to take a swing at his own father. Then suddenly Jason grabbed his face and started screaming that he couldn't see."

"That sounds frightening. Alan, is that how you recall it?" I asked.

"I guess so, but let me tell you, if that punk would have tried to punch me, I would have kicked his skinny ass."

"Don't be ridiculous, Alan. He's stronger than you. Besides, you've never hit him and you never will."

As I listened to Jason's parents, I began to form my own theory of what had brought the Rileys to this point. Over the years, Jason's obsessiveness and need to control had helped him to manage his anger, especially toward his father. His decision to get a Ph.D. rather than go to law school was not simply a choice but also an act of rebellion, an expression of anger toward his father, who had been controlling Jason throughout his life.

Obsessive, controlling individuals often need to avoid direct expressions of anger because they feel it is too dangerous and could become explosive, which is how Jason might have felt when the argument with his father escalated. When Jason finally confronted his father and unleashed his pent-up rage, he was on the brink of physically harming him, and that was unacceptable—at least at an unconscious level. To stop himself, his mind made him believe he was blind. That way, he could no longer strike out and hurt his father.

It seemed to me that Jason was suffering from hysterical blindness to keep from punching his father. With classic hysterical conversion symptoms, the mind suppresses uncomfortable or unacceptable feelings and thoughts and converts them into physical symptoms. The physical symptoms have both a primary and secondary gain. The primary gain is the avoidance of some conflict or feeling. In Jason's case, he avoided striking his father and suffering the consequences of that action. The secondary gain of the hysterical symptom is the attention and comfort the patient receives as a result of the hysterical illness. Both the primary and secondary gains associated with conversion hysteria serve to reinforce the physical symptoms, making them persist, sometimes for months or years. As with most acute-onset illnesses, whether they have a psychological or physical origin, a rapid intervention is usually most effective and can prevent the emergence of chronic problems.

If my theory was correct, then I needed to help Jason consciously acknowledge his anger toward his father and find a way to express it without physical violence. Expressing his anger would detoxify it, making it less dangerous, and eliminate the primary gain of his hysterical blindness. I felt my best shot was to get all the Rileys into the room and help them confront their issues. One in the morning was an unconventional time to have a family session, but the key players were here, and I felt a sense of urgency.

We all pulled up chairs around Jason's gurney, and I helped prop him up into a sitting position for our makeshift family meeting.

"I know it's late and everybody's tired," I began. "But we need to talk about what made Jason lose his sight tonight."

"So the tests came back positive!" Jason said.

Ruth piped in, "You see, Alan? Things aren't always what they seem."

"You're right about that, Mrs. Riley," I said. "But the tests were negative."

"What do you mean?" Ruth asked.

"It's true that Jason can't see, but it's not something physical making him blind, it's his mind making it happen."

Alan spoke up. "So it is all in his head! You can snap out of it now, son. Just open your eyes."

"It's not so easy, Mr. Riley," I said. "The key to Jason's blindness is *why* his mind is doing this to him."

"I don't understand," Alan said.

I wanted to get Jason into the conversation, so I phrased the next question in a way that would appeal to him. "What purpose does it serve Jason to be distracted by this physical symptom?"

As I had hoped, Jason responded, "I think I see where you're heading, Dr. Small. What's your theory?"

My strategy here was to get Jason to express his anger toward his father in a safe way. He didn't necessarily have to understand why he went blind, but we were already down that road and it appealed to his intellectual defenses.

"Jason, for a good portion of your life, you've been angry at your father and you've had no way to express it. You resent his trying to control you."

"That's ridiculous!" Alan blurted.

"Be quiet, Alan," Ruth said. "Let the doctor finish."

I went on. "I believe your father loves you and wants the best for you, but you two see things differently. And the big problem for *both* of you is that you avoid talking about your feelings. If you could learn to talk, you wouldn't feel the need to hit, and it will feel safe."

"That's an interesting hypothesis, Dr. Small, but how do you prove it?" Jason asked.

Before I could answer, Alan interrupted. "The burden of proof is on you, son. Just open your damn eyes."

I ignored Alan's comment. "Jason, let's try this. Tell your father how angry you are at him. Nobody's going to get hurt; I'm here to make sure of that."

Jason laughed. "I'm supposed to just talk about a lifetime of being ignored and controlled, and then forced to stand in for my dead brother."

"Jason, how dare you say that?" Ruth scolded.

"Because it's true, Mom, and Dad knows it."

"What I know is," Alan yelled, "you're not half the man Robert would have been."

"See, Dr. Small? That's exactly what I've been talking about," Jason said.

Alan shook his head. "Tell your shrink whatever you want about me, but I've tried to give you the best life I could."

"I'm sure you have, Mr. Riley," I said. "But before you and Jason can have a real relationship, you've got to grieve Robert's death."

"Don't tell me about grief. I lost my future when that boy died."

"But you still have another son, another future," I said.

"I know that, but Robert was an amazing kid— we had a special connection. He reminded me of myself when I was young. He'd come to work with me on the weekends, and we'd discuss cases. He would have been a better lawyer than I ever was." He paused for a moment as he reminisced, no longer angry but sad. "I did everything for him; I got him everything. Why'd I have to get him that damn sports car?"

"Alan, do you feel responsible for Robert's death?" I asked.

Alan hung his head and covered his eyes. Ruth started to sob.

"Wait a minute," Jason said. "I thought Robert was killed by a drunk driver."

Ruth said, "We only made up that story to protect him."

"What are you talking about?" Jason asked.

His father looked down. "It was *Robert* who had been drinking, and he crashed into a tree."

Jason bolted straight up on the gurney and glared at his father. "You mean you've been lying to me all these years?"

"We didn't want you to hate your brother."

"No, you'd rather I *be* him and grow up to hate you."

"That's not fair," Ruth said. "We love you, and I don't believe that you could ever hate your father."

Jason's face turned red with anger, and I noticed that his eyes were wide open. He seemed to be seeing just fine. "Jason, can see your father right now?" I asked.

He looked at me. "Yes, I can, finally." He turned back toward his father. "But I'm still angry as hell."

"You can see, sweetheart!" Ruth gasped. "Thank God. That's what's important. Darling, please don't be angry anymore."

"Leave him alone, Ruth. He's right to be angry. We never should have lied to him, and if I hadn't pushed Robert so hard and put so much pressure on him, he might still be alive."

The moment that Jason put his anger toward his father into words probably freed him of his psychological need to be blind. The emergency family-therapy session seemed like a miracle talking cure, but soon after the session ended, Jason again clamped his eyes shut and couldn't see again. I admitted him to one of the UCLA psychiatric inpatient units, and we continued family sessions in the hospital for the next two weeks. Jason's father finally came around and said he'd support whatever career choice Jason made. Gradually Jason's psychosomatic blindness cleared up for good.

After his discharge from the hospital, Jason continued his weekly therapy with me. A few months after the hysterical-blindness incident, he entered my office a little late for his appointment, which I interpreted as one of several measures of his progress. He apologized for being tardy and lined up his items in the usual way.

"So how are you getting along with your folks these days?" I asked.

"Dad still needs to be in control of every conversation, and I continue to ignore him. It's typical of the dilemma of the human condition."

I raised my eyebrows, "Typical of the human condition, Jason? Get out of your head and talk about your feelings."

Jason laughed. "Oh, yeah, he pissed me off again when he went on one of his Republican rants last night."

Jason was still obsessive and controlling, but less so, and his therapy had progressed. He was beginning to recognize when he was intellectualizing to avoid feelings. His relationship with his parents was better—he was able to stand up for himself and express his feelings in words, so he had less need to act them out. Eventually, he trusted me enough to try an antidepressant, which reduced his obsessiveness.

"Is it getting any easier to talk with your father when he makes you angry?"

"I guess so."

"What do you think has changed?" I asked.

"All along I felt like there was something wrong with me for being so angry at him. But that night at the hospital when he admitted that he lied and that he was wrong, he became a real person to me, not such a stranger. He became my dad. Not perfect, not infallible. Just my dad, and that's cool."

I was about to explore this more deeply when Jason changed the subject. "By the way, school is going great."

"Oh yeah? What happened with that new class you were trying to get?" I asked.

"Oh yeah, torts," he replied. "I got in and we've got a terrific professor. Did you know that the Latin root of the word *tort* means 'twisted'?"

"Really," I said. "That's interesting."

"We're trying to understand the legal rationale behind decision making. I love that . . ."

Once Jason came to grips with his anger over his father's meddling, he realized that his decision to get a philosophy degree was partly to rebel against his father. When his father backed off, Jason discovered that he did have an interest in law, and he was drawn to it with the same intellectual curiosity that drew him to philosophy. Of course, he still might disappoint his father one day and become a public defender instead of a partner in Riley & Riley, LLC.

When I think about Jason's case, I believe that watching his father come to terms with his guilt over Robert's death was perhaps the most powerful therapeutic moment for Jason. Rather than becoming a crippling and chronic disability, Jason's sudden loss of vision became an opportunity to talk about his true feelings and get closer to his family. He continued with psychotherapy and antidepressants for several years and showed improvement, but many of his deep-rooted obsessive-compulsive traits remained.

Though hysterical blindness is a medical rarity, the conflicts and feelings that fueled Jason's episode are not. How often do we hold back and avoid expressing our anger to preserve a relationship? And what about those people who just let their rage flow out whenever it pleases them? Some get away with it, others learn to keep it in check and suffer, and still others find a healthy way to express it. Jason's question about free will was a profound one. We all have free will, but only when we open our eyes and face the realities of our past and present are we able to make the most of it.

CHAPTER TEN

Brain Fog

Summer 1990

GIGI AND I HAD MOVED TO Studio City, about a forty-minute commute to UCLA. On weekends, we often went to the movies at Universal CityWalk, a replication of Los Angeles within Los Angeles. Why people couldn't just walk down the real streets of Los Angeles made no sense to me, yet there we were, on a Friday evening, eating ice cream and strolling down a simulated street.

We had just seen *Total Recall,* Arnold Schwarzenegger's new science-fiction film about a construction worker who undergoes a false memory transplant that takes him on an imaginary trip to Mars. But things go wrong, and when he comes out of it, he can't tell what's real and what's imagined.

"When he first got back from Mars, there were so many signs that he was from the future that I believed it," I said.

"But honey, before he had that memory implant done, he was perfectly happy living in the present—on Earth. Then he got all paranoid."

"Of course he did. How do you know what's reality if you can't trust your memory?" I asked.

"I don't know; you're the memory expert. I want to go into this shop for a minute." Gigi disappeared into a record store.

As I ate my ice cream and watched the crowds, I kept thinking about those questions. If two realities seem equally true, how would you know which version to believe? Many of my patients struggled with similar issues, whether they were psychotic, demented, or simply having memory problems.

Over the past few years, I had begun to concentrate a large part of my practice on memory issues—not just in older patients with Alzheimer's disease but in middle-aged people who were worried about their increasing forgetfulness. My research was also focusing on early detection of dementia and age-related memory decline, and I was developing brain imaging as a diagnostic tool.

Gigi came back with a bag of CDs and said, "Let's get the car." Thankfully, *she* remembered where we had parked.

The following Monday, I got to the office early and checked my phone machine as usual. There was a message from one of my UCLA mentors, Dr. Larry Klein. He wanted me to see a VIP studio executive, Greg Wiley, who was complaining about his memory. That name rang a bell—I had just read about him in the *L.A. Times* business section. He had been promoted to head of production at a major movie studio.

Two days later he showed up at the office for his first appointment. He was in his mid-fifties, lean and fit, and had an air of authority. He wore an expensive suit and carried a leather briefcase. As we shook hands, he looked me straight in the eyes, but then his gaze flitted about the room, as if he was sizing up my territory. I pulled up a chair across from the sofa, but rather than sitting on the sofa as most patients did, he positioned the other chair opposite mine—he wasn't going to let me forget who was head of production.

Greg crossed his legs, and I noticed his alligator shoes—they probably cost more than my monthly mortgage. Maybe I wasn't charging him enough, but as soon as that thought crossed my mind, I wondered if I felt intimidated by him and was cracking jokes to myself to defend against the feeling.

I had just gotten a new Mr. Coffee machine for the office. I went to pour myself a cup and asked Greg if he wanted some. He declined and pulled an Evian bottle out of his briefcase. "Larry Klein tells me you're the go-to guy in your field. For a newcomer, you've made quite a name for yourself."

"Larry tends to exaggerate." I sipped my coffee.

"Maybe I should hire you away from all this glamour," he said sarcastically, gesturing around my sparsely furnished hospital office.

I smiled and said, "Larry tells me you've noticed some memory changes."

Greg leaned in, suddenly serious. "Now, this is completely confidential, right?"

"Of course," I answered.

"I haven't told this to anybody, not even my wife, but there are moments when my mind doesn't feel as sharp as it used to. And it tends to get worse later in the day and evenings."

"What do you think brings on these episodes?" I asked.

"It could be overwork or stress, I don't know." He took a swig of his water.

"Tell me more about what you're experiencing."

"It's not so much my memory—in fact, most of the time my memory is pretty good. But I have these moments of . . . not confusion necessarily, but my brain starts thinking in slow motion. You know what it's like when you drive through a thick fog at night? That's what it feels like."

"Like a brain fog?" I asked.

"Exactly," he said as he gulped down more water.

"Let me see if I understand this," I said. "When you have these episodes toward the end of the day, your thinking slows down and the thoughts aren't as clear."

"Sort of . . . it takes more time to organize what I want to say, and I suppose it's harder to remember things."

"How often does this happen?" I asked.

"A few times a week . . . maybe every other day."

My mind jumped to an inventory of possible causes for Greg's late-day brain fog. Hypoglycemia was at the top of the list. It also could have been transient ischemic attacks or TIAs, ministrokes that don't lead to lasting brain damage. But when I asked him about his diet and medical history, neither fit. In fact, Greg had just had a complete medical checkup, and his blood pressure, cholesterol level, and glucose tolerance were all normal. I did learn that he had a family history of Alzheimer's disease.

"We used to just call it getting senile," he said. "My grandmother was really out of it, and so was her brother. Now my uncle is totally confused, and his doctor says it's Alzheimer's. I guess that's another reason I wanted to meet with you. Maybe I've inherited a predisposition for it, and it's already starting."

"How old were your relatives when they first showed symptoms?" I asked.

"Probably in their late seventies or early eighties."

"Chances are, what you're noticing now is something different. When Alzheimer's is inherited in families, it tends to begin at about the same age. So at fifty-six, you're way too young," I said.

Greg's worry about getting Alzheimer's was typical for people with a family history of the disease. We all start noticing mild memory changes as we age—it might take longer to recall a name, retrieve a word, or find misplaced glasses or keys. And when someone has witnessed firsthand how these mild mental lapses gradually progress in a loved one, their own forgetfulness can scare the hell out of them, making them worry that they too will have to start labeling their kitchen cabinets. We know that having a close relative with the disease doubles the likelihood of getting it, but it's not an absolute risk factor. Studies have shown that genes account for only about a third of the risk for Alzheimer's disease. Thus, nongenetic factors, particularly lifestyle choices, have a much greater impact than most people realize.

Over the years, these kinds of issues inspired the research and clinical program I developed at UCLA. Our group was doing a lot of research with PET scan technology, and discovered a way to visualize the physical evidence of Alzheimer's disease in living people. Through that invention, we eventually found that the disease begins gradually in the brain, often decades before symptoms begin to show themselves. These observations led us to develop a drug and lifestyle prevention program targeting people at risk in order to protect their healthy brains, rather than attempt to repair neural damage once it sets in.

"But isn't it possible that this brain fog of mine is the subtle beginning of Alzheimer's?" Greg asked.

"It's possible, but not likely," I replied. "Actually, we're doing a study with a new kind of brain scan, positron-emission tomography, or PET. We think it may tell us if someone is going to get Alzheimer's years before real symptoms begin."

Greg looked excited. "Does the study need funding? I control a small family foundation, and I want in."

As much as it killed me to tell a potential donor to put away his checkbook—for now—I said, "I appreciate your generosity, Greg, but I think I can get you into the study without your funding."

"Well, that's a first—somebody refusing a check. I'm impressed. So what else can I tell you, Doc?"

"You mentioned that it could be stress. Tell me more about that."

He laughed. "My job is all about stress. And it's not just stress from keeping the pictures on budget and dealing with prima donna actors. I have to deal with dozens of junior executives competing with each other and clawing their way up the ladder, basically to get my job. Showbiz is just one big party every day."

"Have these mental lapses affected your work?"

"Not yet, but I worry that they will eventually. I mean, in the evenings there are screenings and dinners, I have to schmooze people, and I just don't feel like I'm on my game the way I used to be." He took a sip of water and went on. "Let me tell you, there are plenty of those young sharks coming up, kissing my ass, but really wanting to take my place. And I've got to keep the studio head happy too, so my movies have to make money. In my business, it's not what you've done, but what you've done lately."

I thought for a moment about my own business and reflected on the old joke: Why are academic politics so vicious? Because the stakes are so low. I happened to be in the midst of preparing my dossier for promotion to associate professor—the big leap to tenure. It had taken years, but I was very close now. My peers would be judging my work and making the decision by secret ballot, an old academic tradition. You never knew if someone on your tenure committee might be vying for your job and trying to keep you down. I could relate to Greg's distrust of colleagues who might put their own self-interests before his. I knew I had to remain mindful of this parallel issue that my patient and I shared so it wouldn't cloud my perspective and interfere with my ability to help him.

"Do you have any friends at work that you trust?" I asked.

"I have a couple of racquetball buddies at the studio who I think I can trust, plus my boss and I play together once a week. He really is a friend, and I think he's grooming me to take over his job when he retires." Greg unbuttoned his collar and loosened his tie. "But you know, sometimes it's uncomfortable competing with him on the court."

"Why's that?"

"Well, he's older. And even though he's a hell of a player, there have been a couple of games when I could have beaten him, but I didn't . . . I guess I was afraid."

"Afraid of what?"

"He may be my friend, but he's also my boss. If I piss him off, he could retaliate. He could demote me. But you know? Sometimes when he wins, it's almost as if he's disappointed, like he's waiting for me to step up and beat him like a man."

"So this studio head is your friend, grooming you for his job, and you're ambivalent about beating him at racquetball?"

"Yeah, I guess I am, but it's just a game, and I've always found that competitive sports get me out of my head and help relieve my stress. I used to play basketball, but it's too hard to pick up a game with my schedule."

For the rest of the session, we discussed more of Greg's background. He had been a straight-A student, an immediate success in business, and though his first marriage failed, he got remarried to a gorgeous ex-movie star and now had two teenagers in the best private schools in West Los Angeles. But all these achievements came with a price—he constantly felt a need to stay at the top of his game and watch his back to make sure nobody took what he had worked so hard to get.

We didn't have time that day to really explore his childhood, but I wondered what early experiences might have shaped Greg's lifelong quest for success and control, and his pressing fear about losing his winnings. No wonder he was afraid of Alzheimer's disease. It was the ultimate loss of control, and there was no way to beat it. We could try to detect it early, slow it down and possibly stave it off with medicines and lifestyle adjustments, but eventually, if he did get Alzheimer's, the disease would take over his mind permanently.

I wondered if Greg's worry about the young executive sharks was more than just normal Hollywood competition. If he really did have some type of brain disorder, he might be experiencing more than episodic mental lapses; he might have paranoid thinking. I had seen several cases of early-onset Alzheimer's that started not with memory loss but with psychiatric symptoms. One woman complained of obsessive-compulsive tendencies that seemed to come out of nowhere; another man was referred to me because of sudden-onset panic attacks. Both turned out to have Alzheimer's disease, and the anxiety symptoms were the first signs of the underlying neural degeneration of their mental faculties.

I told Greg I would arrange a PET scan for him. I also asked if he could have his internist send me a copy of his medical records before his next appointment.

Later that day I had a meeting with Larry Klein to help me with my tenure dossier. The first review committee had questioned whether I had enough focus in my research—I'd studied mass hysteria, psychosomatic diseases, brain scanning, and geriatric dementia. Apparently, they wanted to see a thematic trajectory demonstrating how each study led to the next. They also wanted to be sure I had become independent of my mentors as an investigator. So of course, I immediately turned to a mentor for advice.

Larry, often suspicious that others were listening in on his office conversations, had a habit of conducting consultations and supervision sessions during strolls around the West L.A. Veterans Affairs Medical

Center campus. It was the main V.A. hospital affiliated with UCLA, located just west of the 405 freeway. The older buildings were sprinkled across vast lawns, and the north side of the campus had a nine-hole golf course, Larry's favorite spot for conducting business in private. Paranoid? A little, but everybody has their quirks.

As we left the parking lot and headed toward the ninth fairway, Larry cut to the chase. "You've done excellent research your entire career. Now it's just a question of spin." We circled around the ninth hole; I could see the kids at the Brentwood School playing in the yard.

"Spin? What do you mean?" I asked.

"Look at the big picture, Gary. You're an eclectic guy, and you have a methodical way of solving problems. It's reflected in all of your work—whether you're analyzing a bunch of hysterical schoolkids fainting in a recital or figuring out what causes damage to brain neurons in Alzheimer's disease. You just need to show the committee how each question you've answered in your career has led to the next, and where you plan to take it from here." He reached down, picked up a golf ball, and threw it onto the eighth green, nearly getting a hole in one.

"Great shot," I said as I pondered what he had said.

"So what's happening with Wiley? Have you given him your secret screenplay yet?" he asked.

I laughed. "I must be the only guy in Los Angeles who *doesn't* have a secret screenplay stashed in his desk." I found a stray golf ball and tossed it at the next hole, missing the green by twenty yards. "I'm not sure yet. He's having memory lapses and episodes of confusion. It could be early-onset Alzheimer's, TIAs, or some other kind of medical problem, but I don't know. Maybe it's psychological or just plain stress."

"I'm confident you'll get to the bottom of it, Gary. Just like I know you'll figure out how to handle these promotion questions. Remember, never rule out the simplest possibilities."

"I hear what you're saying, Larry, and I appreciate it. But sometimes when a case is unusual or complicated, I don't have the same confidence in myself that you seem to have."

"Gary, becoming a good psychiatrist is not that different from getting comfortable in any role in life—banker, teacher, or whatever. Think about the first time you held your daughter—you must have felt more awkward than the first day you wore a white coat. Everybody feels like they're faking it sometimes. The key is to move forward and make the best decision you can at the moment. Don't be afraid of making mistakes. I've learned the most when I've made mistakes and bounced back from them."

As I drove back to the office, I thought about Larry's advice. I needed to take in the big picture and not overlook the obvious or perhaps simplest explanation—both with my promotion and with Wiley's case. It was interesting that Greg seemed paranoid about his co-workers vying for his job; Klein had a paranoid streak in his personality; and I was worrying about my colleagues sabotaging my promotion. I wondered, when does suspiciousness and paranoid thinking escalate from protecting us from real danger to overtaking our lives and crippling our ability to function? For Wiley, I was hoping I could answer that question quickly. With Klein, I suspected I never would. In my case, I knew those bastards were out to get me.

A FEW DAYS LATER, I RECEIVED GREG'S medical records and pored over them in detail. I couldn't find any abnormalities, not even a suspicious mole on his back. His PET scan also came back completely normal—no evidence of Alzheimer's or any dementia—so I called to give him the good news.

"So what the hell do you think is going on with me?" he asked.

"I'm not sure yet, but we can discuss the possibilities on Wednesday."

"Oh yeah," he said. "Can you see me later in the day, maybe five-thirty? My racquetball game changed to midafternoon."

I checked my schedule, "Okay, that works for me. I'll see you then."

I hung up and pondered the possible causes for Greg's mental lapses. For now, Alzheimer's was ruled out, but a normal PET scan doesn't mean he'd never get the disease in the future—details I wouldn't get into over the phone. In fact, had his PET scan been abnormal, I would have waited to give him that news in person as well.

At about ten-thirty that evening, I climbed into bed with a stack of journals and the best intentions of reading them when Gigi came out of the bathroom in her flying-toaster PJs.

"So what's up at work?" she asked.

"You know, the usual: tenure freak-out, committee meetings, crazy people."

"No, I mean it," she said. "Any interesting cases?"

"Well, there is this patient, some movie mogul who's getting fuzzy-headed in the afternoons and evenings."

She brightened. "Ooh. Do you think you can give him one of my spec screenplays to read some morning before the fuzz sets in?"

I laughed. "No. Now do you want to hear about this or not?" She sat on the bed and looked at me expectantly while rubbing in some hand lotion. I continued, "So I haven't figured out the cause yet. It's not Alzheimer's, and he's not having little strokes."

"Maybe he's depressed. Is he married?"

"Hilarious. Yes, and he's in his second marriage, to a much younger, trophy wife. So watch yourself." She hit me on the head with a pillow, got under the covers, and picked up her novel.

Gigi's question made me think more seriously about whether or not Greg might actually be depressed. As a demanding studio exec, he had to keep up a tough exterior, but he might be hiding a vulnerable and depressed side. And when somebody has a clinical depression, there's often a diurnal pattern or daily cycle to the symptoms. Patients some-times report ruminating only at night or early in the morning. However, arguing against depression was Greg's complete lack of a sleep disorder or weight change.

A diurnal pattern could often be a clue to a psychiatric diagnosis, and not necessarily depression. For example, anxious people have trouble fall-ing asleep while those who are depressed wake up in the night and can't fall back to sleep. We are all diurnal by nature—more active during the day than the night. And beyond that, most of us consider ourselves either morning people or night owls. Our levels of alertness throughout the day are determined by our biologically driven circadian rhythms, reflecting peaks and valleys in hormone levels that cycle during a twenty-four-hour period and are influenced by our daily habits, including sleep patterns, diet, exercise, and medication use.

Greg's symptoms came on at the end of the day and the evening, a clear diurnal pattern. I wondered whether a physiological condition was initiating these symptoms as the day went on. Perhaps a twenty-four-hour cardiac halter monitor would reveal an arrhythmia that could have been causing decreases in blood flow to the brain. But I also had to consider the possibility that an external event was setting off his mental fatigue. His anxiety about the competition at work had become a theme in our sessions. Maybe some daily stressful situation, an interpersonal conflict with a co-worker, a particular meeting with a junior executive or even his boss, could be triggering mental fuzziness in the afternoon and evening.

Wednesday rolled around and I was still mulling over Greg's differential diagnosis. I got a call from his assistant, Tracey, saying Greg had a late meeting and wondered if they could send a car and bring me to the studio for our five-thirty appointment. And of course, I would be duly compensated for my time.

I immediately thought of the benefits of seeing Greg in his natural habitat, which might give me some clues as to what was causing his stress. I also have to admit that the idea of cruising up to the studio in a limo and rubbing shoulders with movie stars was appealing. As I considered running home and changing into something more hip, I snapped myself out of it and replied to Tracey, "That can work, but I won't be free until five-fifteen."

Most people get excited in the presence of celebrities and other important people, and psychiatrists are no exception. In 1964 a psychiatric journal first described the challenges of caring for the rich and famous in an article on this VIP syndrome. Whenever VIPs—whether they're rock stars, politicians, or other well-connected individuals—seek medical care, they don't always get the best. In fact, often their care is substandard. Important patients may attempt to micromanage their physicians, and some doctors may be too starstruck to disagree with the patient. There have been doctors of VIPs who have been known to overmedicate, underdiagnose, and even get lured into their patients' social lives.

At that point in my career, I had taken care of enough VIPs to know about my own emotional reactions to them and the importance of remaining impartial and professional. And even though some VIPs impressed me—after all, I am human—I simply didn't let those feelings affect how I dealt with my patients.

At 5:45, my town car pulled through the studio gates and my driver simply waved to the guard as he drove me toward the main building and parked in front. There were huge soundstages scattered behind the main offices, and lots of people hurrying about. The driver told me Mr. Wiley's office was on the third floor, and he'd be waiting for me when I returned.

Once I entered the building, it was quiet. I rode the elevator up to the third floor, and the doors opened into a large sitting area with several sofas, overstuffed chairs, and coffee tables strewn with industry magazines. Tracey jumped up to greet me and offered coffee, tea, or water. I asked for water, and she brought me a chilled glass. She said Mr. Wiley was on his way up and would arrive in a moment.

I glanced at the *Hollywood Reporter* and noticed that *Total Recall* was still grossing big at the box office. The elevator opened and Greg sprang out in his racquetball clothes. He was sweating profusely and taking the last swig from a large Evian bottle. He motioned for me to follow him into his office and tossed the empty bottle into the trash. Tracey closed the doors behind us.

As I looked around the office, I was impressed by its size and its Art Deco décor. He grabbed another water bottle from the fridge in his bar and invited me to sit down on a couch. He sat across from me on another.

"I really appreciate your coming over here this afternoon." He paused to wipe his face and neck with a towel and swig some more water. "I'm sorry for the late notice, but it's been a crazy day."

"No problem, Greg."

"Man, I had an incredible game today. I kicked the asses off two guys from development." He leaned forward and spoke in a quieter voice, "But I have to tell you about this weird feeling I got on the court today."

"What kind of weird feeling?" I asked.

"You know how I said that sometimes I can beat my boss but I don't?" I nodded and he continued, "Well, I got the feeling today that these punk development guys were letting *me* win. There were a couple shots that were gimmes, and they didn't take them. You think they're trying to push me out?"

Was Greg's suspiciousness escalating to paranoia? I recalled strolling around the golf course with Larry Klein because of his suspicions about others listening in, but in Greg's case, his fears seemed to be intensifying rapidly—was he going off the deep end?

"Look, I'm not in show business, Greg, but it seems unlikely that somebody from development would have a shot at your head-of-production job." I was trying to give him a dose of reality, but he didn't seem to hear me as he guzzled down more water.

He toweled off again as he walked over to the closet and changed his shirt, almost as if he'd forgotten I was there. He sat back down and asked, "What were we talking about?"

"Your racquetball game."

"Oh yeah? Forget it," he said. "You know, I'm feeling a little bit slowed down right now. What do you think is causing this mental fogginess?"

"I was wondering if you have a regular afternoon meeting with somebody who gets under your skin and that may be triggering your episodes. You've been talking about your stress and competition at work, and your mental lapses always occur later in the day."

He thought for a long moment, "Sorry, Doc, it's this brain haze slowing me down." He paused, then continued, "Actually it's my *morning* meetings that are really stressful. That's when we look at the numbers and see how the pictures are performing. And Mondays are the worst, right after the weekend, or Tuesdays if it's a three-day. In fact, I have the least stress in the afternoons—that's when I play racquetball." Greg tilted his head back and finished off his Evian.

Something suddenly occurred to me as Greg put the empty bottle on the coffee table. "How many of those do you drink a day?" I asked. He had a blank look in his eyes and didn't respond. "Greg? Greg, can you hear me?" I was worried. He was having difficulty focusing on our conversation. "Greg?" I practically shouted.

"What?" he asked.

"I said, how many bottles of water do you drink a day?"

"I don't know," he finally answered. "I drink a lot when I play ball. I sweat like a pig."

As Greg walked over to the bar to grab another water bottle, my leading diagnostic theory for his mental lapses suddenly shifted from work-stress to polydipsia, also known as compulsive water drinking. The relatively rare condition can lead to water intoxication or poisoning. What happens is that the amount of water that the patient ingests exceeds the amount the kidneys can excrete. As a result, the body's sodium level dives, which can lead to a variety of symptoms, including confusion, disorientation, and psychotic behavior. If left untreated, the mental symptoms escalate to acute delirium, drowsiness, and even coma. When severe, the illness can be fatal. During my residency in Boston, I treated a chronic schizophrenic who had psychogenic polydipsia. We had to watch her constantly so she wouldn't sneak over to the water fountain and suffer an episode.

Greg's water intoxication was different and associated with over-exertion and heat stress. Some athletes are at risk for water poisoning, but they can usually avoid it by consuming sports drinks with added electrolytes rather than straight water during practice and events. It's critical to recognize the condition quickly to prevent severe hyponatremia, or low blood-sodium levels, which can cause cerebral edema or brain swelling.

Once I realized the potential danger Greg could be in, I knew I had to act quickly. I followed him to the bar and said, "Stop, Greg. Don't drink that water. I think I know what's causing your brain fog."

He was holding another chilled Evian and said, "Great, I want to hear all about it. I just need another sip of water—I'm thirsty as hell." He lifted the bottle, and just as he was about to drink, I grabbed for it and knocked it out of his hand. It spilled everywhere.

Greg backed away. "What the hell is your problem?"

"It's the water," I said. "You're drinking so much that it's poisoning your brain."

He laughed as he grabbed a dry towel. "That's the craziest thing I've ever heard. Water's the healthiest thing you can drink."

"Do you have a clinic or infirmary here at the studio?" I asked.

"Of course we have a medical clinic."

"Okay, prove me wrong. Let's get you a blood test right now and see if your sodium level is low."

He picked up the phone. "Tracey, get the nurse over here right now. I need a blood test, *stat*." He put down the phone and smiled. "I always wanted to say that. I'm kind of tired, Gary. I think I've got to lie down on the couch for a few minutes."

His fatigue only worried me more since it's another sign of low blood sodium. "Once we get your blood drawn, we should get some salt in your system right away." I opened the door and asked Tracey to get us some chips, pretzels, and Gatorade from the commissary.

As I waited for the nurse to come, Greg remained spaced out on the couch, eyes open but not speaking. In what seemed like much longer than the five minutes it actually took, Tracey finally escorted in a studio nurse carrying a blood-test kit. I motioned her toward Greg, and she quickly tied a tourniquet around his upper arm and drew ten cubic centimeters of blood into a test tube. I gave the nurse my card and instructed her to have the lab call me with his electrolyte results as soon as they became available, probably a couple of hours later. Tracey placed a basket of assorted chips, crackers, and pretzels on the coffee table, along with four bottles of Gatorade, as she left with the nurse.

I opened a pack of saltines and urged Greg to eat a few. After downing a pack of crackers, he sat up and grabbed some pretzels. Halfway through the bag, he said "Man, Gary, that was one of the worst episodes I can remember. You came all the way over here for a session, and I completely spaced out." He took a sip of Gatorade and made a grossed-out face.

I was relieved that Greg had snapped out of his fog. His rapid turn-around convinced me that my diagnosis was correct, but we'd have to wait for the blood results to know for sure. It was getting late, and I wanted to head home. I told Greg to take a break on the water and the racquetball for now.

Later that evening, I got a page from the lab with his blood results. As I had suspected, his sodium level had been abnormally low. His medical records hadn't shown any abnormalities because his earlier blood tests had never been taken after one of his games when he drank water excessively.

I felt triumphant—I had finally figured out the cause of his mental lapses. The clues had been there, but I just hadn't pieced them together until I saw him after a game. I had to actually witness my patient in the midst of a potentially fatal episode of water intoxication before the correct explanation came to me and I took action. Had I been too distracted in my search for an elusive interpersonal trigger, some kind of work stressor, when I should have been digging deeper for a medical cause?

Earlier in my career, I probably would have been tough on myself about taking so long to discover Greg's polydipsia. But my years of practice had given me some perspective. I knew that cases like Greg's were complex. Sometimes we never do figure them out. When I discussed the outcome with Larry Klein, he patted me on the back and praised me as if I was some kind of diagnostic hero. It felt good.

A FEW WEEKS LATER, GREG RETURNED TO my office for a follow-up visit. Dressed in his racquetball clothes and carrying a duffel bag, he was clear-eyed and eager to get started.

"Gary, believe it or not, thanks to you, my game has gotten better," he said.

"That's great. You look pretty focused for having just finished a game. Any more brain-fog symptoms?" I asked.

"No, thank you very much, and you know how I was throwing games with my boss? Well, guess what? I just beat him, badly, and he loved it. He even hugged me after the game."

"I guess he really is your friend," I said. "How's it going with those junior executives?"

"I don't even care anymore. No one can do my job like me. Eventually, one of those guys will take over when I become head of the studio, and I wish them luck because it's a hell of a lot of work." Greg pulled a towel from his duffel and wiped his perspiring brow. "Man, I'm parched." He reached into his duffel bag and I winced, worried that he'd fallen off the wagon with his water-drinking problem, but he pulled out a bottle of Gatorade, took a swig and said, "This stuff actually grows on you."

Later that evening, I was stuck in Coldwater Canyon traffic as I tried to call Gigi to tell her I'd be late for our Thursday-night dinner. As usual, I couldn't get a phone signal in the canyon. Typical for L.A., the priciest, most exclusive neighborhoods had the worst cell phone coverage. Twenty minutes later, I showed up at La Loggia. Gigi had ordered me a glass of cabernet, and the bread basket was completely empty.

I took off my coat and sat. "Let's have a toast."

We clinked glasses. "What exactly are we toasting, Dr. Small?"

"I think it would be more appropriate to address me as Associate Professor Small," I announced with a big grin on my face.

She stood, put her arms around me, and gave me a big kiss. The waiters applauded. "You know," she said, "something about that associate professor title makes you really hot. Why don't we get a pizza to go?"

As we finished our drinks and waited for the pizza, I told her how I had responded to each of the promotion committee's queries and relished every detail of my victory. Larry Klein's advice—never rule out the simplest possibilities—had paid off with my achieving tenure. It was also the answer to finally diagnosing my patient's drinking problem. Over the years, I've kept that little mantra in mind, and it's served me well.

CHAPTER ELEVEN

Dream Wedding

Spring 1997

IT HAD BEEN A DRY WINTER in L.A., but finally in late March we got some rain. As usual, Southern California drivers went crazy as soon as the first drop fell from the sky. Thanks to a fender bender on the 134 freeway, I was stuck in traffic after giving a lecture in Pasadena. I hadn't eaten anything all day and was just hoping to make it back to the office by the time my new patient arrived at 1:00 P.M.

I whipped into my regular UCLA parking space, hopped out, and grabbed my umbrella. As I opened it, a gust of wind bent it backward and broke it, so I tossed it into a trash can and ran for the building. As I passed the cafeteria, I checked my watch and decided to grab a sandwich on my way up to the office.

I unlocked my office door and hung my soaking raincoat on the hook behind it. I had moved into a bigger space after making associate professor and getting tenure. I had larger windows and more light, a sitting area with a couch and three chairs, and my kids' drawings decorating the walls. I also had an outer office with an assistant answering my phones.

I still had a couple of minutes to wolf down my sandwich, so I squirted some mustard on it, which went directly on my tie. Holding my turkey and Swiss with one hand, I took a giant bite as I pulled off my tie with the other. My intercom buzzed and my assistant announced my new patient, who, of course, was right on time. I asked her to show him in.

The patient was Dr. Bruce Rifkin, a prominent Beverly Hills plastic surgeon. From our brief phone conversation a week earlier, I'd learned that he wanted to meet because he was having trouble sleeping. He also mentioned that he was forty-eight, had never been married, and was now engaged.

"Hello, Gary. I'm glad we were able to get together so quickly. My schedule is crazy, and I'm sure yours is too."

We shook hands and I motioned to the couch. "Please, have a seat, Bruce."

He laid his designer raincoat over the back of a chair and sat down. He was lean, tall, and wore a pin-striped suit, complete with cuff links, pale-blue dress shirt, and matching pocket handkerchief—he looked as if he'd stepped straight out of *GQ* magazine.

"My internist tells me you know your psychopharmacology, and I understand that you also do some geriatrics. As a plastic surgeon, I guess that's one of my specialties too."

I smiled. "Have you ever seen a psychiatrist before?"

"No," he said, "but my family is so nuts that I probably could have used one for years."

"I'd like to hear about that." As always, I enjoyed working with patients like Bruce who had a sense of humor, but I wondered how much of it had to with his anxiety about meeting with me.

"Really, right now I just need your help with my insomnia. I can't seem to get through the night."

"Are you having trouble falling asleep or staying asleep?" I asked. Typically people with clinical depression wake up in the middle of the night and can't fall back to sleep, whereas patients with anxiety disorders have trouble settling down when they go to bed.

"I fall asleep fine. It's staying asleep that's my problem. My dreams wake me up, and I feel tired the next day, especially during long procedures." He rubbed his face and eyes for a moment, then said defensively, "Look, it's not affecting my work, thank God, but I want to deal with it before it gets worse. I could have written myself some Dalmane or Valium, but as a rule, I think it's a bad idea to prescribe for yourself."

Bruce's comment about self-medicating suggested that he was ethical and had a sense of right and wrong. On the other hand, he could be protesting too much and covering up a drug-dependency problem. Many doctors, because of convenience, tend to prescribe medicines for themselves and their family members, which can get them into trouble if they dole out the wrong drugs or dosages for conditions outside their expertise. It can also be the first step to prescription-drug dependence and addiction.

As a group, doctors are less likely to use illicit drugs like cocaine or heroin but more likely to abuse prescription medicines, such as opiates or tranquilizers. Plastic surgeons, anesthesiologists, and dentists tend to have painkillers and sedatives stored right in their office, and the ready availability increases the risk for self-medication and addiction. I made a note to explore Bruce's medication history in more detail, but for now it seemed best to focus on his chief complaint.

"Tell me about your dreams, Bruce."

"Is that really necessary? I thought we could just discuss the best sleep medication for me. I don't want any hangovers or side effects."

"We'll get to that before we finish today, but sometimes understanding what's waking us up can help us sleep better."

"I don't know how talking about my dreams is going to help me sleep. Besides, they're complicated, and it would take longer than fifty minutes." He stood up, took off his jacket, placed it next to him on the couch, and sat back down.

"We have plenty of time," I said. "Let's give it a try."

"Well, what do you want to know?"

"When did you first start having these dreams?"

"I think I've had them off and on since I was a kid, but they've kicked up a little since I met my fiancée."

"Are the dreams connected to your fiancée in some way?" I asked.

"Well, she has a somewhat peculiar obsession."

"Really," I said, my mind racing with dozens of unusual titillating possibilities. "Care to elaborate?"

"Look, Christina is an amazing woman. My parents were ready to give up on me ever getting married. But when they met her, they knew she was the one—even though she's not Jewish. She's beautiful, poised, intelligent . . . and she has this incredible energy. We have a lot of fun together. We travel, play golf, go to the theater."

"She sounds great, but what does she have to do with the dreams?"

Bruce crossed his arms and slumped. "There is this one little quirk of hers, and it's starting to get under my skin."

"Okay . . . what is it?" I was becoming frustrated.

"Christina has this fascination with Disneyland and everything Disney." He went silent and I waited.

"The first time I went to her condo in Santa Monica, I was blown away—the entire place was decorated in Disney themes. Snow White living room, Mickey Mouse kitchen, Little Mermaid bathroom . . . And she has this Pinocchio den. It's so bizarre, I don't even want to go in there."

"Sounds intense," I said.

"You have no idea." He shook his head. "I mean, everybody has hobbies, but this is ridiculous."

"What's ridiculous about it?" I asked.

"There're people who wear Mickey Mouse watches and stuff, it's kind of kitsch, whatever. But I think Christina's hobby borders on obsession. And here's the potential deal breaker: she's actually planning our wedding at Disneyland. Oh, there'll be no chuppah, we'll be exchanging our vows in front of the Sleeping Beauty Castle, *and* Christina will be wearing a replica of Snow White's gown."

Struggling to keep a straight face and restraining myself from asking if he was going as Goofy or Pluto, I said, "I see."

"And did you know that they actually have people who arrange all this at Disneyland? My parents are okay with my marrying a shiksa, but this? It'll kill them."

"So you haven't told them?"

"God no," he said.

Bruce's humor made his narrative entertaining, but he was avoiding any discussion about the dreams that were fueling his insomnia by focusing on Christina's issues rather than his own. I wondered if there had been a deal breaker in his prior relationships that kept him from making a commitment.

"It's certainly an unusual wedding plan," I said. "But maybe you should tell me about the dreams so I can understand the connection."

"Well, they're nightmares really . . . I mean, they start out as nothing special. I might be at work, or back at school when I was a kid, but they all seem to end up the same . . ."

"And how's that?" I urged him on.

"No matter how the dream begins, I somehow become Pinocchio, my nose is growing, and I start turning into a donkey. I wake up in a sweat and I can't go back to sleep. That's it."

"Can you pinpoint the emotion you experience when you wake up?" I asked.

"I feel like an ass." He laughed and I smiled with him. "Seriously, I feel utter terror. It's insane. I'm forty-eight years old, and I wake up in the middle of the night afraid of a cartoon."

"Dreams can be bizarre and make no sense," I said. "What this dream means to you on an emotional level may not be obvious, and may be only partly connected to the actual content of the dream."

The understanding of dreams has been a focus of psychoanalytic theory and practice since the end of the nineteenth century. In Freud's book *The Interpretation of Dreams,* he argued that the actual content of a dream could reveal its hidden meaning. He believed that all dreams were expressions of wish fulfillment. When trying to understand a dream, a psychotherapist often explores the events of the preceding day that might have triggered it. But the dream's actual content is often illusive, disguised or distorted by years of experience and repressed feelings—fear, anger, anxiety, guilt, and more. These distortions can take many forms, such as condensation—the dream stands for several ideas or experiences; displacement—a dream shifts a person's unacceptable emotions or desires to more acceptable ones; or symbolism—an event or character in the dream stands for something else of importance.

"My dreams don't make any sense, that's for sure," Bruce said.

"Let's try to make sense of it and look at last night's dream systematically. What happened yesterday that might have stirred it up?"

"Nothing much. I had dinner at Christina's."

"Anything out of the ordinary happen?" I asked.

"No, not that I recall. I didn't stay over, though. I had an early surgery this morning."

"Did you go into the Pinocchio den?" I asked.

"I generally avoid it. It gives me the creeps," he said. "I mean, look at my dreams."

"So, what did you talk about at dinner?"

"I was describing a procedure I'm developing, a noninvasive face-lift. But Christina kept changing the subject. She wanted to talk about the Mad Hatter wedding cake and her ridiculous idea for the centerpieces."

"Did you tell her how you felt when she changed the subject?" I asked.

"No. I didn't want to upset her. I mean, I love her, and if this Disney-land wedding means that much to her, I guess I'll do it." He looked down, resigned.

"Bruce, this is your wedding too."

"I know, but women are more hung up on the details of all this wedding stuff."

"But it's important that this wedding means something to you too," I said.

He looked up. "You think it has something to do with my dreams?"

It was the perfect moment for the standard psychiatrist question. "What do *you* think?"

Bruce was pensive for a moment, then spoke. "I'm not sure, but from what I know, I suppose that Pinocchio and the donkey represent some fear of mine, since I wake up in a cold sweat."

"Perhaps you're lying to yourself about something. Lying like Pinocchio did when his nose would grow," I added.

"Are you saying I'm lying to myself about wanting to get married?" he asked, worried.

I thought that was a big jump, but maybe right on the nose, so to speak. "I don't know, Bruce. Maybe you just don't want to have the wedding at Disneyland."

"Well, that's for sure. And I suppose I am sort of lying to Christina by not telling her."

"I think as we get a better handle on what your dreams mean, it will be easier for you to talk about those kinds of feelings with Christina."

"It's not like we don't talk about things," he said. "It's just that I'd rather avoid certain topics than cause a scene."

Despite his initial defensiveness, Bruce was warming up to the idea that talking about dreams and feelings could help. He had made a lot of progress in just this first session. His initial reason for seeing me was to get a sleep prescription, but now he was willing to explore possible psychological causes for his problems. He was even able to come up with a plausible interpretation for his recurring dreams, but I suspected that he had deeper emotional issues stirring them up.

Before our session ended, I wrote Bruce a prescription for a short-acting benzodiazepine, since his sleep problems sounded more like an anxiety disorder than a depression. I suggested that he only use the medication if he really needed it to sleep before a long procedure the next day. I encouraged him to not only let himself have his dreams but to also jot down notes about them when he woke up—that way he'd remember the details better and we could discuss them at the next session.

The rain stopped on the weekend, and Gigi and I took the kids to our favorite breakfast place in Studio City, just down the hill from our house. After having our fill of pancakes and eggs—every way but thrown at us—we were walking to the perfect parking space I had found only four and a half blocks from the restaurant, to avoid the three-dollar parking charge.

Gigi and our five-year-old, Rachel, were up ahead, looking in shop windows, and I was walking with Harry, our three-year-old. He must have been two steps ahead of me—just out of my grasp—when he tripped on a crack in the sidewalk and fell down, hard. He started wailing. He had bloody knees, hands, and elbows, and much to Gigi's horror, on his forehead was a "definite scar for life" (which completely disappeared in two months).

As we drove home to get him cleaned up and bandaged (no stitches necessary), I realized how lucky it was that this first bad fall had happened in front of us. If he had fallen while under the care of one of our mothers or a babysitter, we probably wouldn't have left either of the kids with anyone for the next twenty years. Even though I got defensive about it not being my fault that Harry hurt himself on my watch, we made sure not to argue in front of the kids. We both knew from Gigi's voluminous library of child-rearing books that remaining calm and united was key to minimizing any psychological trauma for the kids when they got hurt or during a crisis.

I wondered about Bruce's early-childhood traumas and what experiences might be contributing to his current nightmares and apparent fear of commitment. After all, he was forty-eight and had never married, although he told me he had been close to getting engaged several times. I knew that to help Bruce, I needed to explore his early memories and discover how they might be connected to his dreams.

The following week, I had my geriatric-psychiatry training-committee meeting at lunch just before Bruce's scheduled appointment. I was in charge of recruiting and training the young psychiatrists who wanted additional experience in geriatrics. There were always challenges in finding good candidates for these much needed positions, in part because of ageism—many doctors avoid treating older patients because they're often complicated, time-consuming, and more likely to die during treatment than younger patients. The faculty had some good ideas on how to attract candidates that year, and I was happy to have time to eat a decent lunch without ruining my tie before Bruce showed up.

I returned to my office and found Bruce sitting in the waiting area. The fact that he was early could have been a sign of his eagerness to get back into his dream work. I figured he had the afternoon off because he was dressed in country-club casual, including sweater carefully draped around the shoulders. I opened the office door, and he went for the couch while I took my chair.

"So, how did your week go, Bruce?"

"I only took the medicine a couple of nights, when I thought I might really need it. It worked great—no hangover, nothing."

"That's good," I said. "What about the other nights?"

He reached into his pocket and pulled out a small spiral notebook. "I made some notes on my dreams."

From what I could see, the pad looked completely filled with illegible surgeon scribbles.

Bruce continued, "You were right. When I jotted down my thoughts as soon as I woke up, I remembered more details. And the dreams don't all end exactly the same."

"Let's start with last night's dream. What do you remember?"

"It was a bit strange. I was in the operating room, but instead of being the lead surgeon, I was assisting my father, who's not even a doctor."

"What does, or did, your father do?" I asked.

"He's an investment banker who just retired a couple of years ago. So it was weird that he was in the O.R. with me."

"Anything else strange about the dream?"

"Yes. I was handing Dad a sponge, and he slapped my hand really hard."

"How did you react?"

"I got furious. I was only doing what I was supposed to do, and he attacked me out of nowhere. And I never meant to get him angry."

"What happened next?"

"He threw me out of the O.R., and my nose started growing."

"What were you feeling just as your nose began growing?" I asked.

"I felt like a kid again—as if I had never been to med school and had lied my way into the O.R. My nose kept growing, and I began turning into a donkey. Then I woke up." Bruce seemed upset as he put away his notebook.

"Have you dreamt about your father before?"

"Probably, but I don't remember anything specific."

"Does this dream remind you of any early experiences with your father?" I asked.

Bruce took a deep breath and settled back on the couch. After a moment he replied. "Dad only hit me once in my life. The rest of the time he really didn't pay much attention to me."

"What do you mean?" I asked.

"His clients loved him—he was charming and attentive, but when he got home, he'd have a couple of drinks at dinner, then just watch TV and fall asleep."

"So when did he hit you?" I asked.

"I must have been in kindergarten. He was supposed to pick me up from school, but it was pouring rain and he didn't show up." Bruce looked tense and rubbed the back of his neck. "My friend's mother offered me a ride—she said it was silly for me to stand outside in the rain. So I got in her car and she took me home."

"Then what happened?" I asked.

"He came home about a half hour later, furious. He had been driving around in the rain, frantic that someone had kidnapped me." Bruce paused, somewhat choked up, then regained his composure. "I can remember him standing over me, yelling that I was an idiot. He grabbed me and threw me over his knee, pulled off his belt, and whipped the crap out of me."

"That must have been terrifying." Bruce didn't seem to hear me—his mind was elsewhere. "Bruce, are you okay?" I asked.

"I just remembered something else. I don't think I've ever recalled this before . . ."

"Go on," I said encouraging him.

"That night, our family went to the temple for some event. My parents dropped my sister and me off at the rec room, where all the kids gathered to watch a movie."

"Where did your parents go?"

"I think they went to a lecture in the chapel."

"So what happened after your parents dropped you off?" I asked. He looked upset. "Take your time, Bruce."

"I can remember sitting there with my sister, kind of nervous—I'd never been to the movies before. I remember the folding chairs they had set up were uncomfortable and my butt was still sore from the beating. And the movie really scared me."

"Do you recall what movie it was?" I asked.

"*Pinocchio!*" he blurted out.

LATER THAT EVENING AFTER THE KIDS WENT to bed, Gigi and I were hanging out in the den. The TV news was on low, and Gigi was working on her laptop. I was ruminating about the difficulty I was having recruiting geriatric trainees. Gigi was giving me an occasional "uh-huh" or "mm-hmm." I found myself getting annoyed because she wasn't paying full attention to me. I immediately thought of Bruce's father, whose clients adored him because he always gave them his full attention, but at night he tuned out and paid little or no attention to his family.

Clearly, it's impossible to pay full attention all the time. Gigi loved me and was interested in my life, but at that moment she was focused on something else. If I had asked her to put her computer down and listen, I'm sure she would have. I tried to imagine how it would feel to live with someone who didn't care about me or was unable to focus on my emotional life.

For some people, it's a personality disorder such as narcissism that makes it difficult for them to experience empathy. They get so wrapped up in their own needs that they never learn to respond to the needs of those around them. For others, it can be a psychotic illness, depression, or a variety of other personal problems that keep them from getting close to other people.

After Bruce's realization about the traumatic events surrounding his seeing the movie *Pinocchio,* his nightmares began to subside. As I continued to work with him, I learned that his father was not only a narcissistic personality but also an alcoholic, although a high-functioning one. He didn't drink during the day, but at night the booze helped him escape from his personal demons and kept him from having to connect with his family. Although Bruce's father only hit him that one time, he had unpredictable rages that perpetuated Bruce's fears. In Bruce's mind, his father was a powerful, judgmental, and emotionally distant figure. Bruce craved the love and caring that his father seemed to give to his clients, and felt that he was a disappointment as a son, not the real boy that his father probably wanted. The fact that Bruce saw the Disney movie right after his father beat him unconsciously linked Pinocchio to this traumatic event. And the theme of the movie seemed to capture many of Bruce's personal struggles that haunted him in his dreams—Pinocchio too wished to be a "real boy" that his father would pay attention to.

I suspected that these unresolved issues had kept Bruce from getting too close to other people and making a commitment, until now, at age forty-eight. Perhaps it was no coincidence that his fiancée had an obsession with everything Disney. Often in life we seek out what we fear the most as a way to overcome that fear and resolve our underlying conflicts.

I turned to Gigi and said, "Honey, if you can take a break, I'd like to talk to you. I need your advice."

She smiled. "Sure," she said, and put her computer aside.

THE FOLLOWING THURSDAY I GOT INTO THE office early to proofread a research paper before my session with Bruce. I got so caught up in the task that I lost track of time and suddenly my assistant buzzed me—Bruce was there.

I opened the door and saw Bruce standing with a pretty woman in her mid-thirties, wearing a pink, lightweight Chanel suit and low heels. Bruce said, "This is my fiancée, Christina."

"I'm delighted to meet you, Dr. Small," she said, smiling.

"Nice to meet you too," I said.

"Sweetie, meet me back here in about fifty minutes, okay? Then we'll go shopping," Bruce said.

"Oh, can't I come in and just chitchat for a few minutes? I've never been in a psychiatrist's office." Before Bruce or I could say anything, she glided into the room and sat on the couch. Bruce, apprehensive, joined her. Christina's cheerfulness was infectious, and I wasn't sure if she was hypomanic or just had an incredibly upbeat personality. She certainly brightened a room. "Bruce tells me that you're an excellent doctor," she chirped.

"Thank you. I understand you do charity work, Christina."

She described how she had become involved in her family's foundation after graduating college back East and was now chairing its board. The foundation gave away about five million dollars a year to nonprofits in music and the arts. Bruce listened, his admiration apparent.

"Is there anything you wanted to talk about in particular?" I asked Christina.

"First, I wanted to tell you how thrilled I am that Bruce is in therapy," she said. "It's wonderful—he's sleeping better, and he's been in such a good mood."

"It's true," Bruce injected. "It's amazing what a good night's sleep can do for you."

"So, how are the wedding plans going?" I asked.

Christina brightened. "We're so excited! It's going to be a fairy-tale wedding. Has Bruce filled you in on the details?"

Bruce leaned forward and clasped his hands, "Of course I've told Gary about the Disneyland thing."

She politely turned to him. "What do you mean by 'Disneyland *thing*'?"

"You know, the Snow White thing, the Sleeping Beauty Castle, all of it," Bruce said.

Christina looked hurt. "You said you were fine with it."

"I am, sort of, but there're so many other options we haven't even considered," he said.

"So you're not pleased with how I'm planning this wedding, Bruce?"

He hesitated, then said with trepidation. "I just think my parents were hoping for something a little more traditional . . . maybe more Jewish?"

She was surprised. "You never mentioned a word of this before."

"I didn't want to hurt your feelings," he said. "I know how important this wedding is to you."

"And it's not important to you?" she snapped.

He took her hand. "Of course it is. I love you."

I spoke up. "It's clear that the wedding is important to both of you, but it's also important to be able to discuss your feelings about the details."

"Dr. Small, since I was a little girl, I've always wished for a perfect Snow White wedding."

"Why do you think that is?" I asked.

"I guess because it was so special to go to Disneyland with my father. I can remember him walking me through the Sleeping Beauty Castle and holding my hand. It was magical. I know he would want this for me."

"Did your father pass away?" I asked.

Christina looked away sadly. "When I was ten he got pancreatic cancer and was gone in three months." Bruce leaned over and wrapped her in his arms to comfort her.

"That's a young age to lose your father," I said.

She pulled herself together. "Yes, it was hard, but Mom remarried, and he's a wonderful man. And I've got my Bruce." She smiled at Bruce and gave him a kiss on the cheek.

I wondered if Christina had become emotionally stuck at age ten when her father took her to Disneyland for the last time. Her attempt to create the perfect fairy-tale wedding could be an expression of an unfulfilled wish to reexperience the closeness she felt with her father. It also could partly explain why she was marrying a man nearly fifteen years her senior.

"I can see why getting married at Disneyland might be important to you," I said.

"It was just a dream of mine; my life doesn't depend on it. I'm more concerned that Bruce never told me he was unhappy about the idea."

I looked at Bruce. "What about sharing some of your dreams with Christina?"

"Yeah. How about it?" she asked him, growing annoyed.

Bruce stood and looked out the window. "Sweetie, one of the things I've been discussing with Gary is a recurring nightmare I keep having."

She softened as soon as she sensed him starting to open up. "Really, sweetheart? Tell me about it."

"They're kind of crazy and embarrassing," Bruce said.

"You don't have to be embarrassed with me. I love you."

"I know . . . Well, at the end of every dream, no matter how it starts,

I become Pinocchio and I'm turning into a donkey. Then I wake up and can't get back to sleep."

"Wow," Christina said. "I had no idea . . . I'm so sorry, darling. No wonder you hate my den." They both laughed.

Bruce went on, "The whole thing is complicated and has to do with my father."

"What happened with your father?" she asked.

"It's sort of a long story, but the one day that he hit me when I was a kid happened to be the day I saw the movie *Pinocchio*. The movie scared the hell out of me. But now thanks to therapy I can see that somehow in my mind, there's a weird connection between these events."

"Bruce, getting married at Disneyland has been a dream of mine since I was little, but you know what?" she paused and sat forward, "I'm grown-up now, and you mean much more to me than some Fantasyland Castle or Snow White dress. All you had to do was tell me how you really felt." Bruce moved next to her on the couch and they hugged.

For any psychotherapist, dream interpretation can be a powerful tool. The actual Pinocchio story is rich with metaphors relating to Bruce's life. His relationship with his father stirred up a lifelong wish to be seen and treated as a real person and not a wooden puppet without feelings. He never learned from his father how to deal with the complexity of a close relationship, and as in most Disney stories, there was no strong mother figure in the picture. Bruce's mother stayed in the background and always took his father's side, no matter what.

Bruce's choice to become a plastic surgeon might have been an attempt to create perfection in his own life, what Freud would have called sublimation, or a way to redirect his unconscious feelings of imperfection into something constructive. Had Bruce not opened up to Christina about his struggles and fears, he might have used the Disney wedding as a "deal-breaker" excuse to flee yet another relationship. As he stopped lying to himself and Christina, the dreams of Pinocchio's growing nose subsided, along with the bad-boy image of becoming a donkey.

Christina's desire to have her wedding at Disneyland might have been an attempt to repair the abandonment and loss she experienced when her father died. In her mind, she was trying to re-create the closeness and magical feelings she recalled having with her father.

It seemed to me that Christina's interest in everything Disney was more of an obsession than a hobby. But how many of us have pastimes that border on obsession, whether it's poker, golf, or collections of cherished possessions from baseball cards to shoes? Sometimes we embrace these passions and even define ourselves by them; other times we might feel ashamed and keep them a secret. The key to feeling comfortable with ourselves and others is to accept our idiosyncrasies and enjoy them without becoming obsessed.

The next week Bruce returned for his solo session. He looked well rested and upbeat.

"The session last week with Christina made a huge difference in our relationship," he said. "We got out of the Disneyland contract, she hired a wedding planner, and we're even having a rabbi perform the ceremony."

"So, where are you going to have it?" I asked.

Bruce grinned. "At my parents' temple!"

"And Christina is okay with all of these changes?"

"She's more than okay. She's been a doll. Ever since I opened up to her about my feelings, we're so much closer."

THE WEDDING WENT SMOOTHLY, AND BRUCE CONTINUED in psychotherapy for the next year. They bought a new house and hired a decorator known for her minimalist style. Christina put her Disney paraphernalia into storage, and Pinocchio made only an occasional appearance in Bruce's dreams.

A few months into the marriage, Christina got pregnant. Bruce was thrilled, but his nightmares returned. During therapy we discovered that his dreams were now triggered by anxiety that his child would not be raised as a Jew. After a few couples sessions, he finally expressed his feelings to Christina. And true to their dynamic, once he revealed his hidden fears and worries, she felt closer to him. She agreed to send their children to Hebrew school, as long as they could still have a tree at Christmas.

CHAPTER TWELVE

Gaslight

Summer 1999

OUR FAMILY HAD MOVED FROM THE San Fernando Valley to a house in Bel Air, overlooking UCLA. I was enjoying the shorter commute, as well as living up in the hills. It was beautiful and quiet, and you didn't feel like you were in the city. And since it was so close to campus, many of our neighbors worked at the university as well.

Early on a crisp Sunday morning, I took our dog, Jake, for a walk up the street to get a view of the ocean. Jake was panting as we approached the top of the hill, so I slowed our pace, not for a moment acknowledging that I was completely out of breath myself. As we rested, I saw Bob Martin, another UCLA psychiatrist, planting hydrangeas in his front garden. He waved, and I went over to say hello.

Bob was an expert in cognitive-behavioral therapy or CBT, a goal-oriented form of treatment based on the idea that a patient's own thoughts, rather than external events, situations, and relationships, cause their feelings and behaviors. By systematically changing how the patient thinks, the therapist can improve how the patient feels and behaves. During sessions, the therapist uses a structured approach that can be applied to several different psychiatric disorders.

It often seemed that a psychiatrist's style of therapy reflected his personality, and Bob's perfectly organized and meticulous garden was no exception. As Jake leaped into Bob's flowers and shrubs to sniff around, I could see the terror on Bob's face. I quickly pulled Jake's leash and brought him back to me, and Bob relaxed.

After discussing tulips and petunias more than I could bear, I shifted the conversation to psychiatry. We got into a friendly debate about the pros and cons of different forms of psychotherapy.

"I know that CBT helps a lot of patients," I said. "But don't you ever wonder if those thoughts you alter or even extinguish so quickly might be better off explored and understood?"

Bob laughed. "That's what I love about you, Gary. You think therapy should last forever."

"No, I just think it should last as long as it takes."

While we were talking, I lost track of Jake, who was now inspecting Bob's lawn, having just left a large present. I pulled out my handy blue bag to scoop up the specimen, and Bob nearly swallowed his tongue as he ran for the garden hose.

"I'm really sorry, Bob, but a beautiful, well-groomed lawn like yours is hard for Jake to resist."

Bob hosed down the offending area. Just then, Jake spotted a white poodle coming toward us and yanked the leash, pulling me up the hill. I managed to say good-bye as I yelled "Heel!" to Jake while he dragged me along.

The next day Bob called me at the office. He couldn't still be upset about his lawn, could he?

"Bob, I'm so sorry about my dog's behavior in your garden yesterday."

He laughed. "Don't worry about it, Gary. It was nice to get a chance to talk. I'm calling because I know a couple who could use some help, and I think you might be the right person for them to see."

"I appreciate it. What can you tell me about them?" I asked.

"Well, I know the wife," he said. "She's a psychologist with a busy practice in Brentwood. She's married to a businessman. Now with their kids grown up and out of the house, she's complaining that something's not right in the marriage."

"I'd be glad to see them. Have them call me."

The next week I had an appointment to see Susan and Raymond Wagner. They came a few minutes late, and as they entered the office, Ray complained about the parking. He was lean, in his early fifties, with salt-and-pepper hair; he wore yachting attire. Except for the clothes, he looked like he could be my older brother. Susan appeared a few years younger. They sat at opposite ends of the couch and stared, waiting for me to take the lead.

I began. "Bob Martin said I might be able to help you. Why don't you tell me what's going on?"

"We got married when Susan was an undergrad and I was getting my M.B.A.," Ray said. "Our youngest just left for college last fall, and as far as I'm concerned, we're having a great time."

I looked at Susan and said, "So, how does it feel to have an empty nest?"

"Not bad. We're both busy with our careers and have a very nice life, but for the last couple of years, I've felt some distance between us. I just don't feel as happy in the marriage as I used to."

Ray shook his head. "Whoa . . . honey, I don't know where all this is coming from," Ray said, and then turned to me. "Frankly, I don't see why we both have to be here. Susan's not happy, I get that, but shouldn't *she* be seeing someone rather than the two of us?"

Susan looked at him, frustrated. "Ray, we have a *marriage* problem. That involves both of us. Why do you insist on being in denial about it?"

Ray raised his arms in resignation. "If you say so, sweetheart, then tell the doctor what you think the problem is."

"Fine," she said. "First of all, Ray spends all his free time on that stupid boat of his—"

"It's a yacht, dear," Ray interrupted.

"Whatever. You know I get seasick just looking at it." She turned toward me. "I mean, when he first got the thing, he'd take it out for a few hours on Sundays, and it was no big deal. But now he's gone all weekend for yacht races and whatnot. And the weekends spill over to Monday nights."

He balked. "You *know* I do business on the yacht. I close deals up and down the coast—it's how I make my living. Besides, it isn't every weekend."

"Yes, lately it is," she said. "And when you're away, you hardly ever call and I feel lonely. It seems like that yacht is more important to you than I am."

"That's ridiculous. When I'm in town, don't we have a great time together? Don't we feel close?" He moved toward her on the couch and took her hand.

She softened. "It's true. When you *are* home, it's good." She shook her head. "I hate when I hear myself complain—I sound like one of those disgruntled housewives I see in my practice. They're always bitching about not getting enough attention from their husbands." She paused and looked away. "I feel embarrassed."

"Why is that?" I asked.

She looked at me. "I shouldn't be so insecure. I'm a psychologist—I treat people with these kinds of problems all the time."

"But therapists are people. We both know that a degree on the wall doesn't make us immune to personal problems," I said.

"Look, I realize that after thirty years of marriage, getting some space and having separate interests can be healthy for a couple. But something just doesn't feel right to me."

Ray looked at her with compassion. "I understand, sweetheart, and I know that it was hard for you when all the kids moved out."

"It's not as bad as I thought it would be." She turned to me and said, "My work is rewarding, and when Ray is around, we enjoy our time together. We see friends, go to movies, take walks . . . I just can't get on that boat, and he knows it." She looked pensive. "So I have to wonder, why did he go out and get it?"

Ray replied, "You know that my father had a yacht, and I've always loved the water. I never had the time or money when the kids were young, but now it's a tremendous source of relaxation for me, and it's great for business. When you wanted to become a psychologist and leave the kids with a nanny, I was fully supportive. I just wanted you to be happy."

"I know," she said. "I get it. This is *my* problem. I just can't figure out why I'm so uncomfortable."

"Is there anything else besides Ray's yacht that might be stirring up these feelings?" I asked.

After a long silence, Ray said, "Think about this, Susan. You have three sisters, and none of them has a career."

Susan looked at him. "What's your point?"

"My point is that in your family, the girls were discouraged from pursuing a career. Let's face it, college was a place to find a husband." He turned to me. "I'm not saying this to be critical, but I wonder if being angry about my yacht isn't really what's bothering her. I think she may feel guilty about being the only girl in her family to have a career."

Susan paused and then said, "That's interesting. I never made that connection before. Let me think about it."

I was impressed by their level of psychological sophistication. I might have expected it from Susan, who had professional training, but Ray was insightful as well. Though he was defensive about coming to the session, he seemed sensitive to her concerns, and she responded well when he reached out to her. In fact, I thought Ray might be on to something; Susan's jealousy over his yacht could stem from deeper issues—perhaps her identity as a wife, mother, or therapist. Maybe she was brought up to believe that success meant being a good wife and mother and a career as a psychologist just didn't fit the family mold. Perhaps marriage counseling wasn't the answer. Maybe Susan would do better with individual psychotherapy. On the other hand, Susan's feeling that Ray cared more about his yacht than about her could be a clue that something else was going on. Were there other reasons behind Ray's buying a yacht at that time? It seemed strange, since the kids had left home, the two of them had more time to spend together now, and he knew Susan would never set foot on it. Middle-aged men do have affairs, which could explain the boat and Susan's discomfort. Ray appeared to love his wife and was concerned about her welfare, yet sometimes when he spoke it seemed rehearsed and insincere—but maybe that was just his communication style.

"You know, I don't know why I pushed us into couples therapy today, Dr. Small," Susan said. "I mean, Ray's a good husband and I've just been in a weird place lately."

He put his arm around her. "There's nothing to be embarrassed about, sweetheart. Your problems are my problems too." Susan was comforted and went on to talk about their early courtship during school. Soon after they got married, she dropped out of college and had their first child, while Ray pursued his career and became successful at start-up companies, making a small fortune.

As the session ended, we talked about next steps. Despite their ambivalence about couples therapy, we decided to give it a short trial run and made an appointment for the following week.

I DIDN'T THINK MUCH ABOUT THE WAGNERS until the weekend when Gigi and I were hanging out on lounge chairs in the backyard, watching the kids play Marco Polo in the pool. Gigi was leafing through a travel magazine and stopped on a photo of St. Bart's, showing beautiful people strolling past a line of yachts. She held it up to me and said, "Look how packed in these yachts on St. Bart's are. They look like sardines."

"What would you think if I went out and bought a yacht?" I asked.

"I'd think you'd either won the lottery or were secretly related to a Kennedy."

"I recently saw a couple where the wife hates boats, but the husband went out and bought one anyway."

"Why did he do that?" Gigi asked.

"He's always wanted one. Now the kids are grown and he can afford it."

Gigi dropped her magazine and raced to the pool to break up a

Styrofoam-sword fight that was getting too rough. She came back and said, "Do they do anything together?"

"Well, yeah," I answered. "But he's gone almost every weekend on his yacht, and she's getting insecure about it."

"I can understand that. I hate it when you travel too much. It's lonely—even with the kids around." She looked at the pool. "Especially with the kids around. Would you mind?" she said as she pointed to our daughter, who was pummeling our now crying son with a pool noodle. I got up and confiscated the offending noodle, then threw in a couple of beach balls to distract them.

Lying back down on the lounge, I said, "They've been married thirty years. Their kids are grown, and he just wants to do something he's always dreamed of. What's wrong with that?"

"Nothing, I guess," she said as she went back to her magazine.

"Don't you think that having separate interests strengthens a relationship?" I asked. "I mean, as long as they're there for each other when they need to be."

"Yeah . . ."

"So why shouldn't a husband be able to have a hobby?" I asked.

"There's nothing wrong with a hobby, but it would be nice if it was something they could do together. Has this patient invited you out on his yacht?" she asked.

"Are you kidding? That would be so inappropriate," I said as I realized that a part of me would like to go out on his yacht.

"You want to know what I think?" Gigi asked.

"Of course."

"I think you're biased. I think you're siding with the husband. What's the term for that again? Reverse transference or something?"

"The term is countertransference, and I'll take it under advisement, Dr. Gigi."

Later that afternoon I thought about the possibility that I was having a countertransference reaction that might be distorting my impression of what was going on between Ray and Susan. Freud used the term to refer to the therapist's emotional responses to a patient during psychotherapy.

An effective therapist has the capacity for empathy and will experience countertransference feelings but should not allow them to interfere with the therapy. In fact, for therapists who maintain perspective on these reactions and their distortions, countertransference offers an important opportunity to explore the patient's inner emotional world. It helps the therapist understand how the patient's behaviors affect others, and how the patient can create dysfunctional interpersonal patterns.

If Gigi was right about my countertransference, then what was it about Ray or Susan that might be distorting my perspective? Perhaps I was overidentifying with Ray because of his physical resemblance to me. Maybe I yearned for more time alone to pursue my own hobbies. Was I looking to escape the dog-walking, kid-watching weekends? I didn't think so—I loved being with my family and wouldn't trade it for anything.

Or maybe my countertransference had to do with Susan. Perhaps I felt uncomfortable seeing another mental health professional experience such doubts and insecurities about her personal life. Treating other therapists can be tricky—it can bring up feelings of insecurity that the patient might know more than you, or you might identify so much with the patient that you become blinded to his issues.

THE FOLLOWING WEEK, SUSAN AND RAY RETURNED for their second session. She looked tired and stressed. As we got started, I asked Susan how she was doing, and Ray answered for her. "Not well, Dr. Small. She's getting worse."

I turned to Susan and asked, "What's going on?"

"I don't know . . . I can't stop thinking about Ray, the yacht, why he really bought it . . . I mean, what's he really doing on that thing? It's even distracting me at work."

"So you're having trouble trusting Ray?" I asked.

"No, I don't know why I'm so suspicious. It's like I'm having a bizarre conversation with myself. It's better when he gets home in the evening and we're together. But then it happens again the next day." She shook her head and looked away. "Jesus, I sound like I'm depressed."

Ray spoke up. "Maybe Susan needs medication, Dr. Small."

"It's possible," I said. "But we don't want to jump into medication too quickly. Let's find out more. Susan, what's your appetite been like?"

"It's down, and you don't have to go through the list of depression symptoms. I have a lot of them. I do appreciate your holding back on the medicine, because I still think we have a marriage problem that isn't resolved."

Ray sighed. "Not again. And what would resolve it, Susan? My selling the yacht? Wouldn't it be less drastic for you to take a couple of Prozacs?"

She glared at him. "I don't appreciate your tone, and no, I don't think taking Prozac is easier than finding a real answer to our problem."

He shook his head. "Darling, *we* don't have a problem. You do."

"Let's slow down a bit," I interjected. "It sounds like we're back to the basic disagreement about who's got a problem and how to go about fixing it. Susan is worried about the situation and may be depressed. But *why* she's feeling this way, and how to help her, is still unclear."

"Look, I love my wife dearly," Ray said as he turned to Susan. "And even though I need it for business, and it's been my lifelong dream to have a yacht of my own, if your happiness depends upon it, I'll sell it right now."

Ray's professed love for Susan seemed sincere, but his perfunctory offer to sell his yacht didn't ring true. I wondered if he was holding something back.

She looked at him tenderly. "Honey, no one is saying you have to sell your yacht, but Dr. Small is right. Let's slow things down and try to get a better idea of what's going on. Maybe it does have to do with the way I was brought up, but we need to be able to talk about it."

We did talk about it for the rest of the session, and I began to see a pattern of how Susan and Ray interacted. Every time she got anxious and expressed her concerns about the relationship, he initially got defensive but then came around and was able to calm her and bring them back together. At times he struck me as a regular family man who really cared about his wife. But other times he seemed a bit too polished and ready with an answer for everything. Something was stirring up Susan's anxiety now, and I wasn't sure what that was. If it had to do with her career, why didn't this problem emerge earlier? Also, Ray had bought the yacht several years ago, so why was it an issue now? It was hard to believe it all went back to an empty-nest syndrome.

That evening, Gigi prepared a fabulous pasta feast for the four of us. The kids and I made pigs of ourselves, and I figured I'd better walk off the extra carbs. No one wanted to join me and the dog, so I took off up the street with Jake in tow. The sun was about to set, and as I caught a breathtaking view of the hillside and ocean, I heard my neighbor Bob say, "I didn't know that they let psychiatrists out after dark."

"Didn't you get the memo about our special night passes?" I asked.

"Hey, did the Wagners ever call you?" he asked as he crossed the street toward me, obviously not wanting Jake back in his yard.

"How well do you know them?" I asked.

"Well, like I said, the wife has a busy Westside practice. I met the husband once at a fund-raiser. You know, I shouldn't say anything, but . . ."

"But what?" I asked, curious to get a colleague to weigh in.

"There's something about him. I mean he's very personable and everyone seemed to be drawn to him at this event, but I don't know."

"What is it?" I asked.

"I just don't trust the guy," Bob said.

"Really? Why not?"

"He was flirting with other women every time his wife's back was turned. Anyway, what's happening with them?" he asked.

"You know, the usual midlife marital issues." I didn't want to give up too much, to avoid breaching my patients' confidentiality.

Bob was about to ask me another question, but his cell phone rang and he had to take the call. I waved good-bye and headed home. Hearing Bob's misgivings about Ray's character began to fuel my own.

At their next session, Susan showed up alone. Ray had to handle a business emergency down the coast. She sat across from me on the couch, and we looked at each other, professional to professional.

"Have you ever wondered why Ray has so much business out of town?"

"No. Why should I?" she asked.

I cut to the chase. "Do you think Ray is having an affair?"

"No," she said. "I think he's just taking a vacation from our marriage, which I don't appreciate."

"Have you ever directly asked him?" I asked.

"Of course not. I don't think there's another woman; I think he's just lost interest in me."

I was in an awkward position. I had outside information from my neighbor that supported my own suspicions about Ray's infidelity. My guess was that he was a pro at covering it up.

Susan went on for the rest of the session praising Ray for his many virtues. She didn't want to talk about her depression and seemed to minimize the loneliness she felt whenever he was away.

THE NEXT WEEK I WAS PREPARING A lecture for an international Alzheimer's meeting in Europe, so I tried not to schedule too many patients. As I was sorting through my presentation, my assistant buzzed me and said that a Francesca Wagner was waiting to see me, but she didn't have an appointment.

"I'm really busy right now. Could you schedule her to come back another time?"

"I tried that, but she insists on seeing you now," Laura said. "She says she drove up from San Diego and only needs a few minutes of your time."

I checked my watch and said, "Okay, give me a minute and I'll be right with her." I closed my PowerPoint file and straightened up the desk before buzzing Laura to send the woman in.

Francesca looked to be in her late twenties and resembled Penélope Cruz with a few extra pounds. She walked briskly into the office, took a seat in front of my desk, crossed her arms, and glared at me. She seemed angry, and I had no idea why.

I tentatively asked, "What can I do for you?"

"I'll tell you what you can do for me, Doctor. You can stop screwing up your billing and sending statements to people who never came to see you." She paused and took a breath before continuing her rant. "Or maybe you're pulling some type of insurance scam and sending out phony bills to see what comes back."

"What are you talking about?" I asked. "I'm not following you."

"Do you have any idea how much this can mess up people's lives? It can cause fights, break up marriages—and for what, a few bucks from an insurance company?"

I was getting worried. This woman seemed unstable. How did she pick *me* out? Was she dangerous? She could be psychotic and have a knife or a gun in her purse. I tried to remain calm and figure out what was going on, but her intensity and anger were clouding my thinking.

"I'm sorry, Ms. Wagner, I still don't know what you're referring to."

"I'm referring to this." She pulled a piece of paper out of her purse and slammed it down on my desk so hard that I jumped. It was my bill to Susan and Ray Wagner. I quickly checked the address, and it matched the one in my records. So how had this woman gotten it? Was she a relative? Did the post office screw up? And why was she so angry about it?

"I'm not sure how you got this bill, Ms. Wagner, but it wasn't intended for you," I said, relieved that all of this was probably just a clerical error.

"You're damn right it wasn't," she said.

"So why do you have it?"

"I found it in my husband's coat pocket when I picked up his dry cleaning." She folded the bill back up and put it in her purse.

"Maybe it was from another Ray Wagner's jacket," I said, grasping for a plausible explanation.

She looked at me indignantly. "I live in San Diego. My dry cleaner is in San Diego. The bill is addressed to a Ray and Susan Wagner in Los Angeles for couples therapy. What kind of con are you trying to pull?"

"Listen, Mrs. Wagner, I'm not pulling any con, but let's try to figure this out. Would you like a glass of water?" She nodded and I got up to pour each of us one. She was starting to calm down.

I sat back down. "Now, you said you're from San Diego?"

"That's right. My husband, Ray, and I live in La Jolla with our baby."

"So your husband, Ray, had this bill in his coat pocket?" I asked.

"I already said that. But I'd like to know who the hell Susan Wagner is," she said as her anger started building again.

I made an effort to sound calm. "Francesca, tell me about your husband."

"He's a successful businessman and a wonderful father." She brightened when she spoke about him.

"And how long have you been married?" I asked.

"Two years now. It was very romantic—we got married on his yacht."

I felt like a brick just hit me on my thick head. I understood why this Francesca Wagner was so pissed off, and why Susan Wagner had been sensing there was something not quite right in her marriage for the last couple of years. I couldn't tell Francesca about Susan—I was bound by confidentiality. The only way Francesca was going to get to the bottom of this was by talking with Ray.

"Francesca, there's no fraud or clerical error, but there's not much else I can tell you. It sounds like this is something between you and your husband, and I think you should ask him about it."

She stood, angry again. "So you're going to stonewall me and just tell me to talk to Ray. Well, I can't do that because he's away on his yacht again, and his cell phone doesn't work at sea."

That didn't make sense—I thought cell phones worked at sea. I remember that Gigi and I called my parents at least three times during our cruise to Mexico while they were watching our kids.

"I'm sorry, Francesca," I said. "There's nothing else I can do."

She grabbed her purse and stormed out of the office. I suspected that she wouldn't be able to confront Ray until the weekend, when he left Susan for one of his so-called business trips. But I had a session scheduled with the Wagner couple I knew the following day, and I could hardly wait to confront Ray about this misplaced-bill incident.

Ray was quite the operator. Not only had he conned Susan and Francesca, but he had pulled me into his ruse as well. Had my countertransference partly blinded me to his sociopathic maneuvering? He sure had me going—shrewdly dictating my therapeutic responses. Susan should be on meds, Susan should have her own psychotherapy, Susan should explore her career ambivalence, Susan should do this and Susan should do that—but Ray was a saint with a heart of gold and deserved his time alone on his boat. It was one thing for Ray to pull the wool over my eyes for a few sessions, but he had managed to dupe Susan, a trained psychologist, for years. He had been so smooth that I had actually fantasized about going on his yacht.

I knew why Ray had been able to fool everyone for so long. He was a quintessential sociopath. Sociopaths, or what psychiatrists call antisocial personalities, have lifelong patterns of deceitfulness for personal gain. They lack remorse and empathy and are wizards at rationalizing away how they hurt and mistreat others. Usually people think of sociopaths as being habitual criminals—thieves, thugs, and murderers. However, intelligent sociopaths sometimes never get caught and can end up running major companies or billion-dollar Ponzi schemes. It's the less organized sociopath who can't hold down a job, is unable to sustain a long-term relationship, and often ends up in jail.

When a relatively successful sociopath like Ray gets caught, those he's fooled are initially shocked and outraged—they can't believe that this person whom they trusted for years has betrayed them. They experience shame because they feel they should have known better or sooner. Ray was skilled in recognizing his victims' emotional needs and fulfilling them in order to get what he wanted. Neither of his wives—at least the two I knew about—wanted to believe that he was capable of living a double life, so they ignored the clues and were quick to embrace his rationalizations.

Most of us have come into contact with people who have sociopathic tendencies—that's one reason we usually take time to get to know people before we trust them. And even people who do have the capacity for empathy might act in an antisocial manner on occasion, whether it's fudging on an income tax return or not bothering to go back and pay for a magazine that was forgotten at the bottom of a shopping cart.

However, no one knows what causes extreme sociopathy, which

afflicts 6 percent of men and 1 percent of women. The condition begins in childhood, kids who set fires or torture animals are sociopaths. It persists into adulthood with chronic lying and cheating, and lasts throughout life. Depending on the severity of antisocial personality disorder, some of the symptoms can be treated with medication, psychotherapy, or both. However, when sociopathy is severe, there is no cure.

If, as I suspected, Ray was a true sociopath, why did his bigamy start so late in life? Perhaps he had been cheating on Susan throughout their marriage and gotten away with it. Maybe the empty-nest syndrome or some type of midlife crisis escalated his behavior to a new level of deceit. I didn't know if I would ever get answers from Ray—he was pretty smooth at avoiding the truth.

I FOUND MYSELF CLOCK WATCHING BEFORE THE Wagners' appointment, anticipating my showdown with Ray. At five after, I got worried that they wouldn't show, but my assistant buzzed and said my appointment had arrived. I opened the door and saw only Susan standing there.

"Is Ray running late?" I asked.

"He won't be coming."

"Oh, no?" I was disappointed.

"I need to sit down. Then I'll fill you in." She headed for the couch.

I took my chair and noticed that Susan's demeanor had changed. She seemed serious but confident.

"I feel like a giant weight has been lifted," she said. "If I was depressed, I'm not anymore."

"What are you feeling?" I asked.

"Rage," she said. "That son of a bitch has another family. Can you believe that? *I* need therapy? *He* needs jail."

"What happened?" I asked.

She laughed bitterly. "I had a little visit from Mrs. Ray Wagner number two, who has an adorable one-year-old son, by the way. Apparently, she's been enjoying Ray's charms Fridays through Mondays. Oh, and she *loves* yachts. I've spent thirty years living with a liar and a cheater, a goddamn sociopath. Who knows how many women he's wooed or married during our relationship."

"Susan, I wanted to tell you that this other Mrs. Wagner visited me yesterday too. Apparently she discovered one of my billing statements in Ray's jacket pocket," I said.

"Yes, I know," Susan said bitterly. "She told me all about it. It's infuriating, but it's confusing too. I feel so embarrassed. How could I not have known for so long? The man I thought I was married to, raised three children with, never really existed. And you'll love this—he actually tried to tell me it was my fault because I was too involved with my work and not paying enough attention to him."

"So what now?" I asked.

"I kicked him out. I've wasted enough of my life with that pompous liar. I never want to see him again. I just feel bad for the kids."

Even though I didn't get my chance to confront Ray, I felt satisfaction from Susan's account of how she dealt with him. I knew that some of my satisfaction stemmed from my own countertransference. My failure to recognize the extent of Ray's deceit may have had to do with my overidentification with him as a happy family man. Also, at some level, I didn't want to accept that a professional therapist—Susan or I—could be duped. But I was gaining perspective on it. In fact, my falling for Ray's scam, even briefly, helped me empathize with what Susan was going through, and I was able to help her gain some insight as well.

Susan continued in psychotherapy with me for the next six months. She kept in touch with Francesca Wagner in San Diego. I wasn't surprised, since people who have been victimized by the same individual often form a bond.

Soon after both Susan and Francesca kicked Ray out, he disappeared from their lives. Susan and I speculated that Ray had started up a new life in some other state or part of the world with who knows how many wives. As a therapist herself, Susan understood that a sociopath like Ray would never change, but she still needed to grieve the Ray she thought she knew and loved for so many years. It took her some time to deal with the shame she felt about ignoring the clues to his infidelity that now had become so obvious to her. Ironically, Ray's theory about Susan's upbringing and feelings about her career had some truth to it, and I helped her get a better understanding of those issues.

I hadn't thought about Ray again until about a year after Susan left therapy. Gigi and I were watching TV in the den. It was one of those rare evenings when she had control of the remote and she was flipping from station to station. I was just about to grab it from her when she stopped on the classic movie channel. I recognized Charles Boyer and Ingrid Bergman.

"Oh, this is so great," Gigi said. "I love this movie."

"What's it called again? I asked.

"*Gaslight.* This guy's such a liar. He actually makes his wife believe that she's the one who's crazy."

I wondered what had ever happened to Ray. I imagined he was still wandering the oceans in his getaway yacht, victimizing various Mrs. Wagners. Maybe the port authorities had finally caught up with him, or perhaps he had been captured by pirates. Little did Ray realize that even on land, he was hopelessly lost at sea.

CHAPTER THIRTEEN

Shop Till You Drop

Winter 2004

IT WAS EARLY DECEMBER AND EVERYONE was preparing for the holiday break. I had just received great news from the National Institutes of Health—a large grant proposal I had submitted was getting funded. That meant that my research staff and I would not have to worry about funding for at least another five years. In the world of research, these are some of the few moments of celebration. When you submit the grand proposal, you worry that it won't get funded; then after you do get funded, you worry that you won't be able to complete the study or, worse, your results will not be what you'd hoped. But tonight was for celebrating. I was taking the family to a hip Japanese restaurant on La Cienega. We all loved sushi, and this was a chance for the kids to try an upscale place.

We were running late because my twelve-year-old, Rachel, refused to go. She had nothing cool to wear. Gigi managed to pull a few things out of her own closet to satisfy Rachel and promised to take her shopping the next week, now that she was in middle school. It never ceased to amaze me how much clothes can mean to some women, even preteen girls.

The next day a woman named Brenda Livingston called. She had been in treatment with me about ten years earlier, when she was in her mid-thirties and in the midst of an ugly divorce. Now she was sobbing into the phone, saying she was in a crisis and didn't know who else to call. I calmed her down and scheduled her for the next afternoon.

That night during dinner at home, Rachel said, "I'm going to Caroline's birthday party on Saturday, and I need to get her a present."

"She's going to be twelve, right?" Gigi asked.

"Uh-huh," Rachel answered.

"Okay, I'll pick her up something nice," Gigi replied.

We finished our meal, and the kids cleared the table and then asked to be excused. Gigi and I stayed.

"What's with you tonight? You seem distracted," Gigi said.

"I'm just thinking about this woman I used to know," I said.

"Great, another woman. I see that this family thing is really working for you."

"It's a woman I used to treat who called me today in a crisis," I said.

"I'll forgive you this time, but you'll have to rub my feet later."

As I washed the dishes, I thought about my former patient. Brenda had been a lot like other career-driven women who have high-powered jobs but whose families and marriages suffer. When I was treating her, she worked sixty-hour weeks as vice president of a large advertising agency. She was at the top of her field, yet she was dissatisfied with her life and she didn't know why. Her way of dealing with her feelings was to overeat.

I remembered that as her marriage fell apart, she became obsessed with eating certain foods according to color throughout the day. Breakfast was brown: coffee, wheat toast, and an occasional bowl of granola. Lunch was white: chicken breast or clam chowder with rice. Late at night she liked to gorge on darker tones—chocolate, brownies, and fudge. Her weight would fluctuate from very thin to overweight. At one point during therapy, she gained almost forty pounds. I recall the humiliation she felt when an associate congratulated her on her "pregnancy."

Brenda's mother had been her nemesis. Brenda could never do anything right in her mother's eyes, yet she lived every moment trying to get her mother's approval. The outfits she wore, the jobs and accounts she pursued, even the men she chose—none of them were ever good enough for Mom. Yet Brenda had a blind spot when it came to seeing her mother's flaws. And then, just when I felt we were making some headway in therapy, she suddenly claimed to be "cured" and stopped coming in.

It's not uncommon for patients to quit therapy when they first become aware of their unconscious conflicts. The painful feelings and memories that might be hiding behind their symptoms can be hard to face. In an attempt to avoid these uncomfortable feelings, their minds often trick them into believing that they are cured and no longer need the therapist. This allows them to continue to suppress or forget what's really disturbing them, without a therapist hammering away at the real problem.

Back when Brenda announced to me that she was cured, I was pretty sure she was running away from feelings she wasn't ready to deal with. In those days, I had less experience as a psychotherapist, and I felt somewhat demoralized by her speedy exit. I knew that premature terminators were often chronic patients who might not have the emotional strength to persevere in treatment. However, in reflecting back on her hasty retreat, I realized I might have pushed her too hard while exploring her problems. I made a mental note of this possible misstep and vowed to move at a slower pace with her this time, if I got the chance.

ON FRIDAY AFTERNOON BRENDA WALKED INTO MY office looking chic and svelte, wearing a black suit. She was blond now, with the latest Jennifer Aniston haircut. She placed her huge designer purse next to the couch and sat down. She was about to light a cigarette when she remembered the no-smoking rule. She smiled. "Hello, Dr. Small. It's nice to see you again. I like that touch of gray in your hair—very distinguished." I couldn't help but crack a smile.

"It's good to see you, Brenda," I said. "So, what's going on? You mentioned some kind of crisis?"

"Yes. I've been married to Richard for three years now, and he's becoming impossible. I don't want another divorce, but he's threatening to leave."

"Why's that?" I asked.

"He thinks I have a problem. Ha. He thinks I have lots of problems. My job, my mother, my shopping . . . Again he's complaining that I spend too much money. Who is he to tell me? I signed his stupid prenup, and I have my own money."

"So he had you sign a prenuptial agreement?" I asked.

"Of course, everybody does these days, but he still freaks out every time I spend a dollar. He says he's just concerned about me, but actually I'm very thrifty. I only shop at sales. Yesterday, everything at Saks was forty percent off, then fifteen percent off that—if you used your Saks First card, which of course I did. What am I, an idiot? I got a gorgeous black Dolce dress for like five dollars . . . okay, around nine hundred, which is like stealing it. And you know what else? And I swear I have never done this in my life, I bought a *purple* Versace for peanuts. I swear to God my closet is stuffed with black and gray suits, and an occasional off-white cocktail dress, but I have *never* bought *anything* purple! Richard should be happy for me. I'm branching out!"

As I listened to Brenda go on about her shopping victories, I envisioned her trying to jam a three-thousand-dollar purple dress in between forty identical black dresses she had probably never worn. I wondered if her eating issues from a decade ago had now been replaced by a new obsession—shopping. More important, I wondered what underlying feelings or conflicts might have led to her current crisis. She was waiting for me to say something.

"That's great that you're branching out, Brenda. Do you think you'll ever really wear that purple dress?"

"I don't know," she replied casually, "maybe in the summer. But it's really cute and it makes my closet pop!"

I smiled. "Are you still working at the ad agency?"

"I'm senior vice president of new accounts now. And with my new position, I make my own hours. Which gives me plenty of time to shop, return stuff I don't like, and shop some more." She laughed.

I was amused as well as concerned by the shopping discussion but wanted to shift our focus to what might be driving this preoccupation.

Perhaps bringing the conversation back to her relationships would help us unravel the conflicts underlying her current crisis.

"What's Richard's issue about you and your mother?" I asked. Brenda's version of Richard's take on the relationship might shed some light on what was really going on.

A general principle of human behavior is that it's easier for us to see something negative in other people than in ourselves. This mental process sometimes guides therapists when they make interpretations during treatment. Often, the traits that disturb us most in others are those that we ourselves possess. It may upset us to see these qualities in other people, but it's completely unacceptable to acknowledge them in ourselves. Richard's complaints about Brenda probably reflected some of his own issues, but the complaints that Brenda had about Richard might lead us to the conflicts behind her current problems.

"Can you believe that a grown man in his fifties is jealous of my eighty-year-old mother? It's ridiculous! Every time I'm on the phone with her, he goes nuts."

"How often do you talk with her?" I asked.

"She calls maybe once or twice a day. So what . . . she's lonely and I cheer her up. Richard says I give Mom more attention than I give him."

I wondered if she did.

She continued, "What a baby. And he's jealous of my job too! He calls my office constantly, saying stupid things like he misses me, but I know he's only trying to insert himself into my work somehow."

"Why would he do that?" I asked.

"Because he just can't stand that I have something going on that doesn't involve him. All day long I'm getting calls from my mother and my husband. I hardly have any time to get any work done!"

As Brenda went on, I recalled a fundamental problem from her earlier therapy that had obviously not been "cured." No matter how many people she had in her life who appeared to care about her—husband, mother, co-workers, friends—she always felt lonely. Part of the issue was that she surrounded herself with people much like her narcissistic and needy mother, who were unable to give her the emotional space to feel independent. My opinion was that Brenda didn't feel deserving of love, so she surrounded herself with people too selfish to deliver it.

Brenda believed that the early death of her father was at the root of all her problems. He had a malignant brain tumor and died when she was twelve, and her mother went into mourning for the next forty years. No doubt her father's death had an impact on her, but I suspected that her mother's inability to feel empathy for Brenda was an even more powerful force behind Brenda's psychological isolation and low self-esteem.

The description of her mother's narcissism and withholding personality was striking. I remembered Brenda telling me about an incident when she was seventeen. She came home a half hour late from a date, and her mother was so furious that she didn't speak to Brenda for a week. During our earlier therapy, Brenda was not ready to grasp her mother's contribution to her problems. It was all about her father dying and her mother's heartbreaking loss, and then Brenda's bastard husband not understanding.

"How does your mother feel about Richard?" I asked.

"Well, she loves that he's a high-profile lawyer. In fact, he's really the first man in my life she's ever approved of. And she's always excited if he gets on the news or something. She brags about it to all her friends. But if I tell her we had a fight or something, the first thing she says is 'What did you do *now*, Brenda?' I hate that. It's as if Richard is all great, and I'm just lucky to have him. She thinks marrying Richard is my finest achievement in life. She doesn't even acknowledge my work."

It looked like Brenda was welling up with tears, so I handed her the box of tissues. She took it from me, appearing embarrassed to have revealed her mother's power over her.

I was beginning to get a sense of what Brenda considered her crisis. She was finally getting her mother's approval through Richard, but her marriage was on the rocks, and now she feared losing that approval. This crisis might be an opportunity for her to understand why she had issues getting close to people—whether it was her husband, her mother, or her therapist. She was in enough pain to be motivated to get help, and it was my job, actually my challenge, to offer that help without frightening her away.

During the rest of the session, Brenda reassured me that her eating struggles were over—she had been at her current weight for the past five years. We discussed a therapy plan and found two regular times to meet each week.

Saturday morning after breakfast, I was getting my son, Harry, ready to go to his friend's house for the day. Gigi showed Rachel the purse she had gotten at the Gap as a birthday present for Caroline. Rachel thought it was cute. They wrapped it together and made a card. I left with Harry to drop him off and did some errands for the house—bought lightbulbs, dog food, and new hedge trimmers. I stopped by the office to catch up on my e-mail, and before I knew it, the day had slipped by.

When I returned home, I stepped into a crisis—Rachel was crying in her room, and Gigi was slamming cabinets in the kitchen.

"Honey, what's going on?"

"Well, Rachel went to the party and everything was fine. Caroline opened up her present and loved the Gap purse. But the next present she opened was a Coach purse," she said.

"Aren't those sort of expensive, grown-up purses?" I asked.

"Yes, it's a ridiculous gift for a twelve-year old," Gigi answered. "But that seems to be what the kids are giving each other on the Westside. So of course, Rachel was embarrassed by her present, and now she's mad at me. I tried to explain to her that the Coach bag was inappropriate, but she doesn't care. She has no clue about value and prices, and she just wants to fit in with her peers."

"Is that so bad? Don't we all want that?" I asked.

"Sure, but she goes to this fancy private school with a bunch of spoiled rich kids, and she has to understand that we don't have that kind of money—and that money isn't everything." Gigi poured a glass of wine and sat down at the table. "Maybe it's our fault for sending her to that school."

"This kind of thing happens at every school," I said. "We've got to teach our kids this lesson sometime. Why not now?"

"I guess, but I'll never give a Coach bag to a twelve-year-old, no matter what."

I was surprised at how early in life shopping becomes an issue, especially for girls. They learn that brand recognition as well as high price stands for greater status, even if it's not a better product. Of course, it's true for men too—show me a guy who doesn't want to wear an Armani suit and drive a Ferrari. We're constantly bombarded by ads with beautiful models using or wearing the coveted items—no wonder even kids want them.

WHEN BRENDA ENTERED MY OFFICE THE following week, she was wearing another designer outfit and black alligator pumps. She didn't waste a minute before complaining about her husband. "Look, I can see Richard for who he is—essentially, an emotionally immature micromanager."

"Did you have any clue of that when you married him?" I asked.

"Of course not. I was in love with him. He treated me like a princess; he never criticized me. But now he doesn't stop with the criticisms."

"That must be hard to live with," I said.

"It can be, but I know how to handle him."

"What about your mother? Does she try to micromanage you?" I asked.

"Of course not. She's just eighty years old and lonely. Is that a crime?"

Brenda was still unable to see any faults in her mother. For some reason, she needed to keep her mother on a pedestal.

"Brenda, it strikes me that you have a hard time seeing any flaws in your mother, as if you have to protect her."

"What are you getting at, Dr. Small?"

"You know, she was very critical of your first husband, and eventually the two of you broke up," I said.

"We broke up because he was a jerk. It had nothing to do with my mother." She started to fuss with her scarf. "By the way, what do you think of this cashmere wrap? I was early, so I stopped at the mall and did some shopping. Isn't it gorgeous?"

It seemed like every time we were on the brink of an insight, Brenda changed the subject, usually segueing into a recent shopping adventure— likely a smokescreen for the real issues that disturbed her. Throughout the initial weeks of therapy, I went easy on my interpretations; probing her unconscious too deeply might stir up more anxiety than she could bear. Instead, I acknowledged her difficulties and frustrations in order to gradually build a therapeutic alliance. Brenda seemed to have no awareness of how she kept people from getting too close, but her ways of maintaining distance were becoming clear in our therapeutic relationship. If she didn't run away from intimacy, she maneuvered others to keep away.

A couple of weeks later, Brenda barged in ten minutes late for her Tuesday-afternoon appointment. She was out of breath and balancing several large department-store bags in her arms. She collapsed on the couch and apologized for being late.

"I actually was early," she said, "so I popped into Neiman Marcus for a few minutes."

"Tell me, Brenda, when you went to Neiman's, how did it feel? What does it *feel* like when you're on a shopping spree?"

She looked at me quizzically. "Well . . . It feels good. I feel powerful . . . energized. *I'm* the one in charge, and everybody around me is waiting with bated breath for my decision. And I don't have the responsibility of an entire ad agency looking over my shoulder. Sometimes I buy things I don't even like just to get that giddy feeling of control over all those salespeople. And when I *really* want something, it's even better. When I touch it and look at it and try it on, I get goose bumps. There's the thrill of the hunt and the catch. It's like sex, but better, at least sometimes." As she spoke, she was entranced. Her face had a far-off look. It reminded me of an alcoholic describing his first drink.

"Does the feeling last?" I asked.

"Well, no, not really. Not after I get home and put the things in my closet. If I wear something new and sexy for Richard, he just wants to know what it cost. I actually end up taking a lot of my purchases back, but it's embarrassing, even though I often feel relieved."

"Really," I said.

"Well, yes, those thrilling catches quickly lose their luster," she said.

I figured that all this shopping and returning must have taken up hours of Brenda's free time and had become an effective way for Brenda to avoid her underlying psychological problems. Apparently, Brenda had replaced her eating addiction with a shopping addiction. The technical term is onio-mania, derived from the Greek *onios*, "for sale," and *mania,* "madness." Her impulsive and obsessive behavior traits had latched onto a new objective—shopping and returning. Brenda was not yet aware of how her addictive tendencies had landed on a new target. The next step in therapy was to help her recognize and understand the pattern. I didn't want her to bolt from therapy again, but I had to go for it and push her a little.

"So, Brenda, do you see any kind of pattern here?" I asked.

"What do you mean?"

"Well, you're no longer overeating, but it seems like you have a new preoccupation—overshopping," I said.

She shifted in her seat, "What are you talking about?"

"You've replaced one addiction with another," I said tentatively.

She looked at me, angry. "You know, you're sounding like one of those TV shrinks. Don't you think your theory is a little too pat, Dr. Small? When I start hearing psychobabble, I just want to quit therapy again."

"I don't think that would be a good idea, Brenda."

"I am *not* a shopaholic, or whatever you call it. It just relaxes me." She reached for her purse, and I thought that was that, she was leaving, but she pulled out her cigarettes instead. "Screw your no-smoking rule." Her pack was empty, so she crunched it up in frustration and shoved it back into her purse. She fished out some gum and started chomping on a couple of pieces.

I was relieved that she hadn't left the office, and not surprised by her defensiveness. Brenda had admitted that she left therapy the first time because of my so-called psychobabble, not because she was cured. Perhaps we had a chance to make some headway here.

"It's hard for any of us to honestly look at ourselves. I think for you, Brenda, it may be tough to admit that you have control struggles. It comes up in many areas of your life—food, clothes, work, relationships."

She looked amused. "You really think you know what makes me tick, don't you?"

"It's worth a shot to consider what I'm saying. Your description of what drives you to shop is a sense of control, but the feeling doesn't last. It doesn't matter what we call it: shopaholism, addiction, compulsion. The first thing to do is admit you've got a problem."

She shook her head and walked to the window. I continued, "Do you see this getting better . . . or worse?"

Brenda put her gum in a tissue and started to pace. "I don't know . . . Of course, Mommy and Richard don't approve. It has *that* going for it."

"In my experience, people don't deal with addictions until there's a crisis and they're forced to. Do you want to wait until you've driven Richard away, you're in debt, and you've possibly put your career at risk?"

Brenda stopped pacing and said, "Of course not. I'm just a worrier and shopping relaxes me. But I admit that when I get home, I feel bad, remorseful even, and I want it all to go away. Richard gets so down on me about my shopping. I figure if he's going to give me so much grief about it anyway, I might as well just shop. Well, that's how I feel with this stupid shopping and Richard's reaction to it. It's gotten to the point where I have to sneak bags into the house. He thinks every minute I'm not working, I'm shopping. And you know what? Maybe it's true." She sat back down on the couch, looking defeated. "I guess I am messed up. I need help, Dr. Small."

I was relieved. Brenda had finally admitted to her addiction and had asked for help. Now we could start working. Within the next two weeks, she began attending a Debtors Anonymous twelve-step program. She told me that at first the meetings seemed hokey, but after a while, talking with other shopping addicts made her feel understood. The others in the group really grasped the highs that came from shopping, as well as the shame and then relief that came from returning. Some of them, like Brenda, had suffered from other addictions, like alcohol or food, and had moved on to shopping. In addition to group meetings and therapy with me, I started her on a low dose of the antidepressant Wellbutrin, which helped lift her mood and quell some of her obsessive behaviors.

The neural pathways in the brain that reinforce dependence on alcohol or drugs also control compulsive behaviors focused on nearly any source of pleasure, including food, sex, shopping, and gambling. When something would trigger Brenda's urge to shop, her brain and other organs would automatically react to the image of the coveted purse, shoes, or dress—her heart rate would slow and brain blood vessels would dilate, a physiological reaction that focused her mind on the object of desire.

Brenda's shopping had all the trappings of a full-blown addiction—just describing a spree brought on a pleasurable rush. These euphoric feelings are linked to brain chemical changes that control all addictive behaviors and involve the neurotransmitter dopamine, a brain messenger that modulates both reward and punishment. The addict compulsively seeks, craves, and re-creates the sense of elation. Dopamine transmits messages to the brain's pleasure centers, causing addicts to want to repeat actions over and over again, even if they are no longer experiencing the original pleasure and are aware of negative consequences. And as any addiction takes hold, the brain's frontal lobe, responsible for decision making and judgment, loses ground. My goal in therapy was to provide Brenda with enough insight and reason to hold the dopamine pleasure centers at bay.

As Brenda's therapy progressed, we delved more into the stressors in her life that made her anxious and triggered her impulse to shop. She also began to see how much she craved her mother's approval, and Richard's as well. Brenda stuck with her twelve-step program, her symptoms improved, and she even quit smoking. I suspected the Wellbutrin helped with that.

It still wasn't clear to me why Brenda's shopping obsession was so extreme. Many women love to shop. I know Gigi certainly enjoyed shopping, and even my preteen daughter was getting into it. But they didn't shop beyond their means and usually only shopped when they needed something. To some extent, they must have felt some of the highs and lows that Brenda described, but they weren't addicts—as far as I knew.

ABOUT EIGHT WEEKS LATER, I TOOK MY regular Wednesday walk into Westwood to have coffee with Charlie Simon. We had been friends throughout our UCLA geriatric psychiatry training, but Charlie had decided to go into private practice. We got together periodically over the years and often reminisced about our earlier, carefree days, when we both had more time and less responsibility. It also gave us each a chance to catch up on what was going on in our respective worlds—private practice versus university life.

Charlie was waiting for me at Starbucks, reading the *L.A. Times* sports section. His neatly trimmed gray goatee matched his thick white hair. He never seemed to age, in part because his hair had turned completely gray in his early thirties.

He took a sip of his coffee. "It's sad . . . this is my midmorning indulgence—a nonfat latte with Sweet'N Low to wash down my Lipitor. I miss those days when we'd sneak off to the Apple Pan, inhale hickory cheeseburgers, and chase them down with pecan pie à la mode. We drank real Cokes back then."

"Charlie, you were already a Tab drinker when I met you. I remember, you liked the chemical aftertaste," I said as I put my briefcase on a chair next to his and went to order an espresso. We chatted about the good old days, family, work, and vacation plans. Charlie pointed to an ad in the paper. "My wife will definitely be hitting this Robinson's sale. She'll probably run into my new patient there, too."

"Oh yeah?" I said.

"I've been treating this shopping addict for the past few weeks," Charlie said.

I flashed to Brenda before she had gotten help with her addiction.

Charlie continued. "This woman shops and returns the stuff like crazy, and still manages to hold down a full-time job." Now I was intrigued. Was there an epidemic of Westside shopaholics hitting Rodeo Drive after work?

"That's weird," I said. "I have a patient who was hooked on shopping and returning stuff after working at her ad-agency job."

Charlie looked me in the eye. "Okay. Ad agency. But did she have an eating disorder before she had a shopping disorder?"

"Oh, man," I said. "You think we're treating the same patient?"

We didn't discuss her by name but exchanged descriptions of Brenda's physical attributes. The similarities were unmistakable.

"Holy shit," Charlie said. "It's got to be the same person."

I couldn't believe it. Brenda was "cheating" on me with another psychiatrist, and not just any psychiatrist, but my old buddy Charlie.

Getting a second opinion during psychotherapy can be helpful when there's an impasse, but this is usually done with the awareness of the therapist. What else was she doing behind my back? My mental ramblings sounded like those of a jilted lover. Brenda was obviously still having trouble facing the truth. But now she was holding it back from me and from Charlie.

"This is definitely a first for me," Charlie said.

"I think I need to have a little discussion with my patient."

Charlie smiled. "Fine, you first."

Walking back to the office, I felt like calling Brenda that minute and confronting her. No wonder Richard and Mommy called her all day. I was learning about yet another one of her ways of manipulating the people around her.

As I crossed the street from Westwood Village onto the UCLA campus, I took inventory of my reactions to Brenda's dual-therapy stunt. I felt angry, used, and like my time had been wasted. She was full of it about her twelve steps to sanity, and she was pulling the wool over our eyes. I knew my responses were coloring my take on Brenda's deception. This was all part of her way of dealing with her discomfort—she would create emotional turmoil in those around her, getting them all worked up about her behavior. In that way, she got them to show concern about her, and she didn't feel so alone.

Thursday afternoon finally rolled around, and Brenda arrived looking professional and calm. We exchanged our usual greetings, and I began, "Brenda, I don't think you've been completely honest with me."

"What are you talking about, Dr. Small? I thought we were making progress. Oh, and I need a new prescription for Wellbutrin."

I smiled. "Is Dr. Simon prescribing that for you also?"

She looked at me, surprised. "What? Who?"

"Brenda, I know you're seeing Charlie Simon as well as me. Please don't deny it."

She laughed. "So you think you know everything about me, right?"

"I only know that you're seeing my colleague Charlie Simon for psychotherapy and you never mentioned it to me."

"What, do you have a little shrink club where you all get together and gossip about your patients? I have a right to see whoever I want. Charlie Simon. Dr. Wells—"

"*Malcolm* Wells?!" I exclaimed.

"That's right. And he's very good."

"Well, who else are you seeing?" I asked in disbelief.

"Jeffrey Sanderson. But he's only an M.F.C.C., so that doesn't really count."

As I sat there trying to regain my composure, Brenda continued, "You know, Dr. Small, when I had that breakthrough with you about my shopping addiction, it felt so good that I craved those flashes of insight all the time. I tried to be a good therapy patient, but those magic moments weren't always there with you. And I got kind of bored with those twelve-step meetings."

"Why didn't you tell me?" I asked.

"I didn't want to disappoint you. Once I started seeing Dr. Simon, the excitement returned. I loved relating my insights about my eating addiction turning into a shopping addiction. I may have embellished things a little about Richard and my mother. Keeping it from you was part of the rush. You know what I mean?"

Just as she had always tried to get her mother's approval, now she wanted mine. But this multiple-therapist quest just seemed like another addiction.

Still shaken, I prompted her. "I'm not sure what you mean."

"Now that I added Dr. Wells and Dr. Sanderson, I have someone to talk to almost every day. It's so great. Besides, it keeps me out of the department stores. That's a good thing, right?"

"Look, Brenda, sneaking therapy on the side is not in the spirit of the two of us working together. It just confuses and diffuses our efforts."

"I don't see how it affects it at all," she said.

"That may be, but I can't see you if you're going to continue with the other therapists. Besides, it appears you've replaced your shopping addiction with a therapist addiction."

"Oh, that's absurd. What do you think I am, a serial addict?"

"Well, it appears so," I said. "This is the first time I've seen someone whose addiction has shifted to multiple psychotherapists, but the same behavior patterns we've discussed before apply here."

She paused for a moment and then said, "Dr. Small, you were the one who helped me face my addictions. I swear I'll stop seeing those other doctors. Maybe we should start meeting more often."

I treated Brenda for a few more years. She was able to work on her need for my approval, which helped her get perspective on her need for her mother's approval. Her relationship with Richard also improved.

I knew from my regular coffee shop meetings with Charlie Simon that at least he was no longer treating her, but unfortunately there was no little shrink club to check for multiple-therapist disorder. Even though I took Brenda at her word that she had supposedly kicked her therapist addiction, I admit that my relationship with her was tinged with uncertainty and I felt distrust—as most people do with ex-addicts. As far as I could tell, she was getting better. I noted that she would wear the same outfit more than once, which I took as a sign of her improved mental health.

CHAPTER FOURTEEN

Mountain Heir .

Winter 2007

"SLOW DOWN! HE'S BRAKING IN FRONT of you," I said with terror.

"I see that, Daddy, and I *was* slowing down," my fifteen-and-a-half-year-old daughter said in frustration. "Why are you always telling me what to do?"

I shook my head in disbelief. "Because I'm teaching you to drive, and I'd like us both to survive it." I really didn't understand why the driving age wasn't raised to twenty-five, when a young person's brain finally has a fully developed frontal lobe. In the six months that I spent teaching Rachel to drive, she became fairly good at it, although my hair turned noticeably grayer.

After nearly sideswiping a parked minivan, she finally pulled up in front of our house to practice her parallel parking. She completed the maneuver and asked, "How's that?"

She was almost a yard from the curb, but I needed to get to the office—with my sanity—so I said, "Good job, honey. Mom can practice with you later."

When I got to work, my first meeting was with a brother and sister, Carolyn and William Dunlop. I knew them from years earlier when I had consulted on an older relative of theirs with Alzheimer's disease. They were extremely wealthy—their grandfather had invested in real estate during the Depression, and now the family business was diversified among several large companies. The Dunlop siblings were in their mid-fifties and had an East Coast, old-money attitude.

My assistant escorted Carolyn and William into my office, which was now part of a suite I kept for my research and administrative staff. It was on the top floor of the Semel Institute and had an impressive view of the ocean and mountains surrounding UCLA. I vacillated between calling it my penthouse and my attic, depending on whether I was trying to impress people or protect my space from academic poachers.

William began, "I'm glad you could see us so quickly, Dr. Small. Thank you again for your efforts on behalf of Uncle Ernest."

"I hope I was helpful. I wish I could have done more. We're still working on better treatments for Alzheimer's, but no major breakthroughs yet."

"I suppose you heard that Daddy passed last year," Carolyn said.

"Yes, I read the obituary. I'm sorry for your loss."

"Thank you," she said. "When you met him, you may have noticed how . . . eccentric he was."

"What do you mean?"

William jumped in. "I suppose that to be so successful, one has to be a bit obsessive, but Father took it to the extreme. It worked in real estate, but in his personal life it became a disaster."

"How so?" I asked.

"Daddy would get up every morning at four-thirty to run six miles," Carolyn said. "Not only did he have forty pairs of running shoes lined up around the walls of his bedroom, but he wrote the purchase date on the heel of each shoe so he could rotate them and make them last longer."

"That does sound a bit obsessive," I said.

"It's not just that," William said. "He was always argumentative and opinionated, and as he got older he became outright paranoid. If you didn't agree with him, then you were out to get him."

"It started escalating when Mother died five years ago," Carolyn added.

I noticed that Carolyn and William spoke like a tag team, taking turns relaying the information and nodding in agreement when the other talked. I asked, "Did your father ever see a psychiatrist?"

"Heavens no," Carolyn said. "We wanted him to come see you, but he was adamantly against it. The mere suggestion of it made him paranoid that we were trying to commit him or something."

William interrupted impatiently. "But that's not the reason we're here today. Carolyn and I are concerned about our younger brother, Henry."

"What's your concern?" I asked.

"We're concerned that Henry may have inherited Father's obsessive-paranoid disorder or whatever it's called."

I didn't know what, if any, disorder their father had, but their brief description suggested several possibilities that could be inherited. No defined "obsessive-paranoid" disorder existed, but people who are obsessive-compulsive might display paranoid symptoms at times. And there are several forms of psychosis that run in families. Some people develop an isolated paranoid delusion later in life, which the English geriatric psychiatrist Sir Martin Roth termed "late paraphrenia." It is more common in women than in men and is associated with declining vision or hearing or both. But their younger brother was probably in his late forties and too young for that condition.

"Hank was the baby of the family, and I adored him when we were little," Carolyn said. "When William was off playing sports, Hank and I would bake chocolate-chip cookies with Daddy, and Daddy would let us lick the batter from the spoon. Hank was really sweet in those days. He would sneak extra cookies in his pockets, and we would share them before bedtime."

"But then he became Father's little favorite, didn't he, Carolyn?" William prodded her. "And you didn't like that too much."

"Well, Daddy did always dote on him," she said. "Here I was the only girl, yet Hank was the creative one, so he was special."

"Never mind that Henry never spent a day using his law degree or helping in the family business," William added. "He couldn't waste his precious time doing real work. He was an artist, a photographer—I think that's part of why Father favored him."

"What do you mean?" I asked.

"Father was all business and exercise, but when he was young he had an artistic side that he stopped pursuing when it came time to take over the business. He studied classical piano in school and even gave recitals. I never heard him play, but apparently he had been quite good," William said.

Carolyn added, "I think Daddy was living vicariously through Hank's art. He built a darkroom for him when Hank was in high school and always supported his artistic pursuits."

"But that's all in the past, Carolyn," William said. "Father's gone now and we haven't set eyes on Hank for over a year."

"Why's that?" I asked, intrigued.

"Because Henry is holed up in a secluded ski chalet in Colorado," William answered. "He never leaves, and he didn't even show up for Father's funeral or the reading of the will. Sometimes he'll take our phone calls, but whenever we invite him to visit or ask to come up there, he insists that he's fine and doesn't want to be disturbed."

"What difference does it make, William?" Carolyn asked. "He probably already knew Daddy was going to make him sole executor of the estate."

"Oh? Your father made him the executor?" I asked.

William turned to me. "Look, we're not here about the money. Carolyn and I are genuinely concerned about our brother's mental health. We know there is a family history of obsession, paranoia, and whatever else, and we want to help him—even if it means he has to be committed."

That would be convenient, I thought. If the sole executor of their estate was in a mental hospital, financial control would revert to them. This plot was thickening like an old Hitchcock movie, and I half expected Janet Leigh to stumble into my office with a knife sticking out of her back.

"So you're not concerned about the money, only your brother's health. What makes you think Hank is paranoid?"

"He's had a suspicious streak all his life," Carolyn said. "He was always Mr. Perfect, and anytime something went wrong, it had to be the other guy's fault. While he was at Dartmouth, he thought the dean had a personal vendetta against him. He went on and on about it for months and eventually ended up in the emergency room. It turned out he'd been high on cocaine for who knows how long. After rehab, he got back to his old self—suspicious but not insane."

"For a while," William added, "after Mother died, Henry cut himself off from the family and moved to the Colorado house. He stayed in touch with Father. But now that he's gone, Henry has no one, and we're concerned."

At the mention of the cocaine-induced paranoid break, my differential-diagnostic wheels started spinning. Chronic amphetamine or cocaine abuse is a well-known cause of paranoia. It was possible that Hank's reclusiveness meant that he was back on drugs. Perhaps his mother's death triggered an initial relapse and then the loss of his father became too much for him to bear without self-medicating. However, someone with a predisposition to paranoia could start believing others were against him as a result of any stressful event or situation. Although drug abuse in college increases one's risk for substance abuse later in life, it was not necessarily the current problem now that he was middle aged.

Carolyn and William had not completely convinced me that they wanted to help their brother rather than just gain control of the money. Having consulted with attorneys on forensic cases over the years, I was impressed by how powerful money could be at suddenly causing, as well as curing, alleged psychiatric illnesses. Maybe Henry was appropriately suspicious of his siblings' motives, rather than paranoid or psychotic.

"So how do you envision me helping?" I asked.

"We want you to diagnose him and get him started on the right treatment, if there is one." Carolyn paused and appeared sad. "Look, I know I've had my differences with Hank over the years, but he's my baby brother and I love him. I'd like to be part of his life."

"We understand you'll need to examine him in person, but he's certainly not going to come down here for a consultation," William said. "You'll need to go to him. We have a jet."

"I'm willing to go there, but if Henry has refused *your* visits, why would he agree to see me?" I asked.

"We anticipated that issue and used a tough-love approach with him," William said. "We got him on the phone and said that if he didn't agree to see you, we would have to take more drastic measures."

"He knew we were threatening an intervention or legal action," Carolyn added.

"How did he respond?" I asked.

"Actually, he was quite agreeable, as long you came to him," Carolyn said. "He even sounded a bit relieved."

Two days later, I was packing my overnight bag for Colorado. As I hurried to get my things together, Gigi stomped around the bedroom putting away laundry. Could she be upset about my Colorado trip? I mean, here I was waiting for a limo to pick me up and take me to the Dunlops' ski resort in their private jet, while she got to look forward to chores and carpooling.

"I just want you to know that it's not fair if you do any skiing without me," she finally blurted. Yep, she was pissed.

"Honey, you know I haven't skied since I sprained my ankle in Vail."

"Oh, yeah," she said with a laugh. "You were going to loosen up in the gym before we hit the slopes, and two minutes later you limped back into the room after tripping on a stair."

"Hey, skip the details. Everyone thinks I wiped out on a black-diamond run."

An hour later I entered the Dunlop jet. A gorgeous flight attendant greeted me and took my coat, "Welcome, Dr. Small. Please, make yourself comfortable. I'll be at your disposal."

As I sat in what appeared to be a small flying living room, I had no problem getting comfortable. We took off and gained altitude quickly. The jet was smooth and silent. The flight attendant brought in a bowl of fruit and a cheese platter and offered me a cocktail. I declined and requested a soda. Now, this was flying—a guy could get spoiled.

As I enjoyed the view, my thoughts drifted to Henry Dunlop. I wondered what I would find when I met him. Would he be a drug-addled opium junkie, or perhaps a hyperactive amphetamine addict? Maybe he was suffering from extreme obsessive-compulsive disorder, constantly washing his hands like another wealthy and disturbed recluse, Howard Hughes. He could also be in a psychotic and paranoid state, and I experienced a moment of anxiety imagining myself entering a secluded fortress of some rich and possibly dangerous loner. But I knew I wouldn't be alone there—his staff included a cook, maid, driver, personal assistant, and bodyguards. I also wasn't convinced that he was psychotic. A classic paranoid would not have been so willing to see me. Somebody in the Dunlop family didn't have the facts straight, and I suspected it might be Carolyn and William.

When we landed, I was chauffeured in a town car, finally driving up a long, winding private road that ended at a large compound. The main building was an elegant marriage of Swiss chalet and modern architecture that I guessed must have been about ten thousand square feet. A half dozen luxury cars were parked in front on a large concrete-and-brick driveway recently cleared of snow.

The driver parked and opened the trunk to get my bag. I rang the bell, and Henry's personal assistant, Ahmed, opened one of the huge, wooden, double-front doors and asked me to follow him as he took my bag from the driver. From the entry foyer, I noticed several stunning black-and-white photographs of what appeared to be the Colorado Rockies. I also got a glimpse of the impressive sprawling interior of the house with its exposed beams, spiral staircase, freestanding fireplaces, and floor-to-ceiling windows framing beautiful views of the mountains.

I followed Ahmed down a long hallway to meet Mr. Henry, as he called him. The hallway was lined with more framed photography, and as we headed toward the back of the house, I noticed that the images changed from lakes and snowcapped mountains to the compound grounds and landscaping and finally to interior shots of the house.

At the end of the hallway Ahmed knocked and then opened the door to an expansive bedroom suite. The sitting area was cluttered with books, magazines, cameras, and photographs. Henry was reading in an easy chair by the far window. He appeared tall and thin, with curly brown hair. He wore wire-rimmed glasses and had a stilted intellectual air about him. He looked up and smiled, "Dr. Small, how was your trip?"

"Fine, thank you."

"Excellent," he said. "Ahmed, please bring us some coffee and water." Henry put his book down and pointed to another overstuffed chair. "Have a seat."

"Thanks," I said, sizing him up. So far, he didn't seem like a crazed, maniacal, paranoid psychotic.

"From what my siblings said about me, you're probably surprised that I agreed to your visit," Henry said.

"They were concerned about how you're doing—they haven't seen you for some time," I said.

"Yes, I'm sure they expressed their deepest concern—speaking in tandem as usual. They've seen eye to eye for years and haven't allowed me into their little club," he said bitterly.

"I'd like to hear more about that," I said as Ahmed came in with the coffee and water.

"Thank you, Ahmed," Henry said. Ahmed left the room and closed the doors quietly behind him.

"My sister and I used to be close when we were little," Henry said. "We had great fun playing games like hide-and-seek, or baking with Father. We made these incredible chocolate-chip cookies. I'll never forget them. But something changed as we got older. Carolyn and William started ganging up on me, and I guess things have stayed that way ever since."

"You must have felt pushed out," I said.

"Yes, I felt excluded, alone," Henry said. "But I suppose it's typical sibling rivalry. I'm sure it happens in all families. I know Father felt sorry for me and tried to make up for it, but I think that only made them exclude me more." He sipped his coffee and added, "They're not really concerned about me, you know; they want something—most likely control of the estate. What did they tell you, that I was lazy? Or maybe they said I was crazy."

"They didn't use either of those terms," I said. "But they did want me to try and figure out what was going on with you, to see if I could help."

"Well, there's definitely something going on with me, but I don't think they have the slightest idea about it." He poured both of us a glass of water and said, "And I certainly hope you can help me. That's why I agreed to see you."

I finished off my coffee. "Tell me what's wrong."

"It's simple," Henry replied. "I can't leave this house."

The phone rang and it was Carolyn. As Henry spoke with her, I noticed the spectacular view outside. I watched an eagle circling a large pine tree, apparently homing in on potential prey scurrying about in the snow. As I listened to Henry, I anticipated the eagle making a dive.

"Yes . . . he's here now . . . He just arrived . . . Fine, I'll put him on the speaker."

"Hello, Dr. Small, it's Carolyn."

"Hello, Carolyn," I said.

"I just wanted to make sure you got there all right."

"Everything's fine," I said toward the speaker. "We're just getting to know each other."

"Look, Hank," she said. "I know you must be wondering why we asked Dr. Small to come up there. It's because we love you and we want to be sure you're okay."

Hank smirked, not buying a word of it. "Thank you, Carolyn."

"Dr. Small, could you pick up, please?" Carolyn asked.

Hank motioned and said, "Go right ahead." He went back to his book. Not the kind of response you'd expect from a paranoid psychotic.

"Yes, Carolyn?" I asked.

"I'm relieved that it sounds civil there," she said. "But how bad is he really?"

"Carolyn, I just got here. The trip was very comfortable, and we're getting along fine. Thank you for checking in."

"All right, I get it, you can't talk right now. I'll go. I don't want to make him any more paranoid than he already is. Call my cell if you need anything."

I hung up and thought about her contribution to the family dynamic. It struck me that it was much more convenient for William and Carolyn to focus on Henry's mental issues than their own. At the moment, Carolyn seemed more paranoid than Henry.

Henry put down his book and looked up at me. "Now, where were we?"

"You mentioned you can't leave this house," I said.

"Right. Every time I try to step out the door, my heart starts racing and I can't catch my breath." He paused. "I feel like I'm going to die, and I'm overwhelmed with terror. In fact, it's gotten so bad, I can't even go into the entry hall without hyperventilating."

"When did all this start?"

"About a year ago. I was in a camera store in town, and suddenly my heart started pounding. I had to sit down so I wouldn't pass out. After about five minutes I was fine. But when I went back to that store the next day, it happened again. After the second attack, I could never go back in there."

"When did it happen next, Henry?"

"Please, call me Hank," he said. "I'm not exactly sure when it happened next, but I remember starting to feel panicked in other places. Restaurants, the bank . . . the attacks seemed random. My doctor checked me out and couldn't find anything wrong with me, so he suggested I get some rest. After a couple of weeks of taking it easy at home, I asked Ahmed to drive me to the bank. But once we left the grounds, my heart started racing so badly that we had to turn around. I haven't been able to leave the property since. I've tried many times to get out, but I know I can't leave the house without having an attack."

Hank's diagnosis was no mystery. He was describing a classic case of spontaneous panic attacks with secondary agoraphobia. These patients initially experience physical and emotional symptoms of panic that seem to come from nowhere and end abruptly. Sometimes there's a physical condition that triggers the attacks, such as a heart flutter from mitral-valve prolapse. Other times the patient has a genetic predisposition for panic.

What Hank described was a typical scenario for a patient with spontaneous panic attacks. He associated the location of the initial attack as its cause, so he avoided that location and other places where attacks occurred. This learned response developed into a phobia about these places, and over time his movements became more and more restricted. Eventually, for patients like Hank, if full-blown agoraphobia develops, they become housebound. I reflected on how Hank's photography display in the hallway gradually transitioned from expansive outdoor scenery to more restricted indoor close-ups, reflecting the progression of his phobias.

Despite their dramatic and debilitating consequences, panic disorder and agoraphobia respond well to treatment, usually to a combination of antidepressants and desensitization psychotherapy. The medication eliminates the panic attacks, and the therapy helps the patient gradually overcome his fears of the outside world.

I spent several hours with Hank that afternoon learning more about his condition and background, before he became too tired to continue. We planned to resume over breakfast the next day, and Ahmed drove me to my hotel.

I entered my luxurious suite at the lodge and saw that a wood fire was already burning. I unpacked, took a shower, and called room service to order dinner and a glass of wine. Settling back on the four-poster bed, I called Gigi to gloat.

"You've been skiing. I can tell from your voice," she said, half joking but with an accusatory tone.

"That's absurd. How can you tell that from my voice?" I asked, feeling guilty for no reason and deciding not to mention the fireplace.

"Because you're tired. You get tired when you ski," she said. "And do you have a fireplace in your room?"

"No, no, that crackling is just a bad connection." She was silent. "Okay, I have a fireplace. And the room is incredible, but you should see my patient's compound! And that private jet! Oh my God!"

"All right, I get it," she said. "I miss you and the kids miss you. When are you coming home?"

"Hopefully, tomorrow evening." I paused, then said, "I have to tell you, honey, all the money in the world can't buy happiness or love."

"Are you okay?"

"I'm fine," I answered. "But it's sad that this incredibly wealthy family is so distracted by their money that it splits them apart and they can't get close. They talk about caring for one another, but they let years go by without seeing one another."

"Do you think you can help them?" Gigi asked.

"I'm going to try. I think the younger brother will get better once he's in treatment. Whether I can help him have a real relationship with his siblings, I don't know."

IN THE MORNING, THE BREAKFAST ROOM AT Hank's estate was sunny and overlooked a ski run below. The meal was a healthy mix of egg-white omelets, fruit salad, and oatmeal.

"You know, the view is spectacular from here," I said as I realized Hank always sat facing away from the windows.

He smiled. "I used to appreciate it more, but since my attacks began, I can't stare out the window too long or my heart starts speeding up."

"This condition has really restricted your life," I said.

He seemed sad. "You know, I've felt alone so much of my life, and now that I want to get close to other people, I'm stuck in this house. Frankly, I'm ashamed of my situation."

"Is that why you haven't told your family about your symptoms?" I asked.

"I suppose so. It's humiliating. I'm a grown man terrified of stepping out my own front door . . . or even looking out the window, for God's sake. If I were stronger, I'd be able to overcome these feelings."

It has always amazed me that people feel such a stigma about their psychiatric conditions. Most people wouldn't feel embarrassed if they had a broken leg and needed help. Despite the remarkable advances in psychiatric diagnosis and treatment, many still believe that mental illness is a sign of personal weakness and something to be embarrassed about.

The effects of these attitudes can be devastating. Patients feel self-doubt and shame, so they isolate themselves. Many who would likely respond to treatment pretend that nothing is wrong and refuse help. They are often rejected by family and friends and discriminated against at work. Health insurance companies have even bought into these biases and routinely provide lower reimbursements for mental conditions compared with physical ones. Advocacy groups such as the National Alliance on Mental Illness (NAMI) have made efforts to correct these stereotypes, but there is still a long way to go. Hank's shame about his condition kept him from getting the help he needed.

"Hank, you're not alone in those feelings," I said. "But having a psychiatric illness doesn't mean that you're weak-willed. Conditions like yours, like any medical illness, have a significant physical component. And as you said, a part of you believes I might be able to help you."

"Do you think you can, Dr. Small?" he asked.

"Yes. In fact, I know I can. You have a classic case of spontaneous panic attacks. And as you've described, they come out of nowhere and go away quickly. We can easily diminish or even cure the attacks with an antidepressant like Zoloft or Prozac."

"But what about my fear of leaving the house?" he asked.

"That can be treated too, but differently," I said. "What's happened is that whenever you anticipate being in a place where you've had a panic attack, you avoid it. And you've developed agoraphobia, a fear of leaving your house, which is common in people with panic attacks. We'll get you started on a desensitization program and gradually teach you to remain calm in normal situations."

"I get the medication part," he said. "But I'm not so clear on this desensitizing thing."

"The way it works is you'll literally make a list of places and situations that you currently fear, then rank them according to the degree of anxiety you experience with each, say, on a scale of one to ten."

"So, if walking into my own foyer rates a five, then going to a restaurant would be off the scale, right?" Hank asked.

"Exactly," I said. "You'll learn relaxation exercises, and you'll gradually be exposed to the least anxiety-provoking situations first. As you get comfortable with those, you'll eventually work your way down the list to the scarier stuff. You'll probably start feeling better the first week you take the medication, and soon you'll be able to overcome the phobias."

"So it's psychotherapy with training wheels. Are you going to be able to stay here for this?" he asked.

"I can get you started," I replied. "But I know of several qualified therapists close by who have a great track record with this type of therapy."

"It's definitely worth a try," he said. "I can't keep going on like this. It's no way to live."

"What may be more challenging," I said, "is repairing your relationship with your brother and sister."

"Look," he said flatly, "I have no relationship with them. I mean, it's complicated. I was very close with our father—he used to love it up here and visited all the time. Even when we were little he paid more attention to me. Maybe that's why my sister and I drifted apart."

"All families are complicated," I said. "You said you didn't want your siblings to visit because you were embarrassed about your condition. Maybe they felt snubbed by you."

"How's that possible? They've been snubbing me for years," he said.

"That may be, but you are the one refusing to see them now," I said. "You and your father were very close. Carolyn and William may have envied that connection."

"I guess you have a point," he said.

"In addition to inheriting your father's artistic talent, you may have also inherited a tendency for panic attacks from him."

Many forms of mental illness are known to run in families. Whether it's schizophrenia, panic disorder, or major depression, complex genetic components have been discovered. Usually more than one gene is involved, and environmental triggers come into play as well. Sometimes a relative inherits only a tendency to develop the illness, which might or might not be expressed, depending on life circumstances.

Identifying a genetic contribution to a psychiatric illness can be tricky, since family members with the disease gene might not develop the illness until later in life. One of the earliest psychiatric genetic studies involved Amish families with manic-depressive illness. The Amish were considered an ideal group for genetic research, since they separated themselves culturally from the general population, making it easier to pinpoint inheritance and factor out other influences. There was tremendous excitement when the genetics were first reported, but the results fell apart years later when several of the supposedly unaffected teens experienced manic episodes.

Of the various forms of anxiety, panic disorder has undergone the most genetic investigation. The condition clearly runs in families, and twin studies have confirmed that it can be inherited. I suspected that Hank had inherited his panic disorder from his father and that perhaps his father's eccentricities were a related form of anxiety.

"I inherited my father's traits?" Hank laughed. "That's a good one."

"What do you mean?" I asked, confused.

"I was adopted, Dr. Small. My brother and sister don't know because my father didn't want them trying to push me out of my inheritance."

I laughed. "You definitely know how to keep a secret. But there isn't any controversy over the estate now, so why not tell them?"

Hank smiled. "I suppose it's childish of me to withhold the truth, but Father didn't want to tell, and I guess I do get some pleasure from their envy of how close Father and I were. And the fact that they believe I've inherited his talent and even his weaknesses probably gets their goats too."

"But keeping this secret also serves to keep you apart," I said.

"I hadn't considered that," he said.

After breakfast, Hank's internist came by the house with a copy of his medical records for me to review. I discussed my findings with him, and he performed an electrocardiogram before starting Hank on Zoloft that afternoon. I reached one of the behavior therapists I knew in the area, and he agreed to come up to see Hank the next day to begin desensitization therapy. The rest of the afternoon I helped Hank begin his list of anxiety-provoking situations, as well as determine their rankings.

At that point I considered heading home but felt we had made so much headway, that perhaps one more day would really make a difference. Also, I could meet with the new local psychiatrist and fill him in. Hank understood that his panic disorder was very much a medical as well as a psychiatric condition, and I hoped that some of the stigma he felt around it had lifted. He seemed optimistic about the treatment plan, and the timing might have been right to try to repair the family rift.

"Hank, how would you feel about Carolyn and William visiting you up here?" I asked.

"Well, I'm just starting my treatment," he said. "Do you think it's a good idea so soon?"

"You seem to understand that there's nothing about your symptoms to be embarrassed about. It's really a medical condition—your body is low in the chemical transmitter serotonin, and Zoloft replenishes that serotonin in your brain so you won't feel so panicked."

"That's true," he said.

"I think now might be a good time to have them come up and break the ice, especially while I'm still here."

He thought for a moment, and then said, "Okay. I'll give it a try."

THAT EVENING BACK AT THE LODGE, I called Gigi to let her know I'd be staying another night. The phone wasn't answered immediately, so I thought I would just be able to leave a message. I suppose I felt a little guilty because I was beginning to think about getting in a quick hour or two of skiing while I was up there.

Just as I thought the voice mail would pick up, Gigi answered. "Hello?"

"Hi, honey, how are you?" I asked.

"Good. I got a lot of work done today," she said. "The kids and I are negotiating bedtimes. I thought you were coming home."

"I have to stay another night, babe. I'm really sorry," I said.

"That's okay, I've got to work tonight anyway," she said. "But listen, I'm on a deadline, and I won't have time to get to the market tomorrow. Do you think you could stop for some milk on your way home from the airport?"

"No problem," I said, imagining myself getting off the Dunlop private jet and asking my chauffeur to stop at the 7-Eleven and wait while I ran in.

It was another perfect morning up at Hank's compound, and we were finishing breakfast when Ahmed announced that Miss Carolyn had arrived without Mr. William. I was getting so used to hanging out with Hank, I almost blurted out, "Thank you, Ahmed, that will be all." Instead, Hank replied, "Please send her back here, Ahmed. Maybe she'd like some breakfast."

"I wonder what happened to William," I said.

"He left a message that he couldn't pull away from some important meeting," Hank said.

We could hear Carolyn walking down the hall. "Henry? Hank?" she called out from the hallway. "Are you back here?" She paused at the doorway. She looked anxious, worried about what she might find.

Hank got up to go meet her. "Carolyn, you look terrific."

"So do you," she said. Hank wrapped his arms around her and they hugged. I could see tears of relief in her eyes.

"Come sit down and have some breakfast," he said.

As she put her bags down, she noticed me for the first time, "Dr. Small, I don't know what you did, but thanks so much for getting Hank to let me come up here."

"It was his decision," I said.

Hank passed Carolyn the bread basket and said, "I'm glad you're here. I want to talk to you about things, things I should have told you years ago."

She smiled. "Me too." She reached for her purse and pulled out a bag filled with freshly baked chocolate-chip cookies. "We can share these while we talk."

He took a cookie and his voice cracked. "I haven't had one of these since I was a kid." As he bit into it, he looked happier than I'd seen him yet.

I got the feeling that they wanted to talk alone, so I excused myself and made a few phone calls in the other room. As the day went on, Carolyn and Hank talked, laughed, and cried a lot. The local behavioral psychiatrist arrived, and I briefed him on my findings and the progress we had made. I wanted to get back to Los Angeles in time for dinner with my family, so I told them I would be heading home. They thanked me, and Hank said the jet was fueled and waiting.

As I flew back to Los Angeles that afternoon, I thought about the Dunlops and their complex family dynamic. William might have been the one to pull Carolyn away from Hank when they were young, and to have kept stirring up the rivalry with an undercurrent of greed as they got older and more distant from their father. But they were adults now, and it appeared that at least Hank and Carolyn wanted to act like it.

Growing up in my own family of three kids, we had sibling rivalry too. It seemed we were always bickering about something. Usually it was two against one. The teams would change from hour to hour, but my older sister always remained on the winning team. I thought of my own two kids when they were younger and would fight over who got to sit closest to Daddy on the couch. It's almost as if bickering over a parent's attention, the last French fry, or the front seat was hardwired.

I felt encouraged that at least Hank was on his way to recovering from his agoraphobia. Perhaps with Carolyn's support he would be able to leave Colorado for a while.

I walked into my house at seven and put my things down in the entry hall. Our Labradoodle came charging at me as I heard Gigi yelling out to the kids, "Come on, guys. Wash your hands. Daddy's home and it's time for dinner." She pushed our giant dog aside and gave me a kiss. "I'm glad you're back, sweetie. And you know I was just kidding—you could have skied."

"I know," I said. "But I didn't have time anyway."

"Good. I would have killed you," she said. "I hope you're in the mood for Chinese because I ordered in."

"Chinese sounds fantastic. I'm starved." I followed her into the kitchen carrying a plastic bag with a half gallon of milk in it.

CHAPTER FIFTEEN

Sigmund Fraud

Summer 2008

I PULLED MY TOYOTA HYBRID SILENTLY into a space in the V.A. parking lot by the Brentwood golf course. My old mentor, Dr. Larry Klein, was standing by his car waiting for me. It was a hot July morning in Los Angeles, and the temperature had already reached ninety degrees. Larry, a tanned sun worshipper, was sweating in the sun, rather than taking two steps to the left and sitting on a bench in the shade.

I hadn't seen him for some time. He was wearing his oversize glasses and signature bow tie, and despite losing more of his gray hair, he still looked spry at seventy-one. He glanced right and left—I guessed it was to make sure I hadn't been followed. I wondered if age had worsened his paranoid tendencies, or maybe I'd just forgotten how wacky he was.

"Thanks for meeting me here, pal," he said and gave me a hug.

"No problem, Larry," I said. "What's up?"

"Let's walk," he said as he took off at a good clip, but not quite as fast as in the old days. "I've got a problem, and I can't talk to anybody else about it."

"I'm your man, Larry. What's going on?"

"No, Gary, I mean *talk* . . . on a regular basis."

"Hey, Larry, we're friends. We can talk every day if you want." He stopped and turned to me. "You don't get me. I'm dealing with something right now and it's making me a little meshuga. I need therapy, Gary. And I want you to be my therapist."

I was thrown. Here was the best mentor I'd ever had in my career, and he was coming to me for psychotherapy? What could I possibly tell him that he didn't already know? The man was a genius whom I had kept on a pedestal for twenty-five years. "I can't be your therapist, Larry. I'm your friend, your student."

"Bullshit. You're the only person in this city who I trust, so you're the only one for the job. You have to do it, period. End of story."

I was sweating—not so much from the heat but from the idea of hearing Larry Klein's innermost secrets. "I'm touched, really, that you trust me. And I'd be happy to talk about any issue that's eating at you. But you know that you can't really be in psychotherapy with someone you have a personal relationship with."

"That's a crock—just because Freud said so? Who gives a shit? You've been brainwashed by those psychoanalysts, and I know it, because I am one."

The written and unwritten rule about psychotherapy for as long as anyone could remember was that therapists had to maintain a professional, not personal, relationship with their patients. In social friendships there is a give and take, where both people share opinions, advise, and help each other. A psychotherapeutic relationship is one-sided: the therapist is designated to help the patient only. If the patient knew personal details of the therapist's life, it could interfere with the therapy's natural development of transference and countertransference, and working through those distortions is key to helping the patient heal.

"But Larry, you know me," I said. "You know my weaknesses, my struggles, and I've looked up to you for years. How could there be any meaningful transference?"

Larry stopped and wiped his brow. "Therapy is not all about this transference crap. A lot of good can come from talking with someone you trust, who understands you."

I was about to continue my protests, but he went on. "I don't want to discuss it anymore, Gary. It's a done deal. Think of it this way: you and I are going to have a regular get-together three times a week—we can get coffee, walk the golf course, whatever."

I caved. "Fine. But I'm not taking any money," I said adamantly.

"So what. I'll be making monthly donations to your Center on Aging, and there's nothing you can do about it," he said, grinning.

The next day was Saturday, and I slept in. Stumbling into the kitchen at about nine-thirty, I could hear the kids outside in the backyard already. It was nice to have them around. Now that Rachel was driving and Harry had gotten serious about his skateboarding, they didn't seem to be home much.

Gigi was sitting outside on the patio with her laptop, probably working on her blog for *Psychology Today*. Her editor, who obviously had a sense of humor, called it "The Simple Life." I poured a cup of coffee, grabbed the *New York Times,* and joined her outside in the shade.

"Good morning, baby. Nice day," I said.

"Hi, honey. Ooh, is there still coffee? Give me a sip," she said.

Rachel called out from her lounge chair in the sun. "Dad, come here and help me with this crossword puzzle."

"Can't, honey—too sunburned. Besides, the *L.A. Times* Saturday puzzle is too easy for me. You know that."

"That's funny stuff, Dad," Harry said while wrestling the dog on the lawn. "Maybe you should go on Conan."

"How did you get that sunburn?" Gigi asked.

"It's a long story."

"Well?"

"I'll tell you," I said. "But you can't put it in your blog."

"Oh," she said, smiling. "Like anybody would actually be interested in reading about you." She stopped typing and looked at me. "No, really, what happened?"

"I had a chat with one of my old mentors out on the golf course, and I forgot to wear sunscreen."

"That's a long story?" she asked.

I knew that even without naming names, Gigi would know who I was talking about. I flashed to a recent conference of psychiatric leaders, where many admitted that on occasion, they confided in their wives about their patients. I wanted to get some perspective and I trusted Gigi, so I said, "Look, I'm not going to mention any names."

"Of course not," Gigi replied.

"But of all the teachers I've had in my life, he stands alone. He's a brilliant psychopharmacologist, and he's probably published at least five hundred research articles. He's also an amazing psychoanalyst. He seems to really understand what makes people tick—even the very sick ones. I'm telling you, he's been more than just a teacher and a friend—he's like a father figure."

"What's the story?" she asked.

"He's having some kind of life crisis and wants me to be his 'therapeutic friend,'" I said.

"That's flattering," she said. "Your mentor came to *you* for therapy."

"Yeah, but it's awkward. I mean, I know him and he knows me. How can I be objective?"

"You do it all the time with me and other people. I know I used to give you a hard time for playing therapist when we were younger and you would hide behind that 'how does that make you feel' crap, but now you're pretty good at friend therapy."

She was probably right. When you do something on a daily basis for years, it becomes second nature, part of your personality. "But this guy is someone I've emulated and gone to with my own problems, at least at work. What if I feel weird listening to his private . . . stuff?"

"That's what you do, Gary. I mean, if you were a plumber, and an old friend had a pipe burst, you'd go right over and help him out. That's what friends do. How many times have we called Rob when we needed legal advice or gone to your brother-in-law when the kids needed a dentist?" Gigi went back to her blog.

As I went back into the house to get more coffee, I thought about Gigi's points. Hearing her say out loud what I had been thinking all along reassured me that I might be able to help Larry. I decided to keep some sunscreen and a hat in my car.

After the weekend, Larry and I set up our first regular meeting, but I wasn't allowed to know where it would be. He insisted on letting me know the location at the last minute. I got a message Wednesday morning that he'd be coming to my office. I was surprised that he was comfortable there. Maybe it was because it was the only suite on the top floor of the institute, and he felt that no one would be listening in.

Just before Larry's appointment, I was cleaning up my e-mail in-box, which had become an unending chore in my life. Larry walked in carrying something wrapped in tinfoil. He placed it on my desk and said, "Louise baked this pound cake. It's fantastic. Have some."

When Larry said "Have some," he wasn't kidding. He was like a Jewish mother—you'd better eat it or else. I walked to the cupboard and pulled out some paper plates and napkins.

"Got coffee?" Larry asked.

He knew I always did—that was just his way of saying "Get me a cup." He sat down on the couch while I poured our coffee and brought over the cake. I sat in my chair and asked, "So what's happening, Larry?"

"Well, we both know that I have a suspicious nature," he said.

I thought it was charming how Larry understated things. "I suppose that's true."

"Well, I've gone beyond suspicious now," he said. "I think I might be getting paranoid, but I'm not sure."

"What do you mean?" I asked while stuffing my face with pound cake that really was delicious.

"I think somebody is out to get me, and all my instincts tell me I'm right."

"Larry, I'm not sure why you'd hesitate to follow your instincts. You've always told me to look at the big picture," I said. "By nature, you are incredibly insightful. If you think somebody is out to get you, you may be right. Have you considered that?"

"Of course. But here's why I'm concerned—I've got symptoms. I never used to wake up in the middle of the night and ruminate. I've always slept like a baby no matter what was going on. The queen of England could be downstairs and I'd let Louise entertain her if it was past my bedtime. Now I have trouble sleeping and I'm distracted at work."

"What's distracting you?"

"I'm convinced that a certain someone is trying to set me up and push me out of the psychiatry department."

"Who could do that, Larry? Who has the position or the power?"

"Trust me, it could be done," Larry snapped. "You have no idea how vulnerable we are. One sexual-harassment comment from a former patient or a disgruntled secretary, and your career is over. Or are we supposed to call secretaries assistants now? I can't keep it straight."

"Who is this person you think is trying to get you?" I asked.

"Anthony Wilson, the little bastard," Larry said. "And I helped him get his endowed chair."

I wasn't surprised. Tony Wilson had gone to Princeton, got his medical degree at Columbia, and always thought he was above us mere mortals whose résumés were tainted by an occasional public-university stint. He was manipulative and spiteful, and one of the few people who could get under my skin.

"Look," I said. "I know that Wilson has a reputation as a petty, self-serving bureaucrat, but what's he got on you?"

"Here's what's really keeping me up at night." Larry put down his coffee and lay back on the couch, hands behind his head—assuming the classic analytic position. I instinctively put down my coffee and listened intently.

"I'm under investigation for scientific fraud."

I was stunned. Larry was the consummate obsessive scientist. He was famous for triple-checking all facts. As editor of one of the major biological psychiatry journals, everyone knew that Larry personally read over every submission and always had astute and detailed notes.

"That's absurd. This has got to be some kind of academic political coup. There must be a mistake here," I said.

"Oh, there's a mistake all right," Larry said. "I fucked up."

"How?" I asked.

"The paper in question was published out of my lab, and the first author is a kid I've singled out as a rising star. He reminds me of myself forty years ago."

"So you think because you liked this kid, you let your guard down and didn't triple-check his facts like you usually do?"

"Precisely," he answered.

"Look, Larry, you're human. You're entitled to let a clerical error slip through the cracks once in a while. You've mentored hundreds of young scientists over the years. You can't expect them all to be perfect."

"Look, Gary, I know it was the kid's screwup, but it came out of my lab, so ultimately it's my responsibility."

"This is the first I've heard of this investigation," I said. "How did it get started?"

"Somebody blew a whistle. I don't know who, probably some disgruntled lab tech. And now Tony Wilson is chairing the committee looking into the charges."

"What are the charges, Larry?"

"False data. I should have seen it. The results looked too good. I don't know why I didn't look more carefully before letting him submit it."

"Why do you think you didn't?" I asked.

"That's the million-dollar question, Gary." He paused and took a deep breath. "Sure, I was impressed with this young scientist and assumed everything he did was golden, but I don't know. Maybe I'm losing it." He took a sip of coffee and continued. "I don't have to tell you how the brain ages—you're the expert. Maybe my suspiciousness is morphing into distorted judgments, where I trust the wrong people and have gotten so paranoid about others that I completely avoid them. I thought this kid could do no wrong. I must have gotten too close to him personally and overidentified with him. Thanks to Tony Wilson, that little weasel, I know now that the kid was too good to be true and he falsified his data."

"Larry, nobody's perfect. You can't catch every mistake. Just tell the committee this guy falsified his facts and you missed it. It was a simple oversight and the journal can publish a retraction. Let the blame fall where it should."

"It's not so simple," Larry snorted. "Look at David Baltimore. He had to resign as president of Rockefeller University when his student was caught faking data."

"But Baltimore stood by his student too long. That's where he got into trouble."

"I know you're right. I've got to take care of myself here." He sat up and straightened his bow tie. "We'll talk more on Friday. Maybe Louise will bake her strudel."

For the rest of the day I kept thinking about my meeting with Larry. I was challenged by the complexity of the situation—both his at the university and mine with him. I had trouble concentrating on my work. It was as if I had taken on Larry's symptoms—ruminating about the problems and even starting to wonder if I had stepped over the line and taken on a task that was doomed to fail.

That evening at home, I got on my elliptical machine for a thirty-minute workout. I usually watched CNN, but this time I just wanted quiet to think about the Larry Klein situation. I replayed our session in my mind and tried to focus on his main complaints. He was having trouble sleeping and feeling guilty over his perceived wrongdoings. As I systematically reviewed his list of complaints, I realized that Larry had several symptoms of depression.

To determine whether or not he needed an antidepressant, I used the mnemonic I learned during residency to go through the eight features of major depression: SIG E CAPS. "SIG" is an abbreviation doctors use for *prescribe;* "E" stands for *energy;* and "CAPS" stands for *capsules.* Each letter is an abbreviation for one of the symptoms: *s*—sleep decrease or increase; *i*—interest loss; *g*—guilt feelings; *e*—energy decline; *c*—concentration impairment; *a*—appetite change; *p*—psychomotor disturbance (agitation or slowed movements); and *s*—suicidal thinking. Patients with three or more of these symptoms generally respond well to antidepressants. Larry had enough of them to warrant a trial of medication. This realization made me feel better because there was something concrete I could do to help him.

Being depressed could explain Larry's escalating paranoia. But maybe he had reason to be paranoid. Larry's instincts about people were usually right, and Tony Wilson did have a reputation for being devious and back-stabbing. If I could find out more about the committee's investigation, it would help—but I knew it was off-limits. At the university, there were lots of committees that deliberated in secret, and this was sure to be one of them.

I'd become so lost in my thoughts, I'd been on the elliptical for more than an hour and was sweating up a storm. Gigi came up the stairs and said, "Are you trying to kill that thing?"

I slowed down and stopped. "I guess I was just going for the endorphin high."

"Well, when you're done with that party, why don't you take a quick shower and come hang out with us."

ON FRIDAY MORNING I WAS WAITING FOR Larry in my office, ready to discuss antidepressants, when he barged in carrying a couple of Starbucks lattes and Louise's strudel. "Grab a seat, Larry," I said. "I'll get some napkins."

"Oh, no. We're not meeting in here today. Let's get some fresh air out on the patio."

"Okay," I said, wondering if he thought they'd bugged my office before he got there.

Outside my suite of offices, there was a large deck with round tables, chairs, and umbrellas, and an incredible view of the Pacific Ocean. I sat in the shade, while Larry took a chair in the direct sunlight and put on his giant sunglasses.

"Larry, I've been thinking about our discussion on Wednesday, and it sounds like you may have symptoms of depression."

"No shit, Sherlock," he said. "You've got to try this strudel. It's amazing I don't weigh five hundred pounds."

"Thanks," I said. "Have you thought about taking some Zoloft or Prozac?"

He laughed. "I'm way ahead of you, Gary. After our meeting I started myself on forty milligrams of Cymbalta. I thought the combination of a serotonergic and noradrenergic boost would lift my mood and possibly quiet down my obsessive thinking."

His choice made sense. As opposed to Zoloft or Prozac, which only elevated serotonin to improve mood, Cymbalta also tweaked noradrenalin to diminish obsessive-compulsive symptoms. Not surprisingly, Larry was right on top of the psychopharmacology. I was concerned that he was self-prescribing, but I would fight that battle another time.

"Look, Gary, I told you about the investigation and some of my symptoms the other day, but I didn't get to what's really bothering me."

I couldn't imagine what new bombshell he had to drop today. I hesitated and then asked timidly, "What is it, Larry?"

He finished his strudel and leaned back in his chair before answering. "I feel like a fraud. I always have."

"What do you mean?" I asked.

"As long as I can remember, I've been faking it. I'm not the genius everybody thinks I am. I just act like one."

I couldn't believe it. "Are you saying that throughout your career you've been faking data?"

"Of course not, you imbecile. I may be a fraud, but I have ethics. I'm scrupulous about my data. What I mean is that all I do is take information that's already out there and regurgitate it in different ways."

"So you're saying you put together available scientific discoveries in a fresh way that no one else has thought of before?" I asked.

"I guess you could say that," he said.

"Isn't that the very definition of genius? It's the basic scientific method—you take observations, spin a hypothesis, and test it. Anything that's new and makes the world a better place is at the core of creativity."

"Spare me, Gary. Don't try to make me feel better with a lame philosophical argument about creativity and genius. I've been faking this smart-aleck persona since grade school, and I have it down. Sure, I've got a high IQ—it was 183 when they tested me in the army. But most success-ful con men are also highly intelligent when you test them."

"Larry, you can't con the most brilliant academics in the world for fifty years and get away with it."

"Obviously, you can," he said, "because I've done it. And *that* is my genius. I'm a genius at being a fraud. And I can thank Tony Wilson and his silly investigation for making me realize the truth. And you know, I just don't want to go on playing this game anymore."

"Larry, I think it's your depression talking right now. You're not see-ing things clearly. You know as a psychoanalyst and as a psychopharma-cologist that when your brain biochemistry is off, you tend to see only the negative and your thinking is distorted. Let's give the Cymbalta some time to do its work."

"Cymbalta or no Cymbalta," he said. "I've felt this way since before you were born."

I flashed back to my early days in residency and how I too felt like a fraud when my patients so much as called me *Doctor.* I had to consciously play the part of a psychiatrist even though it felt awkward and unnatural, but eventually those feelings subsided, and with experience I became the doctor I was. Sure, feelings of inadequacy came back from time to time, especially when I ventured into unfamiliar areas of research or practice. I figured everyone must feel that way sometimes. But Larry was talking about his entire career.

"Larry, I've felt like a fraud at times. It's a universal feeling. I think this investigation has made you depressed and now you're seeing every-thing through dark glasses."

Larry took off his sunglasses and smiled. "You've got a point, and I'm already feeling a little better with the meds. But I can tell you, this fraud feeling is not going away."

"You said you weren't going to play this game anymore. What did you mean by that?" I asked, concerned that he might be expressing indi-rect suicidal thoughts.

"Don't worry, I'm way too narcissistic to off myself," he said. "I just might want to scale down some of this academic bullshit pretty soon.

Everyone needs an exit strategy, right? It doesn't mean I'm going to jump off a building or something."

I suddenly looked around the railing of the eighth-floor patio to make sure there were no openings for a would-be jumper to squeeze through. "Oh shit!" Larry suddenly exclaimed. "I completely forgot about a division meeting half an hour ago. Keep the strudel. I've gotta go."

He ran toward the door and the elevators, looking panicked. I'd never known him to get flustered like that or miss a meeting. This investigation had really gotten to him.

Later that afternoon, Larry's assistant called to cancel our Monday meeting because he had a scheduling conflict and would be out of the office that day. This seemed out of character as well, since Larry usually knew his schedule weeks ahead and would have canceled with me far in advance. I wondered if there was more to it. Perhaps Larry was purposely avoiding Monday afternoon's quarterly departmental meeting, already trying to slip out of the academic game.

Departmental faculty meetings of this size were held in the institute's auditorium, and many of us arrived early to mingle in the foyer near the coffee and cookies. I chose my regular cookie—white-chocolate chip— and figured I'd make it up on the elliptical that evening.

Somebody stepped up beside me and said, "Excellent choice of cookie, Dr. Small." That haughty, slightly sarcastic voice felt like fingernails scratching a chalkboard.

"Thank you, Professor Wilson," I said without looking up. "And what fine snack are you opting for this afternoon?" I asked Larry's nemesis.

"Just coffee for me. I'm watching my girlish figure." His tone changed and he leaned in a bit, "Seriously, Gary, if you have a moment, I want to speak with you briefly about a colleague I'm concerned about."

Like most academic psychiatrists, Tony Wilson was complicated. Although he was easy to dislike with his arrogant style, there were moments when he seemed to have a heart and actually care about people. At times I wondered if he might have Asperger's syndrome, a mild form of autism characterized by difficulty reading the normal but subtle cues of a social interaction. It often seemed like he was working very hard at playing the part of a normal person.

"Sure, Tony. Let's sit down in the back before the others come in."

We took our coffees into the auditorium and sat down. Tony spoke in a quiet voice, "I'm telling you this because I know you've been close to Larry Klein for many years and he respects you."

Oh my God, I thought, where the heck was this going? As casually as possible I asked, "What's your concern about Larry?"

"I can't tell you the details or how I learned of this, but I'm worried that Larry may be in the early stages of dementia, or perhaps mild cognitive impairment."

"That's absurd. Larry is still brilliant. Sure he's quirky and suspicious, maybe even a bit paranoid at times, but demented? I don't see it."

"Maybe you're not looking, Gary, or you might be too close to see. But I came to you because you are *the* dementia expert around here, and if anyone can help Larry, it's you."

"Look, Tony, I've got my own sources and I understand there's been some kind of investigation going on. Maybe that's just stressing him out."

"You didn't hear it from me, but I can tell you that there was an investigation but it was closed weeks ago. The data error was a simple oversight and the journal is publishing a retraction. There was no fabrication, no data fraud, and Larry knows it."

The auditorium was filling up, and we had to stop our conversation. "I appreciate your sharing all this with me, Tony. I'll give it some thought and see if there's something I can do."

"Thanks. See you later." Tony got up and took a seat toward the front. I stayed where I was, my mind reeling with this new information.

As the speaker droned on about budget cuts and the latest university regulations, I thought about Larry and all the signs I might have been missing. He was at an age for increased risk of dementia or Alzheimer's disease, and his forgetfulness was showing in his missed meetings and schedule conflicts. I was concerned that I was not paying enough attention to his paranoia—Larry seemed to be ignoring the fact that the investigation was over and he had been cleared. I might have been too quick to assume that depression was the only cause of his symptoms.

Many times people with mild cognitive impairment, a subtle predecessor of Alzheimer's or dementia, show symptoms of paranoia—it's a way of filling in missing information. In fact, even depressive symptoms can be an early indication of progressive cognitive decline. Several studies have shown that older people with mixed symptoms of mood change and memory loss have an increased risk of developing an irreversible dementia.

I was so close to Larry and admired him so much that I had failed to even consider dementia as a possibility—I didn't want either of us to go through that pain. There were treatments, even cures, for depression, paranoia, and obsessive-compulsive disorder. But we had only symptomatic treatments for dementia that could help for a while. Eventually, every patient got worse and succumbed to the disease.

This was the very reason why I was reluctant to take Larry on as a patient from the beginning. There's an old saying that goes, "The doctor who treats himself has a fool for a patient." In treating someone close to me—a mentor, friend, and father figure—I couldn't allow myself to consider the worst—that he could literally be losing his mind—even though it was right in front of my nose. Unconsciously I must have feared that if someone like Larry could get dementia, then so could I.

The following Wednesday, Larry decided we would meet again at the Brentwood golf course. I got there first and waited in the car with the air-conditioning blasting while I slathered on sunscreen. I also put on a ridiculously large visor that Gigi had dug out of some old beach bag and that I now kept in the car. I was taking no chances with the sun today.

Larry parked right next to me, got out, and pulled a set of ancient golf clubs out of his trunk. "We talk too much," he said. "Let's hit some balls. We'll share my clubs."

The course was a nine-hole pitch-and-putt that I knew I could handle. In fact, I liked the idea of playing a little golf lite to break up my workday. But I wondered why Larry suddenly wanted to play instead of talk.

After he birdied the first hole and I sank my putt, I said, "So I ran into Tony Wilson at the faculty meeting the other day. He said your investigation has been closed for weeks, and the data error was just an oversight. There was no fabrication, and you're in the clear."

"Oh, yeah. I forgot about that, but so what? I still feel like a fraud." Larry took out a driver and in one stroke got his ball onto the next green within three feet of the flag.

"How's the Cymbalta going?" I asked as I drove my ball into the brush.

"Pretty good. My mood is better and I'm less obsessive," he said as he used his handkerchief to meticulously wipe clean the handle of the driver I had just handed back to him.

I thought the game was too distracting for us to have a serious discussion, so I said, "Let's sit down on this bench for a minute."

Larry laughed. "What are you, pooped? You never could keep up with me."

We sat down and wiped our foreheads with our handkerchiefs. "Larry, you know as well as I do that your brain is aging."

"Better than the alternative, my young friend."

"What I'm trying to say is that we don't want to miss anything. It's possible that your shrinking hippocampus and declining neurotransmitters are contributing to some of your symptoms."

"I miss one faculty meeting and you think I have Alzheimer's?" he asked with feigned indignation. "Well, I'd be happy to prove you wrong."

This was going to be much easier than I had anticipated. It was almost as if Larry had planned the conversation to take this direction.

"You're on," I said. "Let's schedule a PET scan and some neuropsych tests."

"Fine," he answered. "But I don't want any run-of-the-mill PET scan, I want that new scan that you and Barrio invented. What is it, FDDNP?"

Larry was referring to the new chemical marker that several of us at UCLA had discovered and patented. It gave an actual measure of the physical evidence of Alzheimer's disease in the brain—amyloid plaques and tau tangles, which are tiny, insoluble, and abnormal protein deposits. Our research had found that these deposits gradually increase in the brain decades before patients experience obvious symptoms of Alzheimer's.

Larry stood up and said, "Well, that's settled. Now let me kick your ass in this game so we can get back to our day jobs."

The following Saturday night, Gigi and I were getting ready for bed. Both kids were sleeping out that evening, and she emerged from the bathroom dressed for the occasion. I was in bed attempting to finish a diabolical crossword puzzle.

"Hey you," Gigi said. "Put down that puzzle and let's seize the moment."

"Sounds good. You look great. Sorry I've been so distracted."

"What's the matter?" she asked, cuddling up to me.

"Well," I said with a sigh, "you know that friend-patient of mine? I got back his test results and PET scan today."

"How bad is it?" she asked.

"Right now it's not too bad, but it's going to get worse."

"I'm sorry to hear that, honey."

"It's really quite remarkable. Here's a genius who had an IQ over 180, and now he tests at 140—still in the upper one percentile of the population."

"So he's off the short list for the Nobel Prize, but he still probably reads quantum-theory books for fun," she said, trying to cheer me up.

"But his PET scan shows that his brain is full of plaques and tangles. His prognosis isn't good—he's going to go downhill, probably soon."

Larry's case was typical of individuals who were highly intelligent and developed Alzheimer's disease. They had enough cognitive reserve to be able to mask their early memory changes. Instead they tended to show mood and personality changes that could range from anger and agitation to depression and social withdrawal. Eventually, however, both the cognitive and behavioral symptoms got worse over time.

"It must be tough for you, honey. I know he's your friend."

"And now I have to tell him what's happening."

Gigi kissed me on the forehead. "That's Monday. Right now it's Saturday night, so let's relax. What's on our TiVo list?" She picked up the remote, turned on the TV, and said "Ooh, we've got two new episodes of *Entourage*. What do you say?"

I grabbed the remote from her and shut off the TV. "Forget *Entourage* and turn off the lights."

THE FOLLOWING MONDAY, WHEN I TOLD LARRY about his test results, he took it well. In fact, he didn't seem surprised at all. That day I started him on an anti-Alzheimer's drug called Aricept, which helps not only with the cognitive symptoms but with the mood and personality changes associated with the illness. Once he was stable on Aricept, I added a second drug, Namenda, which has similar effects and works well as part of a combination treatment. I made sure that the medicine didn't bother his stomach—if it did I could always switch him to an Exelon patch.

Larry and I kept meeting but cut back to once a week. He became less paranoid, and he was now fine with meeting only in my office. For a while he almost seemed like he was back to his old self. After a few months, he decided to take a break from our friend therapy.

About six months later, Larry came in for a midmorning meeting. He arrived right on time and grabbed himself a cup of coffee before getting comfortable on the couch. He looked like he had lost a couple of pounds, and I wondered if his medications were suppressing his appetite. Aricept and Cymbalta sometimes did that.

"Well, Gary, the Tony Wilsons in this place will think they've won, but I've decided to retire."

"What? When?" I asked in disbelief.

"Today. Fuck 'em."

"Have you thought this out, Larry?"

He wagged his finger at me. "Your problem, my young friend,

is you think too much. Anyway, Louise is thrilled. We're going on a cruise."

I laughed. "You hate cruises. You said they were like being in a prison that could sink."

"Yeah, but with Cymbalta on board, I can pretend I'm having fun." He smiled impishly. "You know I'm good at faking it. Besides, Louise deserves something after putting up with me all these years."

"Larry, before you just up and retire, why not take a leave of absence, go on your cruise, and think about it when you get back. No matter what your PET scan shows, I'm sure you still have an IQ of at least 140 and a lot to contribute to psychiatry."

"Look, you and I both know my clock is ticking. Those plaques and tangles are eating up my brain. I could be a total veg in six months."

Hearing Larry say that suddenly made it seem real. I felt a rush of sadness, but I kept myself together.

Larry noticed I was upset and got more serious. "Look, pal, I know it's been hard for you to take me on as a patient, but you're one of the few people in this world that I trust."

"I appreciate that—it means a lot to me," I said.

"Well, I've been grooming you all these years, and it just happens that dementia is one of your areas of expertise. I have to confess, I suspected for a while that something like this was going on."

I took a deep breath as his last few statements sank in. "You always were one step ahead of me, Larry."

"But that's going to change, and we've both got to come to terms with that," he said.

"You know, Larry. You've always been like a father to me."

"Well, you've been like a son, a psychiatrist, and a friend when I needed you most. You helped me to let go of *my* need to control everything. I feel like now I can move on with what's left of my life." He stopped and took my hand. "You have to do the same thing."

I was overcome with sadness and didn't know what to say.

Larry stood and said, "I love you, pal. I gotta go."

I held back my tears as he quickly left the office.

As I expected, Larry failed to take my advice and retired from UCLA that afternoon. I got a few postcards from his Mediterranean cruise, and it sounded like he was truly enjoying it and not just faking it.

WHEN HE RETURNED, LARRY CLOSED UP HIS lab. He still showed up at faculty meetings and teaching conferences from time to time. Our strolls around the Brentwood golf course became less frequent, and I went back to being his old friend rather than his therapist friend.

Aricept and Namenda seemed to hold Larry steady for the next year, but eventually he began to decline. It was hard to watch him slip away, but in his own way, he had prepared me for it.

When I think back on my relationship with Larry over the years, and how much he taught me about my profession and about myself, I know that defining therapeutic and personal boundaries is essential. Those boundaries allowed me to be the best therapist, husband, father, and friend that I could. But in the end, my mentor taught me how boundaries sometimes have to be stretched in order to help those we care about.

What was most unusual about Larry's case was the complexity of our relationship, which temporarily clouded my vision so much that I missed a diagnosis in my area of expertise. In fact, he was so bright that despite his impending dementia, he recognized it before I did.

In many ways, what I experienced with Larry was not much different from what many adult children go through as their parents age. They have to face the psychological confusion that occurs when their roles reverse and they need to care for their own parents. Many respond with love and empathy, but others experience anger, frustration, and guilt.

After his retirement, Larry occasionally mentioned that he still felt like a fraud, yet now it didn't seem to bother him. It became a recurring philosophical debate for us. After a while, he came around to see it my way—that those feelings were universal. But I wondered whether I had really convinced him or perhaps his progressing dementia just made him more agreeable. Soon Larry's cognitive impairment got so bad that we had to stop our walks and eventually Louise had to get twenty-four-hour help at the house. It became hard to visit him and watch my mentor-hero disappear before my eyes.

Even after Larry passed away, I kept his lessons in mind. Whenever I make a correct diagnosis, tolerate my own anxiety, or mentor my own students, I feel Larry with me. And no plaques or tangles will take that away—I hope.

AFTERWORD

WHEN I THINK BACK ON THE unusual cases I have dealt with throughout my career, I'm surprised by how many there were and how hard it was to decide which ones to include in this book. Some were unusual because of the rarity of the diagnoses; others were noteworthy because of the complexity of the relationships and situations. Many had an element of medical mystery, and as a young psychiatrist I sometimes found myself stumbling upon the correct diagnosis and treatment without even realizing it.

Each of these unusual cases—whether it was a mute, naked woman standing on her head or a man who thought he would be more comfortable with only one hand—also contained an element of the usual issues that we all struggle with at some point in our lives.

Of course, most people don't obsess about chopping off an extremity, but who doesn't occasionally feel discomfort about his body weight or perhaps how his hair looks? It's certainly out of the ordinary to meet someone who believes she's had sexual intercourse with you because you merely looked her in the eye. Yet many of us have had experiences with strangers or acquaintances who are intrusive. Perhaps it was someone whose gaze lingered too long or a co-worker who touched you inappropriately on the arm.

And many of us have had the uneasy experience of dealing with somebody who suddenly starts acting crazy—it could be a relative with hidden alcoholism who begins to unravel or a colleague who flips out with acute mania during a staff meeting. We all wonder how to respond during those awkward moments, how we might help the person who's off kilter, and how we can deal with our own emotional reactions to these events.

Often our first instinct is to run, but if we can get beyond our fears and anxieties, we have an opportunity to understand their pain and show compassion. When we do express empathy and compassion, it not only helps the person who is suffering from a mental problem, but it also helps us to feel more human.

Many people who could benefit from seeing a psychiatrist choose not to because of their fear and denial. We spend years of our lives in school and college studying any number of topics, yet the idea of taking a few hours to study ourselves seems foreign to so many. It's not surprising that we sometimes go to extraordinary lengths to escape our psychological pain in our attempts to feel accepted, valued, and loved.

Much has changed in medical education since the days of my early training in psychiatry. Doctors callously discussing cases on elevators and in hallways within earshot of families and other patients have become rare occurrences. The stereotypical "know-it-all" doctor is being replaced by the physician as a partner in healing. Medical students are now required to take courses on effective listening and empathic abilities. Although most people rank technical skill as the leading quality they seek when choosing a doctor, studies show that those technical skills are most effective when delivered with sensitivity and understanding.

The field of psychiatry continues to evolve. With continued discoveries of safe and effective medicines and growing appreciation that talk therapy works, psychiatry is moving into the future as a respected medical specialty that benefits both the mind and the body. Almost all of us will face emotional struggles during our lives. Whether we use humor, denial, or some other defense mechanism to cope with these struggles, taking some moments to reflect on how our minds work usually brings us insight and relief.

NOTES

PREFACE

xii *In any given year, an estimated one in four adults*—National Institute of Mental Health website: http://www.nimh.nih.gov/health/publications/the-numbers-count-mental-disorders-in-america/index.shtml.

CHAPTER I: SEXY STARE

5 *The term stands for young, attractive, verbal*—Kimm HJ, Bolz W, Meyer AE. The Hamburg short psychotherapy comparison experiment. The patient sample: overt and covert selection factors and prognostic predictions. *Psychotherapy and Psychosomatics* 1981;35:96–109.

9 *Freud took the position that the therapist should be impenetrable*—Gelso CJ, Hayes JA. *Countertransference and the Therapist's Experience: Perils and Possibilities.* Lawrence Ehrlbaum and Associates, Mahwah, NJ, 2007, p. 62.

15 *He said that transference was one of the most*—Goldberg ST. *Using the Transference in Psychotherapy.* Jason Aronson Publishers, Lanham, MD, 2006; Bloch, S. (ed). *An Introduction to the Psychotherapies.* Oxford University Press, New York, NY, 2006.

18 *Borderlines are patients whose psychological state*—Friedel RO, Hoffman PD, Penney D, Woodward P. *Borderline Personality Disorder Demystified: An Essential Guide for Understanding and Living with BPD.* Da Capo Press, New York, NY, 2004.

19 *Her EEG revealed no evidence of temporal-lobe epilepsy*—Geschwind N. Personality changes in temporal lobe epilepsy. *Epilepsy & Behavior* 2009;15:425–33.

CHAPTER 2: THE NAKED LADY WHO STOOD ON HER HEAD

22 *an unfortunate but traditional rite*—Small GW. House officer stress syndrome. *Psychosomatics* 1981;22:860-9.

25 *I had come up with my own mnemonic*—Cassem NH, Murray GB, Lafayette JM, Stern TA. Delirious patients, in *The MGH Handbook of General Hospital Psychiatry*, 5th ed. Edited by Stern TA, Fricchione GL, Cassem NH, Jellinek MS, Rosenbaum JF. Mosby, St. Louis, MO, 2004, pp. 119-34.

28 *If somebody injects too much insulin*—Fishbain DA, Rotundo D. Frequency of hypoglycemic delirium in a psychiatric emergency service. *Psychosomatics* 1988;29:346-8.

31 *Today, on-call hours are limited*—Meltzer DO, Arora, VM. Evaluating resident duty hour reforms: More work to do. *Journal of the American Medical Association* 2007;298:1055-7.

CHAPTER 3: TAKE MY HAND, PLEASE

40 *He taught a small seminar entitled "Autognosis"*—Stern TA, Prager LM, Cremens MC. Autognosis rounds for medical house staff. *Psychosomatics* 1993;34:1-7.

41 *It helps to maintain "detached concern"*—Halpern J. *From Detached Concern to Empathy: Humanizing Medical Practice*. Oxford University Press, New York, NY, 2001.

52 *"Apotemnophilia"* —Money J, Jobaris R, Furth G. Apotemnophilia: Two cases of self-demand amputation as a sexual preference. *The Journal of Sex Research* 1977;13:115-24.

52 *Dysmorphophobia was first described by an Italian psychiatrist*—Gilman SL. Creating Beauty to Cure the Soul. Race and Psychology in the Shaping of Aesthetic Surgery. Duke University Press, Durham, NC, 1998.

53 *Patients suffering from BIID*—Frare F, Perugi G, Ruffolo G, Toni C. Obsessive-compulsive disorder and body dysmorphic disorder: A comparison of clinical features. *European Psychiatry* 2004;19:292-8; Müller S. Body integrity identity disorder (BIID)—Is the amputation of healthy limbs ethically justified? *American Journal of Bioethics* 2009;9:36-43; Bayne T, Levy N. Amputees by choice: Body integrity identity disorder and the ethics of amputation. *Journal of Applied Philosophy* 2005;22:75-86.

55 *Anafranil*—Gitlin MJ. *Psychotherapist's Guide to Psychopharmacology*. Free Press, New York, NY, 1990.

CHAPTER 4: FAINTING SCHOOLGIRLS

58 *although these epidemics were*—Small GW, Nicholi AM. Mass hysteria among school children: Early loss as a predisposing factor. *Archives of General Psychiatry* 1982;39:721-4.

61 *"Essentially, the sixth-graders were"*—Ibid.

62 *In fact, he was describing typical features*—Small GW, Borus JF. Outbreak of illness in a school chorus: Toxic poisoning or mass hysteria? *New England Journal of Medicine* 1983;308:632-5.

64 *I studied several episodes*—Small GW, Borus JF. The influence of newspaper

reports on outbreaks of mass hysteria. *Psychiatric Quarterly* 1987;58:269–78; Small GW, Propper MW, Randolph E, Eth S. Mass hysteria among student performers: Social relationship as a symptom predictor. *American Journal of Psychiatry* 1991;148:1200–5; Small GW, Feinberg DT, Steinberg D, Collins MT. A sudden illness outbreak suggesting mass hysteria in schoolchildren. *Archives of Family Medicine* 1994;3:711–6.

65 *Examples of bizarre explanations*—Johnson DM. The "phantom anesthetist" of Mattoon: a field study of mass hysteria. *Journal of Abnormal and Social Psychology* 1945;40:175–86; Medalia NZ, Larsen ON. Diffusion and belief in a collective delusion: The Seattle Windshield Pitting Epidemic. *American Sociological Association* 1958;180.

65 *My Boston-suburb elementary school outbreak had its own*—Small GW, Nicholi AM. Mass hysteria among school children: Early loss as a predisposing factor. *Archives of General Psychiatry* 1982;39:721–4.

66 *A decade later I studied*—Small GW, Propper MW, Randolph E, Eth S. Mass hysteria among student performers: Social relationship as a symptom predictor. *American Journal of Psychiatry* 1991;148:1200–5.

70 *Almost exactly two years after*—Small GW, Borus JF. Outbreak of illness in a school chorus: Toxic poisoning or mass hysteria? *New England Journal of Medicine* 1983;308:632–5.

72 *As I reported in the* New England Journal of Medicine—Ibid.

CHAPTER 5: BABY LOVE

78 *Pseudocyesis, also known as false or hysterical pregnancy*—Small GW. Pseudocyesis: An overview. *Canadian Journal of Psychiatry* 1986;31:453–7; Sobrinho LG. Prolactin, psychological stress and environment in humans: Adaptation and maladaptation. *Pituitary* 2003;6:35–9

85 *I continued to read up*—Small GW. Pseudocyesis: An overview. *Canadian Journal of Psychiatry* 1986;31:453–7.

CHAPTER 6: SILENT TREATMENT

87 *Few young psychiatrists were looking to work with seniors*—Jarvik LF, Small GW (eds). *Psychiatric Clinics of North America*, Issue on Aging, vol. 5, no. 1, 1982; Small GW, Fong K, Beck JC. Training in geriatric psychiatry: Will the supply meet the demand? *American Journal of Psychiatry* 1988;145:476–8

90 *Scottish psychiatrist R. D. Laing*—Boyers R. *R. D. Laing and Anti-Psychiatry*. Hippocrene Books, New York, NY, 1974.

90 *Stanford psychologist David Rosenhan*—Rosenhan DL. On being sane in insane places. *Science* 1973;179:250–8.

90 *Psychoanalysis has helped many*—Gabbard GO, Gunderson JG, Fonagy P. The place of psychoanalytic treatments within psychiatry. *Archives of General Psychiatry* 2002;59:505–10; Leichsenring F, Rabung S. Effectiveness of long-term psychodynamic psychotherapy: A meta-analysis. *Journal of the American Medical Association* 2008;300:1551–65.

93 The illness afflicts about 1 percent—Jamison KR. *An Unquiet Mind: A Memoir of Moods and Madness.* Vintage Books, New York, NY, 1997.

97 Alan Gelenberg's classic—Gelenberg AJ. The catatonic syndrome. *Lancet* 1976; 1:1339–41.

97 The other articles described the safety—Sherese A, Welch CA, Park LT, et al. Encephalitis and catatonia treated with ECT. *Cognitive and Behavioral Neurology* 2008;21:46–51; Fink M, Taylor, MA. *Catatonia: A Clinician's Guide to Diagnosis and Treatment.* Cambridge University Press, New York, NY, 2003.

CHAPTER 7: THE SHRINKING PENIS

108 Freud viewed sex as our primary social activity—Freud S, Brill AA. *The Basic Writings of Sigmund Freud.* Basic Books, New York, NY, 1995.

111 Psychosis is defined—International Early Psychosis Association Writing Group. International clinical practice guidelines for early psychosis. *British Journal of Psychiatry* 2005;187:s120–4.

116 In medical settings, gallows humor—Small GW. House officer stress syndrome. *Psychosomatics* 1981;22:860–9.

117 Many patients with both mood and psychotic symptoms—Malhi GS, Green M, Fagiolini A, Peselow ED, Kumari V. Schizoaffective disorder: Diagnostic issues and future recommendations. *Bipolar Disorders* 2008;10:215–30.

CHAPTER 8: WORRIED SICK

120 A major part of any insight-oriented therapy—Goldberg ST. *Using the Transference in Psychotherapy.* Jason Aronson Publishers, Lanham, MD, 2006.

127 Although stress and diet can contribute—Marshall BJ, Warren JR. Unidentified curved bacilli in the stomach of patients with gastritis and peptic ulceration. *Lancet* 1984;1(8390):1311–5.

129 Medical studentitis—Kellner R, Wiggins RG, Pathak D. Hypochondriacal fears and beliefs in medical and law students. *Archives of General Psychiatry* 1986;43:487–9; Moss-Morris R, Petrie KJ. Redefining medical students' disease to reduce morbidity. *Medical Education* 2001;35:724–8

131 Minuchin often worked with nuclear families—Minuchin S. *Families and Family Therapy.* Harvard University Press, Cambridge, MA, 1974.

136 Cases of Munchausen's by proxy—Meadow R. Munchausen syndrome by proxy. *Archives of Disease in Childhood* 1982;57:92–8.

CHAPTER 9: EYES WIDE SHUT

149 With classic hysterical conversion symptoms—Murphy GE. The clinical management of hysteria. *Journal of the American Medical Association* 1982; 247:2559–64.

CHAPTER 10: BRAIN FOG

158 Studies have shown that genes—Small GW. What we need to know about age-related memory loss. *British Medical Journal* 2002;324:1502–5.

158 Our group was doing a lot of research with PET scan technology—Small GW, Kepe V, Ercoli LM, et al. PET of brain amyloid and tau in mild cognitive impairment. *New England Journal of Medicine* 2006;355:2652-63.

165 In 1964 a psychiatric journal first described—Weintraub W. "The VIP syndrome": A clinical study in hospital psychiatry. *Journal of Nervous and Mental Disorders* 1964;138:181-93; Parker-Pope T. When the patient is a V.I.P. *The New York Times,* August 27, 2009.

168 my leading diagnostic theory—Hiramatsu R, Takeshita A, Taguchi M, Takeuchi Y. Symptomatic hyponatremia after voluntary excessive water ingestion in a patient without psychiatric problems. *Endocrine Journal* 2007;54:643-5; Farrell DJ, Bower L. Fatal water intoxication. *Journal of Clinical Pathology* 2003;56:803-4.

168 psychogenic polydipsia—Rae J. Self-induced water intoxication in a schizophrenic patient. *Canadian Medical Association Journal* 1976;114:438-9.

CHAPTER 11: DREAM WEDDING

174 doctors are less likely to use illicit drugs—Hughes PH, Brandenburg N, Baldwin DC Jr, et al. Prevalence of substance use among U.S. physicians. *Journal of the American Medical Association* 1992;267:2333-9.

176 In Freud's book The Interpretation of Dreams—Freud S, Brill AA. *The Basic Writings of Sigmund Freud.* Basic Books, New York, NY, 1995.

CHAPTER 12: GASLIGHT

188 cognitive-behavioral therapy—March JS. Cognitive-behavioral therapy, in Sadock BJ, Sadock VA (eds). *Comprehensive Textbook of Psychiatry, 8th ed.* Williams & Wilkins, Baltimore, MD, 2005, pp. 2806-13.

194 Freud used the term—Gelso CJ, Hayes JA. *Countertransference and the Therapist's Inner Experience: Perils and Possibilities.* Lawrence Ehrlbaum and Associates, Mahwah, NJ, 2007.

201 Sociopaths, or what psychiatrists call antisocial personalities—American Psychiatric Association. *Diagnostic and Statistical Manual of Mental Disorders.* American Psychiatric Association, Washington, DC, 1994, pp. 645-50.

CHAPTER 13: SHOP TILL YOU DROP

216 These euphoric feelings are linked to brain chemical changes—Kalivas PW, Volkow ND. The neural basis of addiction: A pathology of motivation and choice. *American Journal of Psychiatry* 2005;162:1403-13.

CHAPTER 14: MOUNTAIN HEIR

225 Chronic amphetamine or cocaine abuse is a well-known cause—Cherland E, Fitzpatrick R. Psychotic side effects of psychostimulants: A 5-year review. *Canadian Journal of Psychiatry* 1999;44:811-3.

230 a classic case of spontaneous panic attacks—Bienvenu OJ, Onyike CU, Stein MB. Agoraphobia in adults: Incidence and longitudinal relationship with panic. *British Journal of Psychiatry* 2006;188:432-8.

233 *National Alliance on Mental Illness*—http://www.nami.org/.

234 *One of the earliest psychiatric genetic studies involved Amish families*—Egeland JA, Shaw JA, Endicott J, et al. Prospective study of prodromal features for bipolarity in well Amish children. *Journal of the American Academy of Child & Adolescent Psychiatry* 2003;42:786–96.

235 *Of the various forms of anxiety, panic disorder*—Smoller JW, Gardner-Schuster E, Covino J. The genetic basis of panic and phobic anxiety disorders. *American Journal of Medical Genetics* 2008 15;148C:118–26.

CHAPTER 15: SIGMUND FRAUD

246 *To determine whether or not he needed an antidepressant*—Bender S, Messner E. *Becoming a Therapist: What Do I Say and Why?* The Guilford Press, New York, NY, 2003.

246 *SIG E CAPS*—SIG E CAPS was devised by Dr. Carey Gross at Massachusetts General Hospital as a mnemonic for the criteria of major depressive disorder.

252 *Several studies have shown*—Alexopoulos GS, Meyers BS, Young RC, Mattis S, Kakuma T. The course of geriatric depression with "reversible": A controlled study. *American Journal of Psychiatry* 1993;150:1693–9; Devanand DP, Sano M, Tang MX, Taylor S, Gurland BJ, Wilder D, Stern Y, Mayeux R. Depressed mood and the incidence of Alzheimer's disease in the elderly living in the community. *Archives of General Psychiatry* 1996;53:175–82.

254 *Larry was referring to the new chemical marker*—Small GW, Kepe V, Ercoli LM, et al. PET of brain amyloid and tau in mild cognitive impairment. *New England Journal of Medicine* 2006;355:2652–63.

255 *anti-Alzheimer's drug*—Alzheimer's Disease Medications Fact Sheet: http://www.nia.nih.gov/Alzheimers/Publications/medicationsfs.htm.

AFTERWORD

260 *Doctors callously discussing cases on elevators*—Small GW. That boorish, insensitive, loudmouthed, crass physician in the elevator. *Journal of the American Medical Association* 1985;253:2645.

260 *Although most people rank technical skill*—Dibbelt S, Schaidhammer M, Fleischer C, Greitemann B. Patient-doctor interaction in rehabilitation: The relationship between perceived interaction quality and long-term treatment results. *Patient Education and Counseling* 2009;76:328–35; Kim SS, Kaplowitz S, Johnston MV. The effects of physician empathy on patient satisfaction and compliance. *Evaluation & the Health Professions* 2004;27:237–51.